The

LIBRARIAN'S Guide to
NEGOTIATION

Winning Strategies for the Digital Age

Beth Ashmore,
Jill E. Grogg, and
Jeff Weddle

Information Today, Inc.
Medford, New Jersey

First Printing, 2012

The Librarian's Guide to Negotiation: Winning Strategies for the Digital Age

Copyright © 2012 by Beth Ashmore, Jill E. Grogg, and Jeff Weddle

Library of Congress Cataloging-in-Publication Data

Ashmore, Beth, 1976-
  The librarian's guide to negotiation : winning strategies for the digital age /
Beth Ashmore, Jill E. Grogg, and Jeff Weddle.
       pages cm.
  Includes bibliographical references and index.
     ISBN 978-1-57387-428-1
1. Acquisitions (Libraries) 2. Acquisition of electronic information
resources. 3. Libraries and electronic publishing. 4. Library administration-
-Decision making. 5. Communication in library science. 6. Negotiation in
business. I. Grogg, Jill E., 1972- II. Weddle, Jeff. III. Title.
    Z689.A82 2012
    021--dc23
                                                                    2011049609

Printed and bound in the United States of America.

President and CEO: Thomas H. Hogan, Sr.
Editor-in-Chief and Publisher: John B. Bryans
VP Graphics and Production: M. Heide Dengler
Managing Editor: Amy M. Reeve
Project Editor: Barbara Quint
Editorial Assistant: Brandi Scardilli
Book Designer: Kara Mia Jalkowski
Cover Designer: Amy Romanofsky Schneider
Copyeditor: Bonnie Freeman
Proofreader: Barbara Brynko
Indexer: Candace Hyatt

www.infotoday.com

Contents

Foreword, by Maria Collins v

Introduction vii

Chapter 1 **Translating Negotiation Expertise
for the Library World**............................. 1

Chapter 2 **Negotiation Advice From Library
Leaders and Vendors**........................... 21

Chapter 3 **The Power and Pitfalls of
Consortial Negotiation** 45

Chapter 4 **Negotiating in Times of
Economic Stress**.................................. 63

Chapter 5 **Negotiating With Funding Sources
and User Communities**......................... 85

Chapter 6 **Playing Hardball: When to Get
Tough and When to Walk Away** 119

Chapter 7 **Negotiating in the Era of Publisher
Consolidation and the Big Deal**........ 143

Chapter 8 **EResource Management,
Workflows, and Standardization** 163

Chapter 9 **Negotiating in the Age of Open
Access, Open Source, and Free
Internet Resources**............................. 183

**Appendix A How to Research a
            Forthcoming Negotiation**.................. 205

Appendix B Useful Resources 211

**Appendix C Sample Licensing and
            Negotiation Checklists**..................... 217

**Appendix D Digital Tools, Netiquette,
            and Negotiation** 221

**Appendix E Theory in Practice:
            Understanding Communication** 227

Bibliography... 235

About the Authors 243

Index.. 245

Foreword

Taking the mystery out of negotiation is a pretty tall order, but that is exactly what *The Librarian's Guide to Negotiation* achieves. Negotiation situations abound across the library profession involving multimillion dollar contracts with STM publishers, government funding for public libraries, and the evolution of the scholarly communication environment. These complex topics provide a few of the focal points for the discussion of negotiation throughout the guide, but also embedded are descriptions of essential skills required for effective negotiation, such as listening, preparation, and building context. Even if you are unaware of it, all of us use negotiation techniques throughout our daily lives.

Take my middle son, Christopher, for instance. Throughout his life he's participated in a series of negotiations to gain the upper hand with his older brother and to outwit his little sister. If you have interacted with eight-year-old boys, you are well aware of the variety of toys that are marketed to this age group: trading cards, transforming battle balls, puzzle erasers, fighting marbles, mini figures ... : The list goes on and on with new toy lines replacing each other before parents can even begin to figure them out.

My son, however, has an intuitive understanding of toy trends. He knows what's in and what's out. He collects the latest toy wonders as birthday and holidays gifts and then supplements them with his meager allowance. Once the fascination of a toy line begins to fade, it's time to negotiate. He assesses his collection with serious intent, determines the trading value for these items and begins wheeling and dealing at school. As I prepare his book bag each day, I'm constantly asking him, "Where did you get this?", recognizing that I didn't buy the latest treasure tucked away in his bag. "Oh," he says, "I traded one of my Star Wars mini figures, but

I only traded my duplicates." Even without steady financial resources he has figured out a way to acquire the latest craze while demonstrating many of the strategies threaded throughout the guide by Ashmore, Grogg and Weddle.

He definitely understands how to take advantage of "tough economic times" by evaluating what he really needs and giving up what is no longer important. His understanding of current toy trends and the needs of his friends (or customers) at school allow him to make win–win trades—hence, the perfect negotiation. He's done his homework and kept his ear to the ground for trading opportunities.

Christopher serves as an analogy to many librarians: He's enthusiastic, he's bright, he's tech-savvy, and he has no money. Librarians have waded through library school and entered the job market to find themselves in the midst of an information revolution. Technology and the explosion of electronic resources are quickly reshaping the role and potentially the value of the library for students and researchers This constant flux within the library environment makes it ripe for negotiation. With each negotiation, a librarian gains an opportunity to influence change. In my roles as project manager, supervisor, department head, author, and editor, my ability to negotiate has proved critical to my success.

Like my son, some librarians have an intuitive sense of how to negotiate. However, many lack awareness of how to influence others and shape the direction of their work despite possessing raw talent and superb technical skills. *The Librarian's Guide to Negotiation* builds this awareness by detailing library-specific examples of negotiation across a spectrum of contexts. The authors detail interviews with experts who discuss tactics and best practices, and they also incorporate models and theory from non-library-related literature throughout the guide. Awakening librarians to the importance of negotiation is the value proposition of this book. If librarians cultivate the skills described in this guide, just as I have seen in my son Christopher, mastering the art of negotiation will seem like child's play.

—Maria Collins, head of content acquisitions
and licensing, North Carolina State University Libraries

Introduction

Let's begin with two basic premises. First, for the practicing librarian in the 21st century, negotiation is a basic job function, and negotiation skills are a basic job requirement. Nowhere is that truer than in dealing with digital content and services. Some of the worst elements that initially appeared in digital license agreements, such as vendors unilaterally terminating access at the first hint of breach, may have become less common. Other unreasonable terms persist, however, requiring skilled and alert negotiation to eliminate them.

Moreover, negotiation is a skill needed by all librarians, not just the librarian charged with purchasing digital content and making it available. Negotiation exists in the library in many guises and cuts across all areas of service, both public and technical. Therefore, knowing how to negotiate successfully remains a valuable and necessary skill for any librarian.

The second premise underlying this book's approach to negotiation is the recognition that, for most librarians, negotiation is scary. If you are reading this introduction, chances are you can identify with this statement. Why do so many of us find the prospect of negotiation intimidating? For starters, we don't think we are very good at it. There is an impression that negotiation is something for which one either has a natural proclivity or doesn't. For those of us who don't feel like natural negotiators, this leaves us out in the cold. Librarians receive very little (if any) formal negotiation training, perhaps only sink-or-swim, on-the-job training in negotiation tactics after negotiations have already begun. Library schools may not offer negotiation classes. Therefore, little opportunity exists for the average librarian to have the bargaining process demystified.

"What, me negotiate? Not going to happen. I'm not good at negotiation. I don't like to negotiate. I'm not going to do it." Sound like you or someone you know? Well, big surprise, most of us negotiate every day. Most librarians, at least those engaged in public service, have at some point in their training or practice engaged in the art of question negotiation, a skill that lies at the heart of the effective reference interview. Practitioners who have chosen to go the technical services path most likely negotiate issues with any number of people during their daily work lives.

The art of negotiation is, at its core, communication, and developing skill in this art is a journey. Just as a baby learns to walk, a child learns to hit a baseball, or a library-school student learns to decipher a MARC record, it helps to move through a set of logical steps on the road to mastery. Becoming a skilled negotiator is no different.

Negotiation stirs emotions: desire, enthusiasm, frustration, anger. Few catalog records or reference questions can get a librarian as invigorated as the prospect of getting a good deal on a resource or successfully negotiating new funding for a program. While these feelings can make negotiation a very satisfying experience when it goes well, failure can spell disaster both professionally and emotionally.

Finally, we tend to avoid negotiation because it is conflict. In so many interactions within the library, librarians feel as though they are working in concert with their users, administrators, and even their vendors. Negotiation, on the other hand, often appears to involve conflict, and many of us avoid conflict at all costs.

How will this book help? While there are, admittedly, natural negotiators, just as there are natural researchers or organizers, these skills can be learned. By learning the preparation process and techniques used by effective negotiators, you can reduce much of the anxiety related to negotiation and redirect your energy into more positive and useful activities. We provide you with the necessary context for negotiations in the library world. We also provide perspective on how the internet and the ubiquity of technology have changed the negotiation landscape for librarians. We examine the importance of recognizing the perspectives of the major stakeholders in preparing for negotiations. Finally, since a single book can't cover all the possible negotiation situations that an information professional might encounter, we include additional resources that can address specific issues in more depth.

Why should you care? Unless your job description includes license negotiations for electronic resources or software or other similar products, you might be wondering whether this book holds much value for you, but the fact is that negotiation is everywhere. Even if you are not the kind of person who tries to bargain with the salesperson at a department store, there's no denying that we all negotiate with ourselves, our family, our co-workers, and others more times a day than we can count. "Mommy, do I have to eat four green beans or five?" "Can I give you my conference report next Monday instead of Friday?" "How about we spend Thanksgiving with your parents and Christmas with mine? Then we can switch next year." Everyone can benefit from being a more effective negotiator, particularly librarians engaged in purchasing digital sources and services. Chances are, if your library is not negotiating for the resources and services it purchases every year, then your library is overpaying and failing in its duty to serve as a good steward of the funds allocated to it.

The chapters of this book can be read in order or as need and interest require. Certain ideas or concepts appear in multiple chapters because they play a large role in negotiation theory or the library world. While some of the content deals with information on negotiation theory and practice in general, all the chapters will be of value to those who negotiate for digital content and services.

The digital revolution has put a greater number of librarians in the position of needing to negotiate, and that trend is accelerating. For example, libraries are experiencing an explosion of electronic books similar to the explosion of ejournals that began in the mid-1990s. Paula Hane reports in her "Review of the Year 2009 and Trends Watch—Part 2," that "2010 will probably be a tipping point for the ebook" and that ebook sales are "growing at an explosive rate."[1] In addition to all the intricacies of ejournal acquisition, delivery, and management, ebooks offer a greater complexity: They can be delivered via PCs, iPads, smartphones, Kindles, NOOKs, the web, and more. Many ebook vendors offer options such as patron-driven acquisition, which gives patrons an expanded role in a library's collection development. Ebooks can be purchased outright or on a subscription basis, which changes the very notion of a monograph.

The practice of collection development is radically changing. In the print world, use of material was not the primary determination of what was purchased and retained. It was certainly important, but it did not drive the collection decisions the way that usage statistics and other use data analyses drive decisions in the digital world. Librarians can now use evidence-based analysis to justify expenses. These sorts of considerations about digital content and more are examined in the context of negotiation.

We hope that this book will provide the tools necessary to help librarians build confidence in their ability to negotiate well with all partners. Most of all, we hope that librarians will feel the need to put these concepts and skills to work. Just as with other skills in the library world—the reference interview, MARC bibliographic coding, collection development evaluation, and so forth—negotiation is a skill that improves greatly with frequent and plentiful practice.

The unknown future of the information industry makes negotiation a key skill for present and future librarians. Librarians in the future will likely have more partners rather than fewer, and partnerships require negotiation. We live in a Google world, with Facebook, Twitter, mobile computing, smartphones, iPads, and streaming audio and video—all available to users *everywhere*. We need to adapt ourselves, and quickly, and give users the information and services they want, when they want it, on their terms.

As Barbara Quint wrote in a 2010 *Searcher* magazine editorial, "We've got to turn the word 'library' from a noun describing a place or an institution to a verb describing a function or an app. The verb has got to mean finding the best information on a subject. It's got to mean archiving information safely and permanently. It's got to mean reaching out to qualified information professionals for the essential support and protection of users' interest that only we supply. ... We need to see ourselves as serving the world and not just narrow clients. And we need to get started now. There's no time left to waste."[2]

To shift a noun to a verb and accomplish all that Quint enumerates will necessitate good negotiation skills because we cannot do it alone. We will need to partner with a variety of entities and individuals. And at the end of the day, only good negotiations can create good relationships.

Endnotes

1. Paula Hane, "Review of the Year 2009 and Trends Watch—Part 2," January 7, 2010, accessed December 6, 2011, newsbreaks.infotoday.com/Spotlight/Review-of-the-Year--and-Trends-WatchPart--60486.asp.

2. Barbara Quint, "Searcher's Voice: Long Thoughts, Big Dreams," *Searcher* 18, no. 6 (July/August 2010), accessed July 19, 2011, www.infotoday.com/searcher/ jul10/voice.shtml.

Chapter 1

Translating Negotiation Expertise for the Library World

There is no shortage of books providing negotiation advice—a shocking statement for the first chapter of a book on negotiation, but a true one nonetheless. Some of the more strident titles claim that there is a lot of difference among all of these books; however, that perspective probably has more to do with author and/or publisher pocketbooks than actual negotiation playbooks. Yes, playbooks! Do not be misled. Negotiation is a sport. As a sport, much of what one finds in the best-selling negotiation books are examples of plays, er, deals, and how you can use the same tactics at your negotiation table. Depending on the background of the author (sports agent, political scientist, corporate bulldog), these examples can seem either applicable or downright nonsensical to the average librarian-reader. To make sure that librarians get their moment in the negotiation spotlight, we'll show how advice from a few well-known negotiation experts can apply in the library world. Since these works rely heavily on examples to illustrate their points, this chapter will include a number of examples of ways these techniques and concepts could help librarians negotiate with a variety of library stakeholders. We will also take a look at how technology has changed the way negotiations are conducted in the digital age. Not only do librarians find themselves negotiating for an increasing number of electronic resources; they also find themselves using an increasing number of electronic tools to prepare and conduct the negotiation process.

Do Your Homework

The one piece of advice that is the most consistent across negotiation guides is the importance of preparation and research before you begin negotiations. Ronald Shapiro and Mark A. Jankowski, authors of *The Power of Nice*,[1] lay out seven steps to ensure that your preparation is comprehensive: 1) Identify pertinent precedents, 2) Identify alternatives, 3) Clarify interests, 4) Identify deadlines, 5) Define strengths and weaknesses, 6) Identify your ultimate goal (best possible outcome), and 7) Recruit a team. We can apply each of these seven steps to the library world:

- *Identify pertinent precedents.* What kinds of deals have you done with this vendor in the past? Is this a renegotiation for a particular database or ejournal package, or a new relationship? What about other vendors that serve this same market or offer similar products? What information can you discover about deals with institutions similar to yours or consortia you might join? This step might involve emailing fellow librarians at similar institutions, checking listserv archives, or just old-fashioned web searching for deal details.

- *Identify alternatives.* This step can involve identifying alternative products, but in the case of content available only from a single vendor, it may also include coming up with your Best Alternative to a Negotiated Agreement (BATNA), which we will discuss in more depth in the next few chapters. For a quick example, imagine that a librarian is looking to acquire a new, highly specialized database that a few vocal faculty members want for their research. Before sitting down to negotiate for this database, the librarian would want to project costs for setting up individual user pay-per-search or pay-per-article accounts for the faculty interested in using this database. While this setup would not be ideal, any deal to acquire this database for all users should be better than the alternative of a small number of individual user accounts.

- *Clarify interests.* It may seem obvious, but you need to know what it is that you hope to achieve through this negotiation. It is important to put your interests "down on paper" (or a digital equivalent) as clearly as possible. During the heat of negotiation, it can be easy to become distracted by the task of defending your position, but doing so may not always serve your interests. When negotiating a license for digital content, remember that a license is written by an attorney, and it is his or her responsibility to use the license to control the risk incurred by the vendor. It is your responsibility to control the risk incurred by your library or parent institution. Clarifying your interests ahead of time allows for a more fruitful and dispassionate negotiation. Moreover, if in the heat of the moment you lock yourself into a particular position, you may not be able to see when your interests are being met. It may be that your interests could be met, just not in the way that you had considered.

- *Identify deadlines.* Anyone who has received an email from a vendor at the end of the year that offers an excellent deal if you just sign the contract by December 31 knows that deadlines can be a powerful force in negotiation. Technology has made these kinds of last-minute bargains even more popular because email, PDFs, and click-through licenses have made it that much easier to turn a decision into a contract. Sadly, such deadlines can sometimes force either party into agreeing to poor deals. Be sure that any deadlines are real and unmovable before allowing them to dictate too heavily in any negotiation. These sorts of vendor deadlines can seem arbitrary but are often driven by a need to meet quarterly or yearly sales quotas. It is always important for the librarian to ask, "Why such a price difference between June 30 and July 1?"

- *Define strengths and weaknesses.* Librarians sometimes see themselves as having more weaknesses than strengths, particularly when dealing with large publishers or funding agencies, or when negotiating for exclusive content. The key is not to overestimate the strengths of those with whom you are competing for budget dollars. Libraries are a huge market for many vendors, and that factor should not be underestimated. Libraries represent an essential service to the communities they serve. Take the time to write out your strengths and weaknesses. If you are business-minded, feel free to do a SWOT (Strengths, Weaknesses, Opportunities, Threats) analysis of the situation, but at the very least, identify what leverage you have in the deal. Also, identify which forms of communication play to your strengths. A sales representative may know that his or her strength lies in in-person or phone negotiations and may try to steer negotiations to these formats, but if that's not your comfort zone, use email for those conversations. Asynchronous communication such as email gives you the opportunity to craft your responses and clarify your concerns, and unlike the phone and in-person deals, email provides a record of what has been discussed and decided.

- *Identify your ultimate goal (best possible outcome).* When you clarify your interests, you know what you hope to get out of the negotiation. When you identify your best possible outcome, you know what it would look like to have those interests fulfilled. This is not to say that this outcome is the only acceptable outcome, but it is a yardstick to assist you in measuring how close you are coming to satisfying your interests. This is also a way to identify the difference between a good deal and a great deal. When the negotiations are going well and needs are being met, don't be afraid to ask for it all.

- *Recruit a team.* While negotiating on your own can have its advantages, having a team can allow you to take advantage of the expertise within your organization, as well as provide opportunities to practice your negotiation skills prior to meeting with the other party. Technology makes a team a feasible option. The ubiquity of tools such as Skype for videoconferencing has made it possible to pull a team together for a meeting regardless of physical location. For example, when negotiating a big deal with a large publisher in a university setting, you might have a team that includes legal counsel, contract administrators from the purchasing office, experienced teaching faculty and researchers, and upper-level library administrators.

The Digital Download on Negotiation Basics

Many popular mass-market negotiation guides were written long before tools such as email and videoconferencing became so ubiquitous and easy. Most of these books envision boardrooms rather than chat rooms, so some of their advice seems rather old school and not very relevant to the fast-paced cycle from request for proposal to closing. But as with many things in life, knowing a little old-school theory to go with your new-school tools can be just the right mix for success.

Take for example the process of researching your opponent's product and comparing it with other competing products. There was a time when the bulk of this research would have required calling multiple vendors and requesting price and product information, which would have probably been supplied either over the phone (without accompanying documentation) or via fax or snail mail. The digital age has brought some of this information online, freely on vendor websites or slightly mediated through requests-for-quote forms. Negotiators can check forums, blogs, and listserv archives and communicate with large communities of other librarians to determine and to compare competing products and deals. In the end, everyone can come to a negotiation with more information, a situation that all negotiation experts recommend.

The ability to share and edit official contract and license documentation in an online environment has also greatly enhanced the speed with which a negotiation can be completed. Face-to-face meetings and messy, marked-up, faxed contracts are no longer the status quo. While email communications can seem immediate, thus adding to the speed with which a negotiation can take place, it is important to note that email, at its heart, is a form of asynchronous communication. Just imagine taking the last phone conversation you had with a vendor and, instead of having the discussion immediately, leaving each statement made as a series of "phone tag" voicemail messages. It would be infuriating, but email can function like phone tag in a negotiation. One question gets answered and another is raised until you have a monstrous email thread covering days. Although technology accelerates modern life, it has its own way of slowing things down, as well. It is important to know when technology is an obstacle. Ultimately, while technology has significantly changed the way two parties negotiate in practice, it has not changed the underlying give-and-take of the process. The key is to make the technology work to your advantage.

Trust the Orange

Another recurrent theme in many of the most popular negotiation titles is the need for good negotiators to be open to creative solutions. Sometimes this just means discarding the idea that if my opponent is winning, I must be losing. This perception can be tough to shake, so authors often use stories or games to illustrate the power of creative solutions. One of these stories is the Parable of the Orange. The story goes that two people are negotiating for an orange that they both want. After much haggling, they finally agree to share the orange, with each getting half. The first person takes half of the orange, throws away the fruit, and keeps the rind to garnish some cocktails. The second person takes the other half, squeezes the juice into a glass, and throws the rind away. Both parties still wish they had gotten the whole orange instead of just half. The moral of the story is that if the two parties had focused on communicating their interest in the orange (the rind versus the juice) instead of focusing solely on their own position ("Give me that orange!"), both would have been able to get all that they wanted rather than settling for half.[2]

Although it is sometimes presented a bit differently, the parable teaches us to always look for instances of mutual gain. Roger Fisher and William Ury, authors of the seminal book on negotiation, *Getting to Yes*, see inventing "options for mutual gain" as key to any negotiation and have defined a four-step process for identifying mutual gain opportunities. The first step is to avoid "premature judgment" of the ideas being offered.[3] This is where brainstorming comes into play. Typical brainstorming sessions can involve a fair amount of evaluation of the ideas being offered, so the key to looking for mutual gain involves setting some ground rules, such as welcoming all ideas. Rare is the librarian who has not encountered the "negative Nelly" colleague—the person in any committee meeting or brainstorming session who is highly critical and seems ready to sabotage any new idea. Shapiro and Jankowski, authors of *The Power of Nice*, remind readers that remaining open to ideas and trying to have fun are key elements of any creative endeavor, including brainstorming sessions.

The ideal environment for brainstorming is one in which all participants feel free to suggest ideas without concern for how plausible they might be; that is, without wondering whether the other party would agree to them. In other words, ban the phrase "They will never agree to that." If you think a simple ban may be ignored, set up an electronic suggestion box, a Word document in a networked location, or maybe an online survey where interested parties can contribute ideas without fear of having them shot down. As any blog reader will tell you, people will type things they would never say aloud, but this tendency can work to your advantage when brainstorming. Since participants are not being asked to critique the ideas but merely to come up with them, there is greater likelihood that a creative solution may emerge from the brainstorming process.

What kind of a creative solution merits further attention? The second step in Fisher and Ury's process is identifying those brainstorming ideas that expand available options instead of forcing a particular solution. This broadening of options, or "increasing the pie," is where creative thinking becomes really important. For example, if your users have come to you with the desire for new services or longer hours, it can be tempting to imagine your negotiation ending in either offering new services or not. This binary approach is limiting. Rather than asking "Can we?," the questions should be: "What are our users really asking for? What is the real problem? What are the ways that we could fill this need (including giving the users what they have asked for)?" In fact, in the case of negotiating with your user community or library staff, you might even have an opportunity to brainstorm with your users, or opponents, as it were. The idea of offering an electronic suggestion box to your users might be a little scary at first, but sometimes even the angriest anonymous comment can contain the kernel of a good idea. In these situations, staff and users can benefit from understanding the librarian's or administration's side of the issue, and they can also feel encouraged and satisfied by their involvement in the solutions that result from the process.

This leads to Fisher and Ury's third step in the process—the search for mutual gain. Let's say, for example, your users want to send chat and text message reference questions in addition to asking questions at the physical reference desk and over the phone. This proposition can seem like a zero-sum game. Either the librarians have to provide a new service in addition to their reference desk duty or users have to make do with the existing services provided. However, ultimately both librarians and users want the same thing—excellent point-of-need service that is convenient for users regardless of what technology is used. This leaves the door open to an opportunity for mutual gain.

One possible solution is to take the librarians off the reference desk and have a paraprofessional staff the desk instead who make referrals to librarians when necessary. This releases the reference librarians from staffing the desk while at the same time leaving them available to answer any chat or text message questions, as well as referrals from the reference desk. Library administrators may need to tinker with this solution and evaluate statistics to determine times that demand more than one librarian, but in the best-case scenario, the users get the services they desire, and the librarians shift their workload without necessarily increasing it. This is one example of how shared interests can lead to solutions that benefit both parties. In fact, this solution may lead to additional improvements in the triage of reference services, with paraprofessionals answering routine chat and text message questions and librarians focusing on difficult queries. In this case, instead of ending, the negotiation gets set aside as new information and ideas become available. Technology can be both the problem and the solution, which is not an uncommon circumstance for many librarians.

The fourth step in Fisher and Ury's process is to "make their decision easy." This is where understanding the other side's point of view comes in handy. Present your solution in terms that not only make sense to the other party but also appeal to that party's sense of fairness and legitimacy. This part of the process involves selling to a certain extent, but the idea is simple: Show your offer in the best possible light so that your opponent will have fewer reasons to turn it down.[4]

Ask Questions

To show possible solutions in the best light, you have to know what the other side is all about. The easiest way to learn more about those on the other side of the table is to ask them pertinent questions, but the answers are not always as forthcoming as one would like. That's why, in the hierarchy of important negotiation skills, the ability to ask good questions (and really listen to the answers) is second only to preparation. Jim Camp, author of *Start With No*, sees asking questions as paramount to developing as a negotiator. Camp recommends sticking to interrogative-led questions.[5] These kinds of questions tend to be open-ended and leave lots of room for your opposite numbers to disclose information about their situation and their goals. This is where listening skills come in. Shapiro and Jankowski agree with Camp and offer their own technique for probing, called WHAT.[6] This is where librarians' reference interview skills come in very handy. Look at the other side as your patron and ask the same kinds of useful and clarifying questions that you would use to get to the bottom of research needs. Sure, your opponent may be reluctant, but so are many patrons.

The "W" in the WHAT technique stands for *what, what else, which,* and *why*—in short, all those good words that reporters use to dig into a topic. When the other side takes a position, don't make a counteroffer or disagree with that assessment of the situation. Simply ask why a certain aspect of the offer is warranted or appropriate, or what else might be included in a deal to make it more attractive. For example, if a vendor quotes a price you find absolutely ridiculous for a new database, use the quote as an opportunity to ask how the price was calculated, considering the less expensive resources available. If a content provider offers a less-than-transparent pricing and access model, be sure to ask how the company arrived at that model. For example, an ebook vendor offers unlimited simultaneous users for each ebook purchased by the library. However, for each ebook, the library can only "loan" the item a total of 325 times in a 12-month period. A loan is a 24-hour period and is incurred after a user interacts with the ebook for more than 10 minutes. If the user interacts for 11 minutes and then exits the ebook, the period is still considered one of the 325 loans. How did the vendor arrive at the 10-minute limit? Was it based on user research? Was it a best guess? Is it negotiable?

The "H" stands for *hypothesize* and encourages the reader to offer hypotheticals that provide a chance to probe in a nonthreatening, noncommittal way. When asked to make budget cuts to an already skintight bottom line, use the opportunity to suggest a series of hypothetical budget and service adjustments in order to test the waters and see which options might be the best-received by staff and administrators. Using a spreadsheet can make it easy to compare various scenarios, as well as make it clear up front that you are not committing to any of the scenarios.[7]

The "A" stands for *answers* and reminds us that "the best answers are questions. They lead to more answers."[8] For example, if a vendor asks what cost increase is acceptable for a product, instead of answering, ask what the standard cost increase is for peer institutions.

The "T" stands for *Tell Me More*. Be sure to take the time to listen to answers you have been provided and see where you are still lacking info. In those areas, ask "Tell Me More About…"[9] This probing technique may prove particularly useful if the other side seems reluctant to share information or engage in much discussion, as sometimes happens with public library boards and university administrations. Developing a low-pressure, high-question style can lead to more information than you might normally collect. The best way to collect all this new information is to listen—really listen—and, if you find it difficult not to respond, focus on your note taking. As Camp explains, "note taking removes us from our world and keeps us in our adversary's world. The simple act of picking up the pen or pencil moves us in that direction. As we take notes, our concentration is automatically focused on what is being said."[10] Not only is it a great way to focus on the speaker, it also keeps you busy and alert.

Camp also recommends asking questions multiple times or asking the other side to restate a position.[11] The goal is not to speak too quickly after your opponent has spoken. Be comfortable with silence; your opponent might not be and may seize the opportunity to tell you more about the situation. Not only can the silence allow you a moment to clarify your thoughts, but it can also lead to further disclosures. The last and possibly most useful aspect of asking good questions is that you will be so busy asking, listening, and taking notes that you will disclose only the information you desire to disclose and won't give away too much about your own situation.

Here, too, technology has enhanced our ability to ask questions and listen closely to the answers. In email negotiations, parties can carefully craft both questions and answers and use Sent Mail folders as a second set of ears and hands to keep good notes. Other tools for sharing, commenting, and tracking changes in programs such as Adobe Acrobat and Microsoft Word allow us to take and share notes on the documents themselves.

What's the Alternative?

It is easy to sit in negotiations and think, "This deal has to work! We don't have an alternative." However, this is usually not the case. It is extremely important for a negotiator to recognize that every negotiation has options. Look for what the best possible alternative would be to making a deal. This is the BATNA, and it acts as an alarm bell, warning a negotiator that it might be time to walk away from a negotiation. A BATNA is used in lieu of a bottom line, which can often be too rigid and uninformed by what is learned during a negotiation. For example, if your bottom line is the maximum amount of money you can pay for something, it might force you to walk away from a deal that will save you money in the long run but doesn't meet your bottom line. Instead of saying "This is as low or as high as we can go," figure out the best thing you could do if this deal falls through.[12]

For example, you are in negotiations with a publisher to receive a collection of science ejournals. You know how much you can afford for these titles, and you know the standard license terms your library asks of all vendors and publishers; however, this particular publisher is known for restrictive license terms and high list prices that are well above your suggested price. Before going into negotiations, you may want to determine that your BATNA would be the costs associated with setting up a pay-per-view document delivery service with the publisher or a third-party service. Document delivery would allow users to have access to the titles, but it likely won't be as simple as the click-to-full-text option offered in a site license with the publisher. Fisher and Ury see developing a BATNA as key to going into negotiations confidently. They suggest that a negotiator's power increases in direct proportion to the negotiator's comfort with not reaching an agreement.[13] The better your BATNA, the easier it will be to tell the difference between a good deal and a bad one.

Make an Offer

Many negotiation books differ sharply on when to make an offer. Most agree that you should never make the first offer, although one wonders how negotiations ever move forward if no one makes the first move. More important than not making the first offer is not accepting the first offer! All too often, librarians are quoted a price and begin their internal discussions based on that price without ever questioning the rationale for it or discussing ways to make the deal more palatable (much less proposing an alternative price). Shapiro and Jankowski remind us that "Much is lost for want of asking."[14] As in the brainstorming process, don't be overly critical of your counteroffer. Consider it a jumping-off point without making it insulting. If a publisher bases the price for a discipline-specific collection of eresources on the entire full-time equivalent (FTE) of your constituency, ask whether the price can be based on the relevant FTE subset instead. For those paralyzed by fear of insulting their opponents or appearing naïve, remember that you can use technology to your advantage. Sending an email explaining your institution's tight budget and asking whether 10 percent, 15 percent, or maybe 20 percent could be knocked off the list price saves you from actually having to say the words and gives the opponents an opportunity to "play the good guy." The worst they can say is no.

One thing that can poison the offer–counteroffer process is the appearance of neediness or, in other words, the appearance that you will take any deal offered as long as you get the product. Camp recommends going into negotiations with a blank slate: no expectations, no assumptions.[15] While this approach may seem a little unrealistic for most of us, it's best to go in without the baggage of past deals or of desperation. Neediness is frowned upon because it can kill leverage. *Leverage* is one of those words that scare people away from negotiations, but Richard Shell, author of *Bargaining for Advantage*, clarifies this concept beautifully. He argues that leverage is inversely proportional to how much one has to lose. In other words, if you don't have much to lose, you can leverage like Archimedes.[16]

Librarians often see themselves as leverage losers in many situations dealing with outside entities (vendors, publishers), but this point of view ignores an important point: Unless a publisher has a large consumer market for a product, libraries represent the publisher's biggest and most desirable customer. Once librarians take into account the increasing number of resources available on the open web, we can see the leverage scales shifting in our favor. In other situations where librarians feel they lack any significant amount of leverage, such as in negotiation with funding agencies, the situation itself could breed leverage. For example, in times of tight budgets, library directors and deans usually have more access to administrators and budget makers. This access can be an opportunity to make deals for future projects or allocations once budgets rebound. Sacrifices made now can lead to windfalls later, and in organizations where it can be hard to get a seat at the table, the ear of the administration can be an advantage all its own. Remember that recognizing and gaining leverage is only one aspect of negotiation and a constantly changing one.

Know Thyself

Much is made of personal style when it comes to the literature on negotiation. This is often where librarians tend to feel at a disadvantage, believing that they don't possess the natural skills of a negotiator. Many authorities on negotiation use a scale of conflict-management styles to classify negotiators—Avoiders, Compromisers, Accommodators, Competitors, and Problem-Solvers. A multitude of assessment tools exist (e.g., Thomas Kilmann Conflict Mode Instrument, or TKI; Kraybill Conflict Style Inventory, or KCSI; Myers-Briggs Type Indicator, or MBTI) to help you determine where you fall on this scale, but regardless of where you fall, Shell recommends not fighting it: If you are by nature accommodating, don't try to become a shark, and vice versa. Instead, make peace with the image in the mirror and work toward "using the style you have more effectively."[17] Successful negotiators come in all shapes and sizes.

For example, let's say your natural style tends to be heavy on avoidance of conflict, making negotiation your worst nightmare. Although you feel changes to your library's food and drink policy are warranted, you aren't sure how to start the negotiations with your colleagues. You can avoid actual confrontation by focusing on the facts and collecting as much persuasive data as possible; data that will not only bolster your position but also counter some of the arguments you expect your colleagues to make. When it comes time to sit down, look at the situation as less of a negotiation and more the report of a fact-finding mission. Present your findings and let your colleagues come to the logical conclusion that you desired. Negotiation won, without even throwing a punch.

When it comes to negotiation styles, a team approach can also come in handy. Inviting colleagues with different negotiating styles to join the team allows different members to step forward when a particular style is needed. It also means that the team will need to discuss which approach is warranted and when, a discussion that may require more preparation and practice before heading to the table. Camp takes a slightly different tack, believing that it is your opponent's sense of well-being more than your personal style that will determine how well a negotiation proceeds. Suppose your opponents feel that things are going well and that they are in control of the situation. This can work to your advantage, so you need to do what you can to keep them that way. Camp calls this "the Columbo effect" and suggests that "the wise negotiator knows that only one person in a negotiation can feel okay. ... By letting your adversary be a little more okay, you start to bring down barriers."[18] A caveat is warranted here. Being a little like Columbo, or, in other words, giving your opponent the impression that you are less prepared than you really are, can seem a little disingenuous and could leave the other party feeling tricked, or worse, like an enemy, which does not achieve the good working relationship that will lead to future successful negotiations. In other words, don't break out your trench coat and cigar just yet.

Regardless of its effectiveness as a strategy, the Columbo approach can teach us something important about the kind of questions and careful listening that most experienced negotiators recommend. Asking questions can give your opponents the impression that you don't have as much information as they do, while at the same time helping you to see the situation as they see it. This approach can also take advantage of some of the natural feelings that an inexperienced negotiator might feel. As Rob Walker points out in his article on negotiation tips, "One of the things that makes us feel weak as negotiators—and it's those of us who feel weak that are likely to go looking for advice—is the sense that the other side has more information than we do."[19] If you feel that way, you can use it to your advantage by honing your questioning skills.

You can also use the Columbo effect without feeling fake or unethical when negotiating with a new employer. Both before accepting an offer and after beginning your tenure with a new organization, you may have many opportunities to question policies and practices, claiming legitimate ignorance of the organization. Your colleagues shouldn't feel threatened by the inquiry, and you may be able to ascertain the origins of and reasoning behind a policy you may be interested in changing.

Win–Win or Don't Lose

The term *win–win* has become part of our popular culture, and therefore it is easy to go into negotiations thinking that this type of solution should be your ultimate goal. You might be surprised to know that not all negotiators think win–win is such a great idea— at least not as a sole guiding principle. Sadly, the idea of achieving a win–win deal runs counter to most negotiations. Fisher and Ury observe that "no talk of 'win–win' strategies can conceal that fact: you want the rent to be lower; the landlord wants it to be higher. ... Such differences cannot be swept under the rug."[20] Other experts firmly believe that win–win isn't even a desirable goal. Camp argues that focusing on a win–win solution breeds mediocrity— prizing any deal more than the best possible deal. To Camp's way of thinking, looking for the win–win is a step on the wrong foot. "Negotiating under the banner of win–win, you'll have no way of knowing if you've made good and necessary decisions leading up to the compromise."[21]

Shapiro and Jankowski hedge a bit on the win–win concept by recognizing that "in reality, we're out to achieve all (or most) of our goals, to make a desirable deal. But the best way to do so is to let the other side achieve some of their goals, to make their acceptable deal. That's WIN–win: big win for your side, little win for theirs."[22] Shell spends less time criticizing the win–win approach and more identifying what kind of traps can lead a win–winner down the wrong path. Shell warns of consistency traps, in which your opponent seeks to get you to agree with a series of statements ("You want your users to have access to the most journals possible, right? You want to save money on ejournal subscriptions, right?"). Then the logic trap snaps, and suddenly you feel as if you have to say exactly what they want you to say ("Currently, you are spending $10,000 with us for 10 ejournals, but for just $5,000 more we will give you access to 30 more ejournals. That's quite a deal, isn't it?"). Suddenly, you are signing a contract and you aren't entirely sure just what it is you purchased and whether you got your money's worth, because you got caught in a trap.

As Shell puts it, "You are logically committed to say 'yes.' You have to invent some new reason or excuse to say 'no.'"[23] The fact that you got caught in their logic trap doesn't make this deal inherently bad. You may find those ejournals to be very appropriate and valuable for your collection. The problem is that the trap attempts to obligate you before you have had a chance to investigate all aspects of the deal. There are always questions to ask. Are the extra 30 journals anything you would normally purchase? Do they support programs that you have? Are there any restrictions on the use of these 30 journals that would cause the original 10 to lose value for your users? Is there anything in place to keep them from jacking up the price next year? The year after that? Before you can say yes to this deal, take advantage of available time to ask pertinent questions and hear the answers that can determine whether the deal is in line with your interests and goals. Those 30 new ejournals could include the *European Journal of Fish Eyeball Dissection, Part A, Part B, Part C,* and so forth.

The biggest pitfall of the win–win approach is that it can, at times, prize relationships over getting a good deal. Sacrificing your interests in order to be liked by your opponent is almost never a good idea. Yes, relationships are important, but there is no benefit to a relationship if you are getting taken to the cleaners again and again. One relationship trap to avoid is a reciprocity trap. Shell describes this as "people who make small concessions and then ask for much bigger ones in return."[24] ("We've got the air-conditioning in the reference room fixed so it's no longer 87 degrees in there. In return, we think it would be only fair for the reference librarians to staff the reference desk until 1 AM instead of closing at 10 PM. OK?") Similarly, beware of those who reveal a little information of their own and then ask you to disclose some information too, but then get offended that you won't spill everything you know. Good relationships are important and should not be underestimated, but they are not your only goal.

Tricks Are for Kids

Like just about any other skill, becoming a good negotiator takes time and practice. The advice provided by the experts cited in this chapter is designed to put you in the negotiator mindset and alert you to your own strengths and weaknesses. No matter how much any of these authors tout their abilities to turn you into a top-notch negotiator, they all admit that there are no magic tricks to negotiating. In fact, the two most consistent pieces of advice they provide (other than to read their books) are to be confident in your skills and to practice at every opportunity. Practice may not make you perfect, but it will let you go to sleep at night knowing that you did all you could to get the best possible deal. Most readers who open a book on negotiation would like to finish the book transformed, but instead of a transformation of yourself, a more realistic goal might be a transformation of your perspective. Ignorance breeds fear, and, let's face it, library schools are not noted for teaching negotiation. So take the time to get up-to-date on what the experts say about negotiation. It can be just the thing to make negotiation anxiety a thing of the past.

Endnotes

1. Ronald Shapiro and Mark A. Jankowski, *The Power of Nice: How to Negotiate So Everyone Wins—Especially You!* (New York: Wiley, 1998), 104–105.

2. Rob Walker, "Take It or Leave It: The *Only* Guide to Negotiating You Will Ever Need," *Inc.* 25, no. 8 (August 2003): 77.

3. Roger Fisher and William Ury, *Getting to Yes: Negotiating Agreements Without Giving In*, 2nd ed. (New York: Penguin Books, 1991), 76, 100.

4. Ibid., 11, 57.

5. Jim Camp, *Start With No: The Negotiating Tools That the Pros Don't Want You to Know* (New York: Crown Business, 2002), 104.

6. Shapiro and Jankowski, 126–127.

7. Ibid., 128.

8. Ibid., 129.

9. Ibid., 131.

10. Camp, 151.

11. Ibid., 124.

12. Fisher and Ury, 101.

13. Ibid., 102.

14. Shapiro and Jankowski, 161.

15. Camp, 142.

16. G. Richard Shell, *Bargaining for Advantage: Negotiation Strategies for Reasonable People* (New York: Viking Penguin, 1999), 104–105.

17. Ibid., 9.

18. Camp, 37.

19. Walker, 77.

20. Fisher and Ury, 81.

21. Camp, 9.

22. Shapiro and Jankowski, 5.

23. Shell, 46.

24. Ibid., 73.

Chapter 2

Negotiation Advice From Library Leaders and Vendors

Negotiating is one of the most important skills a librarian can have. Unfortunately, library schools do not uniformly teach the art of negotiation, so many librarians remain woefully unprepared to engage in negotiations. Peter Brantley, on his Thoughts and Speculations blog (www.peterbrantley.com), identifies the ability to effectively negotiate and renegotiate contracts as one of the necessary elements of the successful reshaping of libraries. Brantley goes so far as to say, "Where significant contracts must be re-negotiated … frankly, librarians make poor businessmen and worse negotiators. Acquisitions—the business part of it—should be removed from libraries and placed into central campus purchasing units. … Move the most critical staff—the ones with the most expert or specialized knowledge of vendors—to central campus units and terminate the remaining positions."[1]

Before any acquisitions librarians start packing up their desks, however, they should know that skillful negotiation is something they can learn. In addition, understanding library collections and library users is not something that can be easily transferred to a campus purchasing department and, in fact, could lead to worse deal making when the negotiator doesn't fully understand the interests he or she is trying to represent. This is particularly true when one is negotiating for complex digital resources and services, and A-level expertise is required in order to evaluate and choose the best possible resources and prices, as well as to understand the licensing terms needed to make resources useful and sustainable. In short, a balance needs to be struck. Taking a page from nonlibrary purchasing departments and possibly even involving their unique expertise in the process under the library's direction, could give the library negotiator an advantage—a new member of the team with a different perspective and style.

When it comes to preparing librarians to make good deals, the possibilities for improvement are endless. One of the best ways librarians can begin learning is to listen to industry leaders' perspectives on the current negotiation environment. Chapter 1 cited experts who were master negotiators from outside the library profession. For this chapter, we interviewed vendors, content providers, consortium directors, subscription agents, licensing experts, and librarians to broadly map the negotiation landscape. Each one provided individual slants on fundamentally consistent advice and insights. Most of the comments centered on negotiation for digital content, tools, or services, which is what we traditionally think of when negotiation enters a conversation. However, remember that we engage in all types of negotiation all the time—with user communities; with employees, co-workers, and employers; with funding agencies; with administrators; and more. This chapter will focus on negotiation for digital content, tools, and services, but the lessons learned may apply well beyond these arenas.

Before You Get to the Table ...

First and foremost, almost all the people interviewed advised librarians not to be frightened of negotiation. Without much training in this area, librarians may feel a certain fear of the unknown, but this unknown area is knowable. Librarians charged with negotiation responsibilities must invest in continued training and education—even if their institutions do not overtly support such endeavors. Within the library community, resources, texts, workshops, webinars, and preconferences address negotiation issues, most often in terms of licensing. (See Appendix B for continuing education resources.) The increasing number of online education opportunities also means you can access a wealth of information

Advice From an Expert: Fiona Fogden, Part I

Online Subscription Contract Checklist

It is easy to check a contract to see if it works for your organization and how you want to use it, but what about what the contract does not contain? It is not always possible to get the terms in a contract changed, and you may not be the person to sign the contract, but that doesn't mean reading the contract is unnecessary. It may be that the contract forbids the use of the information in a way that is crucial to your organization. Take into consideration whether the product is aggregated material or content owned by the publisher; this will give you an indication of how easy it might be to get terms changed.

What constitutes the contract?

With an online subscription, the contract can come in many parts; these different parts make up the entire contract. For example, there may be an order schedule, followed by a section of terms and conditions, followed by an appendix, which might encompass a set of agreed variations or details on the charges. It is not unusual for one of these items to be left out, so check that you have everything, and if what you are reading refers to another document, make sure you are happy with the contents of that document, too. A trend becoming more common in these contracts is a reference to web terms. These will also form part of your agreement. Be sure to keep digital or print copies of these terms for future reference.

What to do before reading the contract:

- Be aware of your organization's policies. For example, does your organization have a standard contract you would prefer over the publisher's contract?

- If the contract you are negotiating is a renewal, check on what was discussed last time.

- Have an idea of the prices.

- Talk to the stakeholders or users of the product about how they want to use it, and make a clear note of any preferences. If necessary, ask them questions such as the following:

- Where do you want to use this product?

- Who needs to use the product?

- How does the content from the product need to be disseminated?

When to read a contract:

- If this is the first contract with a particular vendor, it is essential that you read it before the commencement of any subscription.

- There is no hard and fast rule about whether you read the contract before negotiating the price or after, but if you negotiate the price before, always make it clear that the price you have agreed to is subject to the contract's being suitable to your needs.

- Read the contract several times, preferably on different days, as it is very easy to miss things.

Who should read the contract:

- All of the people involved in the negotiation should read the contract.

- Your organization may have a nominated legal advisor who should be involved; check your organization's procedures.

- If you will not be one of the users of the product, involve a user, perhaps asking the user to read the permissions section of the contract.

Since June 2008, Fiona Fogden has been the national information services manager for Baker Tilly, the seventh-largest tax and accountancy firm in the U.K. Prior to that, she was the library and information centre manager at the London office of Baker & McKenzie, LLP. As Fiona Durrant, she published Negotiating Licences for Digital Resources *(Facet Publishing, 2006). When asked what advice she would give to information professionals looking to improve their negotiation skills, she offered the preceding checklist.*

without the time and expense of travel. A librarian completely new to negotiation should invest in education and explore possible mentoring relationships to remedy a lack of skill. Mentors might come from a given user community or institution, or the librarian might need to reach out to state or regional consortium directors or employees. The online environment has made these relationships easier to strike up, particularly for those who may be the sole librarian at an institution. Sue Medina, former director of the Network of Alabama Academic Libraries, advised, "Read, learn, ask for advice. ... Abandon your generous 'I am here to help you' librarian personality and adopt 'It's my money and I am not spending it.'"

When asked for advice on helping librarians learn to negotiate, one librarian commented that the question itself could indicate worrisome problems for the organization. She noted that it may not serve an institution well to assign a green librarian the task of negotiating *all* aspects of a contract. Contracts are, after all, legal documents that require serious thought and review. Unfortunately, all too often negotiation and licensing are viewed as "add-on" responsibilities, rather than core tasks, and are shifted to someone who might not be the best person for the job. Institutions should appoint librarians who have the negotiation skills necessary to get better contracts, better prices, and improved vendor relationships. Chapter 7 explores these issues of workflow.

On the other hand, another librarian noted that involving too many people in a negotiation process can make it a Byzantine endeavor that gobbles up excessive time. This is one area in which technology can actually exacerbate a problem. Anyone who has ever had extensive committee discussions via email knows that they can often take much longer than if the interested parties met face to face. In the case of a large negotiating group or workflow, the librarian is often caught in between the vendor or publisher with whom they are working and a variety of institutional stakeholders, which may include legal and purchasing offices (whose staffs may have signatory authority), and internal library business offices. In short, the internal negotiation process among all the involved parties should not take more time and energy than the external negotiation for which you are preparing. In these situations, effective communication (within the library and within the institution as a whole) becomes the key to improving negotiations and streamlining processes. In a large, complex organization, a simple face-to-face meeting of librarians, purchasing agents, and general counsel can promote confidence in each party, reduce duplication of effort, and contribute to effective and uniform communication with the vendor or publisher.

Regardless of who handles negotiation and licensing within an institution—and it varies widely—introductory or continuing education is essential. Beyond the library community lies a mountain of resources, including training opportunities devoted to the art and skill of negotiation. When asked about his advice for librarians new to negotiation, John Cox of John Cox Associates emphasized that negotiation is, after all, often a quasi-commercial activity. Tapping the commercial sector for training makes sense. Just a quick Google search for *negotiation training* yields many viable options. Using the resources developed for the commercial sector also acculturates librarians to an environment that, in many ways, differs greatly from "library land." While it may seem obvious that libraries are interested in giving away information and vendors and publishers are interested in selling it, it behooves both partners to learn the native dances of the other. At one vendor presentation, for example, a representative presented the price structure of an ejournal package for the coming year, a price significantly higher than in years past. The representative attempted to soothe the librarian audience by explaining that it was the representative's job to go back to the vendor and negotiate on the library's behalf. This tactic represents a fundamental lack of understanding. It is not the representative's job to negotiate on our behalf. It is the representative's job to sell us the product. It is our job to negotiate for the best possible business and license terms. This type of misunderstanding can be avoided if librarians take advantage of resources to help them grow as negotiators.

Advice From an Expert: Fiona Fogden, Part II

Considering the Contract

If you are looking at a contract for the first time, have a red pen ready to mark up what you want to clarify, what you consider unfair, or what you consider incorrect. This way, if you have to review the basic contract again in future years, at least you will be able to tell whether you are looking at the original or the one you managed to get amended. The following are contract terms to consider:

- *What are you being given access to?* Is it what you understood you were getting access to? For example, if you subscribe to only part of a multimodular collection, what happens if someone tries to access other areas? Is access automatically blocked? Can the user view the link but not access it? Or are extra charges automatically made?

- *Who is being given access?* Is it one named user? Is the "you" defined, and does the definition match whom you want to have access? What about people off-site or working from home?

- *How can the material be used?* This is usually key to the value of the contract. Can the material be disseminated to third parties? If you plan to use a federated search, are there clauses preventing this type of use?

- *What is the equality of the contract?* Is the contract fair to both sides, or does it favor one party? Remember, publishers have to protect their interests, too.

- *How does the contract cope with change?* How does the contract address issues such as major changes in content, a merger of your organization with another, or a merger of a vendor with another vendor? Is a take-down clause included, which takes into account compensation for the removal of key content? What if the publisher changes its model of business, such as a subscription web paper becoming a free one? Can you get a pro rata refund?

- *What is the duration of the contract period?* Is it a multiyear deal?

- *Are there notice periods?* Are you required to notify the publisher within a certain time frame of any desire to cancel, for example?

- *What are the liabilities and penalties?* Usually these sections are formalities, but check that there are no unfair liabilities. Some contracts have been known to include penalties if a subscription is not renewed, even if cancellation was done in time, calling the penalty a severance fee or something similar. Check that you do not have to carry out tasks that are too onerous, contradict your organization's policies, or conflict with the way you use other products. Some contracts have been known to require a subscriber to ensure that the vendor's product is marketed internally as the *preferred source* and that other products with similar content sets should not be marketed internally.

Besides focusing on what is in the contract, you also need to consider what has been left out. These omissions might include your rights if content is removed, training provisions, and the use of the product by telecommuters.

If an item in the contract just needs clarification and you are happy with the explanation, then keep the explanation (if you have it in writing) with the contract so that you have the full picture. If you need some wording changed, the changes may appear in the body of the terms and conditions, or they may take the form of a schedule of variations. If the latter, ensure that a provision of the contract states clearly that, if there are contradictions between the schedule and the terms and conditions, the schedule overrides the terms and conditions.

In the final phase of contract negotiation, make sure that you sum up in writing all that was agreed to with regard to the contract. This summary will give you a ready-made contents page for your contract, schedule of amendments, clarifications, and queries, all ready for when you need to do it again next time.

Besides educating themselves, librarians can actually do a number of things to improve their chances of striking a good deal while simultaneously improving confidence in their negotiation skills. While it may seem that negotiations are won or lost at the negotiation table, an experienced negotiator knows that some of the most important work can take place before the scheduling of the first negotiation session.

The average library professional should have no problem following this first piece of advice: Do your research! Nondisclosure clauses in license contracts can make it difficult to get hard numbers on what other institutions may be paying for any given eresource or other product, but a wealth of information is available that can provide a strong foundation for any negotiation. This information includes basic data about a vendor's product line, current subscribers, and longevity in the industry, all of which is usually advertised freely on a vendor's website or librarian-created resource such as lib-web-cats, an international directory of libraries (www.librarytechnology.org/libwebcats). It is also critical to research and to know well the vendor's main sources of competition. Although other librarians will probably not be able to discuss the specifics of their license agreements, they may still be able to provide important insight into what support and training services could be negotiated into licenses to create added value. Often this information can be found by looking at blogs or listserv archives to review the buzz about certain products and vendors. Another avenue for research is the business library and accompanying business librarians—if you are not one yourself. Appendix A offers resources for specific information needs, but in general, proprietary databases such as Hoover's Online, Mergent Online, Business and Company Resource Center (Gale/Cengage), and Business Source Premier (EBSCO) are great places to start.

The research does not stop with digging up dirt on the vendor, as Barbara Quint explained in her 1997 article from the *Bottom Line*: "Know the operational detail and the future directions of what you and your clients need and desire. Identify your own organizational resources and analyze your ability to command or commit those resources."[2] Other forms of in-house research, such as cost–benefit analysis and trials, can keep librarians from entering needless negotiations just because a product sounds as if it could become an essential tool for a particular constituency.

In her 2006 *Information Outlook* article, Debbie Schachter counseled librarians to "consider 'just in case' versus 'just in time' decisions that limited budgets have forced libraries to make for a number of years."[3] The digital age has given libraries a much greater ability to react nimbly when it comes to acquiring resources just in time. Pay-per-view and document delivery increase a library's options for acquisition and allow for greater evaluation before a decision on permanent acquisition. Considering alternatives to acquisition, along with user needs and reactions, can help librarians create lists of "must-have" and "like-to-have" conditions for the license under negotiation. Coming to the table knowing what customers need, as well as what they would like, allows librarians to clearly identify deal breakers. Appendix A discusses how to do this kind of research.

Armand Brevig described another way to interpret the "be prepared" mantra in an October 2008 issue of *Searcher*, "Getting Value From Vendor Relationships."[4] Brevig emphasized the importance general negotiation literature places on "developing a good Best Alternative to a Negotiated Agreement (BATNA)," a term introduced in Chapter 1. He explained, "A BATNA basically identifies the point at which you would be better off not reaching an agreement, because the alternatives are more attractive." At its most effective, a BATNA is explored and agreed upon prior to any negotiations. Beyond its intrinsic value to librarians, BATNA is an example of the type of useful information found in nonlibrary negotiation literature.

Knowing thyself includes more than simply knowing what one wants. It also includes knowing thy organization and thy consortia. In some cases, you may not need a whole new license. Perhaps another unit within the institution already has a contract with a particular vendor for a particular resource. You may have to do a little investigating into departmental labs and purchasing departments, but as Sharon Srodin pointed out in her 2004 *ONLINE* article, "It is often easier (and cheaper) to add your group onto an existing contract rather than drawing up a new one from scratch."[5] Investigating whether a relevant consortium has a deal for a particular resource may seem like a routine step in the acquisition process, but don't overlook it. The sales representative may know of consortia that your institution can join. Chapter 3 discusses the crucial role that consortia play in the library negotiation landscape.

Before beginning a negotiation, examine your own policies and collection development criteria. Being well-versed in the limitations that library and institutional policies place on negotiations may take some guesswork out of the process. Kristine Kenney pointed out in a 2006 *Public Libraries* article that intimately knowing the processes that govern decision making at a particular library or institution gives the librarian an instant answer for an overanxious vendor who asks, "When can I expect an answer?"[6]

Every industry leader interviewed for this chapter, from the subscription agent to the vendor to the content provider to the librarian, resoundingly said that much of the work of negotiation happens before anyone gets to the table. Whether necessarily making a simple list of must-haves and can-do-withouts or creating a more comprehensive BATNA, librarian negotiators must always know what they want and what they need before entering any discussions. Librarians and vendors alike should know as much as they can about the other party. In the long run, this makes for a more even playing field and often a more productive and mutually beneficial agreement.

When to Hold 'Em ...

Once you have a critical mass of research about your organization and that of your opponent, it is time to negotiate, but first, don't call them your *opponent*. The best negotiations create an opportunity

Advice From an Expert:
Rick Anderson, Part I

Negotiating Price

Know that it's OK to negotiate price. Many of us in the library pro-fession aren't especially comfortable with haggling—the prospect of doing so isn't what attracted most of us to this career path, and it's something we rarely did in the print era. But as budgets tighten and patron expectations increase, it's more important than ever to get as much patron service as possible out of each budget dollar we're entrusted with. You may not be able to haggle over every individual journal subscription, but if you're renewing a journal package, a major database, or even a single big-ticket title, it's almost always worth telling the publisher that you want to discuss the price. Remember that this isn't a salary negotiation, in which the worst-case scenario is that the other side will decide not to hire you and walk away. The worst-case scenario in a price negotiation is that the publisher won't move, in which case you'll have to make a difficult purchase deci-sion but won't be any worse off than you were to begin with.

Don't apologize for negotiating. In some cases, your vendor will be surprised when you balk at prices or license terms and may even suggest that you're being unreasonable by doing so. Don't let yourself be intimidated in these cases; that reaction is a negotiation tactic. Explain why you're making an issue of the points under discussion, and repeat yourself as necessary. Sometimes you'll back down or compromise, of course, but always do so rationally and strategically.

Rick Anderson is associate director for Scholarly Resources and Collections at the University of Utah's Marriott Library. He has worked as a bibliographer for YBP, Inc.; as head acquisitions librar-ian for the University of North Carolina, Greensboro; and as direc-tor of resource acquisition at the University of Nevada, Reno. He writes a regular op-ed column for Against the Grain *titled "In My Humble (But Correct) Opinion," and his book,* Buying and Contracting for Resources and Services: A How-to-Do-It Manual for Librarians, *was published in 2004 by Neal-Schuman.*

for both sides to gain something from striking a deal and place neither party in a continual state of trying to abandon negotiations. Quint explains, "A clear perception by both parties of the mutual benefit inherent in the relationship will ensure the smooth and unbroken flow of information service that marks good library operations."[7] The mutual-gain negotiation also recognizes that the library–vendor relationship is a symbiotic one and not as one-sided as either party may perceive it. As Schachter reminds us, "The vendor's intentions are, yes, to earn money, but also to make you a satisfied customer—particularly when competition would only be happy to provide you with their services and products."[8]

As mentioned in Chapter 1, Roger Fisher and William Ury's seminal book on negotiation, *Getting to Yes: Negotiating Agreements Without Giving In*, can teach all librarians an important lesson in separating people from problems. In other words, the vendor or sales representative is not the problem; the deal is. Instead of automatically saying no to a provision in a license, a good negotiator will ask how or why a particular provision is needed or warranted. In a 2001 *Searcher* article, Seymour Satin advised, "Ask them [the vendor's reps] how they came up with the price and how they support it and move on from there. If you attack what they say, you put them on the defensive and they'll probably attack you back, and that gets you nowhere!"[9]

Fisher and Ury call this type of conversation *positional bargaining*, and their research suggests that it gets both parties nowhere fast.[10] Even when positional bargaining takes a more compromise-oriented approach, also known as *soft bargaining*, bad deals can often result. Kara Phillips explained in a 2006 article from *LLRX.com*, "Soft negotiations most often occur among family and friends when compromises are made to maintain relationships. This is problematic, however, because librarians who have long-standing dealings with a particular vendor may find themselves trying to avoid conflict by conceding too much and not communicating their interests."[11] This is when that list you created beforehand, stating your needs and wants in the negotiation, plays an important role. With both parties focusing on the terms of the license, it may prove easier to achieve workable compromises.

A mutual-gain situation does not mean that the parties each get everything they want. Ann Okerson, senior advisor on Electronic Strategies for the Center for Research Libraries and previously associate university librarian for collections and international programs at Yale University, recalls that "Isabella Hinds [a former vice president of publisher relations at the Copyright Clearance Center] used to say that a good negotiation is where both parties leave just a little bit unhappy. I thought this was very wise." Realistic expectations are a critical element to any negotiation—you can't always get what you want, but you might get what you need.

Asked his advice for new negotiators, Dan Tonkery, former vice president of business development, EBSCO Information Services, notes that it is important to recognize that nearly everything in a contract—price, terms, service—is negotiable. However, a critical word here is *nearly*. Remember that, in most situations, some requests or elements will immediately draw a red flag. Jane Burke, former vice president and general manager of Serials Solutions, comments that one of the few nonnegotiable elements is intellectual property: Any contract that takes actual ownership of intellectual property away from the vendor will become a deal breaker.

A good sales representative can become the librarian's greatest ally and source of leverage. As Quint wrote, "Your vendor rep can identify key players and key forces within [the rep's] organization. [Reps] may share the names of other purchasers for similar products and services. … Take advantage of the information and opportunities your vendor rep gives you, but protect them too. If they're good to you, make sure they never, ever look bad to their management."[12] Librarians often have key negotiating resources right under their noses. An institution's purchasing department specializes in deals, particularly the big, intimidating licenses that include lots of zeroes. Tapping existing expertise, as Srodin points out, can sometimes become the key to a successful negotiation. "Purchasing professionals specialize in the negotiation of corporate contracts. They have years of experience dealing with difficult vendors and it's their job to save the company money."[13]

Even with good reps and the proper approach, the price librarians are willing to pay can be much lower than the price vendors are willing to offer. But even this does not have to become a deal breaker. Look for ways to make the price more palatable. Sometimes this means multiyear deals with price caps to facilitate better budgeting and ensure the continuation of access over time. Sometimes adding additional months to the first-year price in order to synchronize renewals can be seductive enough to make signing that first contract feasible. There can be a tremendous amount of wiggle room when it comes to new deals; for a new deal, a sales representative may be open to making a variety of accommodations. As Srodin observed, "Vendors who are extremely inflexible with pricing might be more open to throwing in other services as part of the deal, such as free training, extra technical support, marketing materials or manuals."[14] However, there are times when a deal simply cannot be reached. That's when it is important to walk away.

Advice From an Expert: Rick Anderson, Part II

Pointers on Staying Strong

Don't be manipulated. If your sales rep uses guilt or sob stories to try to get you to buy a product, ask for a new sales rep. If your rep tries to discuss his or her sales goals with you rather than the needs of your library and its patrons, shut down that line of conversation politely but firmly. It's not your job to help sales reps reach their goals. Such behavior is rare, but many of us have experienced it at one time or another.

Pick your battles. Think in a rigorous and dispassionate way about how you spend your time and energy. The purpose of negotiating is to return maximum benefit to your patrons, not to make a point with your vendor, stick it to a publisher you don't like, drive down every price as low as possible, or show how tough and savvy you are. A basic rule of business is that "everything's negotiable." But that doesn't mean that every term and every price is worth the trouble of negotiating. Especially when dealing with license terms, go into the negotiation with a clear and solid understanding of what you can agree to (but would prefer not to) and what you can't (because of legal or institutional restrictions).

Keep it professional. Don't allow yourself to get personally offended by the fact that your vendor is trying to maximize its revenues or its contractual protections. After all, you're doing essentially the same thing for your side. In all of your communications during the negotiation, force yourself to be calm, reasonable, and gently assertive. This can be a real challenge if the vendor seems to be pursuing completely unreasonable prices or terms, but it's worth the effort. While a firm and even stern demeanor can be very effective, losing control is never appropriate and rarely productive.

And When to Fold 'Em ...

There are a number of ways in which negotiations can start on the wrong foot and head straight for an impasse. Even enthusiasm for a product can work against the negotiation process—not unlike the homebuyer who says "We love it!" at first glance. Satin warned, "You should never go into a negotiation and give up some vital piece of strategic information."[15] While this is not a call to be dishonest with a vendor, it is vital to maintain any existing advantages.

For example, time can be an advantage. Deal deadlines can loom large for nervous librarians. Resist the desire to "get this over with." Rushing the process can result in settling for less and making unnecessary concessions, a particularly dangerous situation if some of those concessions came from the must-have list. Quint reminds us, "Sometimes a protracted negotiating process may work to your advantage. The key is advantage. Wait 'til you get all the advantage you can and then use it effectively."[16]

Nothing threatens a librarian's ability to acquire advantage in a negotiation more than a defeatist attitude. Most librarians have been in a meeting or two (or 2,000) in which someone suggests a solution to a problem and is met with a resounding "That will never happen!" or "You're dreaming!" If the solution involved unicorns and a magical rabbit, then the group might have a point, but in a fair number of cases, it does not hurt to try. Take Quint's advice: "If you ever find yourself or your advisors and colleagues telling you that 'Well, they'll never give us that' or 'We shouldn't even ask for this,' blow the alarm siren. Never appear totally unrealistic in negotiation, but let the vendor prove why you can't have the unattainable."[17]

Careful preparation and strategy will still not guarantee you can reach a compromise. Librarians should never be afraid to walk away. "Purchase a resource only when you are comfortable that the deal meets all your library's needs and means. Step away from the negotiations whenever you feel uncomfortable, but keep the lines of communication open," recommends Kenney.[18] Medina and others emphasize the importance of being able to walk away—and the equal importance of walking away on friendly terms. Policies and priorities are constantly shifting; today's unreachable deal may become tomorrow's bargain opportunity. Keeping the door open to future offers is nearly always the path to follow.

Advice From an Expert:
Curtis Robinson

Knowing What You Want

When I've participated in coaching on negotiation, even for people meeting with congressional committees, I've often been shocked that people go into negotiations without a clear answer to this question: What is the desired outcome? No, really—what do you want? If your answer is "more money," then you've failed—how much more money, paid when? If the other side said,

"Okay, how much?" could you immediately answer? This is difficult for an individual, but if you're negotiating for an organization of any size, it's amazing how many different answers you can get—better pay or more job security? Health benefits or days off? If you don't do the hard work up front, then you negotiate without a foundation, and you end up "checking with your people" as part of the process, which extends time, erodes your position as the deal maker, and empowers the other side. Ask everyone involved, "What is the desired result?" Then ask that same question about the people on the other side of the table—do they really hate you and everything you stand for? Chances are, they have competing agendas. It's the most important question, but people "talk around it" all the time.

With more than 30 years of journalism experience, Curtis Robinson has launched more than 20 publications for some of the largest media companies in the U.S., including Harte-Hanks, Scripps-Howard, and Thomson. He is currently founding editor of the Portland (Maine) Daily Sun, *his fourth daily newspaper startup. He has personally negotiated more than 500 vendor contracts and pulled together startup companies in five states.*

We've Come a Long Way, Baby, But …

In terms of electronic resources, librarians and vendors alike have made much progress in learning about one another during the past 10 years. The digital age has raised so many questions about acquisition, access, sustainability, and preservation that negotiations have become increasingly complicated. Negotiating a contract a decade ago for an ejournal or eresource was a far different game from what it is today. Many of us have come to common ground on some initially difficult terms. Okerson notes, "We have solved a lot of licensing difficulties in the last decade; things that used to be hard to get are now fairly easy, like walk-in users." Rick Anderson, associate director for scholarly resources and collections, Marriott Library, University of Utah, comments, "These days most negotiations are not that difficult; almost every publisher now understands that out-of-state jurisdiction clauses, indemnification terms, and institutional liability for end-user behavior are simply not going to fly, and they don't try to push those kinds of terms the way they once did." There is so much common ground that the Shared Electronic Resource Understanding (SERU) initiative has been launched in an attempt to eliminate certain elements of licensing in certain situations. SERU is not meant to replace contracts or negotiation, only to reduce the burden on content providers and librarians alike. It attempts to address the "long tail"—the multitude of publishers with only a few titles. SERU is still in its infancy, and its effectiveness remains to be seen, but its very existence gives evidence of the continually improving relationships among librarians and vendors. SERU is discussed in more detail in Chapter 8.

Some areas, however, remain challenging. Okerson specifically describes three. The first is interlibrary loan or document delivery (ILL/DD). She explains, "One of the things that I think are still very difficult is [ILL/DD] done from the electronic version and transmitted electronically. Many of our licenses still do not permit this. Almost all permit ILL/DD, but you have to print or fax something. You can't just hit the Send button."

The second challenge is long-term access. According to Okerson,

> Most of our licenses say that access will be provided "in perpetuity," but many of us know that for many of our resources, there is no mechanism to facilitate such access. The publisher is happy to try to agree to this, and we are happy to sign it, but unless it is a really standard resource, like the major journals from major publishers, which may be included in Portico, LOCKSS, or a handful of other limited archives, there is no long-term access mechanism or third party provision. It is not difficult to agree to the license language, but it is difficult to have assurance that you will really get that long-term perpetual access. We are signing these things cheerfully, but the terminologies are hollow.

Librarians are not the only ones to find these license terms disturbing. Some vendors cannot commit to perpetual access simply because they do not own the rights to their content. John Tavaska, director of database licensing and vendor licensing, H.W. Wilson, a division of EBSCO Publishing, notes that librarians have become accustomed to asking for archival rights from publishers. What is doable for publishers and other content owners, however, can be more difficult for aggregators. Tavaska also notes that there has been an increase in the number of libraries that ask for similar archival rights for their aggregated database content, which companies such as Wilson cannot necessarily offer as they themselves do not always have archival rights to the content they provide.

The third—and seemingly eternal—challenge is price. Okerson notes that in all reality, publishers still do not have much flexibility when it comes to price. There are some options, as Okerson explains: "We know that if you can get groups of libraries together, such as … Network of Alabama Academic Libraries or OhioLink or … NorthEast Research Libraries consortium, you have a much better shot at getting flexibility. But even with consortia, the biggest publishers—the ones with the most essential resources—do not flex on price hardly at all."

The Digital Download on Pricing Structures

Some pricing structures for electronic resources are as transparent as mud. The pricing structures can be as simple as a scale based on flat full-time equivalent employees, students, other personnel, and so forth of your organization, or involve a multitude of variables. For those publishers that offer packages of their titles—for instance, to consortia—and then offer "access only" options for *all* of their titles, there is the cost of the package itself (usually discounted depending on whether you buy the "premium" package or some smaller subset) as well as the access fee.

To add another layer of complexity, some vendors structure the price of the access fee differently from the package fee. Perhaps the access fee is based on a library's usage, historical spend (amount spent on content in previous years), current spend, and Carnegie Classification of Institutions of Higher Education, which organizes schools by the level of research that is being conducted at the institution. The package fee, on the other hand, is based flatly on full-time equivalents. Additionally, if the contract is multiyear, it may stipulate (based on negotiations between the library and the publisher) a capped percentage increase, perhaps on the access fee, the package fee, or both.

These examples are single fish in an ocean of species. What is critical is that you ask questions if you do not understand. If the publisher or content provider is less than forthcoming, be polite but aggressive and insist that they explain, clearly, how they arrived at a given price.

Work with consortia and other library advocacy groups to lobby vendors for more transparent pricing schemas. One price will never fit all, but one should expect—and get—a rational and fair pricing structure.

Negotiation via consortia is a complex topic in and of itself. It requires a different skill set and a broader understanding of how to accommodate multiple interests. A well-run and organized consortium can be a powerful entity when it comes to negotiating for a group of libraries. When asked how consortia pricing and negotiations have improved or hurt librarians' abilities to negotiate, Medina explains, "Group buying power is a strong negotiating position. If the individual participants commit to stand with the group—and the group has significant buying power (not just dollars—marketing share, too)—this can be a powerful negotiation advantage. Being locked into a group offer can be limiting, especially if the group is for a product available from several vendors and your users prefer another vendor's enrichments." Both librarians and vendors should understand the business model for this type of commercial activity because consortia can play a number of roles for libraries.

Relationships among consortia must also be negotiated. Larger consortia with more staff might provide licensing or billing services for smaller consortia. Additionally, the consolidation of consortia is something to watch; time will tell how the megaconsortia, so to speak, will affect negotiations between libraries and vendors; more on this in Chapter 3.

One final aspect of negotiation and libraries that continues to evolve is the role of the subscription agent. What is the appropriate and most useful role for the subscription agent? Should subscription agents negotiate on the library's behalf? Anderson notes,

> Theoretically, we could give our agents a model license and ask them to use it as a template for negotiating with publishers on our behalf. But in practice, I doubt that's feasible. There will always be terms that we don't anticipate, there will always be exceptions, and there will be serious institutional resistance to making a third party (and a commercial one at that, one that has a vested interest in getting us to subscribe) an agent for our libraries. On the other hand, if we want to implement a non-license agreement such as SERU, vendors can help to put inertia on our side by presenting that preference to publishers on our behalf first, and making it easier for the publisher to simply accept the SERU agreement and move on than to push past it and negotiate their regular license with us. That could be a significant service.

In the end, no one party holds all the cards. Okerson comments that at times librarians do not realize how much negotiating power they do have, with the unfortunate result that a contract ends up containing elements—such as terms or price—not in the library's best interests. Cox echoed this notion and noted that librarians should not be frightened of the process. Cox went on to say that librarians should not hesitate to say "I don't know" at any point during the conversation. Taking the time to investigate, explore, or refer to someone else who might be able to provide an answer reduces the likelihood of "muddling through" a negotiation, which is not in the best interest of either party.

Ultimately, the best negotiators have two key qualities: patience and integrity. Believing that all parties are coming to the table in good faith and are willing to put in the time to broker the best possible deal can go a long way toward achieving success. No negotiation or deal is ever perfect, but being prepared for and savvy about the process can create far less doubt over whether you just bought some worthless swampland in Florida or an essential tool that your users will love.

Endnotes

1. Peter Brantley, "Libraries Re-shaping," Peter Brantley's Thoughts and Speculations, September 9, 2007, accessed July 22, 2011, blogs.lib. berkeley.edu/shimenawa.php/2007/09/09/libraries_re_shaping.

2. Barbara Quint, "Six Rules of Engagement: Negotiating Deals with Vendors," *Bottom Line* 10, no. 1 (1997): 4–10.

3. Debbie Schachter, "The Rules of Negotiation," *Information Outlook* 10, no. 9 (2006): 9.

4. Armand Brevig, "Getting Value From Vendor Relationships," *Searcher* 16, no. 9 (2008): 28+.

5. Sharon Srodin, "'Let's Make a Deal!': Tips and Tricks for Negotiating Content Purchases," *ONLINE* 28, no. 4 (2004): 17.

6. Kristine Kenney, "Negotiating With Vendors," *Public Libraries* 45, no. 5 (2006): 12.

7. Quint, 4–10.

8. Schachter, 8.

9. Seymour Satin, "Negotiating: From First Contact to Final Contract," *Searcher* 9, no. 6 (2001): 53.

10. Roger Fisher and William Ury, *Getting to Yes: Negotiating Agreements Without Giving In*, 2nd ed. (New York: Penguin Books, 1991), 5.

11. Kara Phillips, "Deal or No Deal—Licensing and Acquiring Digital Resources: License Negotiations," *LLRX.com*, November 22, 2006, accessed July 22, 2011, www.llrx.com/columns/deal2.htm.

12. Quint, 4–10.

13. Srodin, 18.

14. Ibid.

15. Satin, 54.

16. Quint, 4–10.

17. Ibid.

18. Kenney, 14.

Chapter 3

The Power and Pitfalls of Consortial Negotiation

In the face of the rising costs and complex licenses that accompany electronic resources, librarians have taken a variety of approaches to negotiating good deals with low bottom lines and a minimum of access restrictions. One of the ways in which librarians have been most successful in this pursuit is through the use of consortia. Consortial deals for resources—electronic and otherwise—offer a multitude of advantages, the nature and size of which may vary depending on the size and makeup of the consortium itself. As with any and all good solutions, there are also downsides to consortial negotiation. Enriched by the insights of some of the top consortial negotiators at work today, this examination of consortial negotiation should shed light on when to join the team and when to go it alone.

Welcome to the Price Club!

The process of purchasing resources through consortia has many similarities to the wholesale shopping club experience. Consortial negotiators represent a large group of libraries and consequently a large group of users. So when they look to purchase a resource, they are, in effect, buying in bulk, not unlike the buyers for a local price club. This has advantages, not only for the libraries within the consortium, but also for vendors looking to get their products out to the market in the most efficient way possible. As Anne McKee, program officer for resource sharing for the Greater

Western Library Alliance (GWLA), explained, "The more you can bring to the table, the better the publishers like it, and the greater the discount."

Ed McBride, who has worked with both consortia and vendors, remarked, "It represents a much larger piece of business for them [publishers or vendors,] so ... they are able to look at the picture as a whole, and in a lot of ways, come up with a better pricing structure. The more market share they can gain from a particular deal—especially if it is a multiyear deal—the better it is for them." On the other hand, McBride noted that not all publishers or vendors, particularly the smaller ones, are keen or even able to offer such discounted pricing for large groups of libraries.

The improved pricing that comes with consortial purchases has ramifications beyond any individual library budget. "A consortial agreement expands access in at least two ways: By negotiating lower prices and redistributing costs, it can make resources affordable for its smaller members; and by offering 'cross access' to content subscribed to by other member institutions, it can make available to each member far more content than would be possible in an individual agreement," according to Ivy Anderson, director of collection development and management for the California Digital Library.

Consortia can bring to the negotiating table those libraries that may never have gotten there on their own, meaning that there is no question of whether the price will be discounted; the only question is how big the discount will be. In a consortial negotiation, any deal struck will be better than list price. Joining a consortial deal relieves the individual librarian—especially an inexperienced one—of the bazaar-like activity of negotiation.

Of course, price isn't everything, though sometimes it feels that way. Unrealistic and draconian licensing terms can make a resource so difficult to manage and use that it is hardly worth the trouble, not to mention the price. Consortia can offer help in this regard as well. Kim Armstrong, deputy director of the Center for Library Initiatives at the Committee on Institutional Cooperation (CIC), explained that by representing a large number of libraries, consortia can push for the progressive licensing terms that many librarians seek. "We can't always predict 5 or 10 years out what is going to be a priority in a license, so we are able to help move along new terms that may not be standard yet in license agreements, but which are emerging for our libraries." Terms such as the right to interlibrary loan, the right to place materials on reserve or in course packs, or the right to deposit materials by an institution's faculty into institutional repositories represent just a few of the license terms that consortia have championed. Once a vendor or publisher has agreed to these terms with a consortium, individual libraries have no reason not to request and even expect the same terms.

Libraries ♥ Cooperation

Librarians are no strangers to cooperation, which made the creation of consortia a no-brainer, even before the popularity of eresources made consortial license negotiations prudent. As Rona Wade, executive director and chief executive officer for the UNIL-INC consortium in Australia, described in a 1999 *Library Consortium Management* article, a variety of groups developed throughout the 1980s with a desire for union catalogs, shared library systems, and reciprocal borrowing. It was not until the 1990s that the negotiation of licensing agreements became a larger part of library consortia's missions.[1]

Libraries often joined consortia for projects well outside the realm of resource acquisition. Librarians may find themselves with memberships in a variety of groups that may appear to have competing interests when it comes to striking resource deals for their members, not unlike subscription agents competing for library contracts. However, this sort of competition is not necessarily troubling. "I am most interested in getting the best price and the best terms and conditions for my libraries," said Terry Austin, coordinator of electronic resource licensing for the University of Missouri Library Systems. "I will check known consortia to meet that end. Likewise, if one of my libraries can do better with another consortium, then they should go that way."

The Digital Download
on Consortial Negotiation

The internet and its accompanying ocean of eresources have enabled libraries to form powerful bargaining consortia. The history of most successful consortia includes a chapter about librarians coming together to leverage the power of the internet and work collaboratively, initially to create a shared web-based catalog or a digital collection. Even consortial lending programs, which existed long before the digital revolution, have been improved in their efficiency and their scope through the use of the internet.

Consortia have really hit their stride in the digital age, and negotiating for digital content has become one of the ways in which they have made themselves essential to the library world. Consortia can push progressive licensing terms that digital innovations make necessary. Issues that never existed in the days before digital resources, such as perpetual access, have benefited from the advocacy of large consortia.

The leadership role that consortia have taken in the creation of digital repositories for their members could portend a future for consortia as content providers. The ramifications of consortia creating and storing unique digital collections have yet to be fully understood or determined. Consortia are well placed not only to assist in the negotiation of this licensing but also to manage the digital access for all partners.

The diverse origins of consortia often assist a library in deciding which group to join for a particular resource. The members of a consortium share a common understanding of the goals of the partnership. If a library belongs to a statewide consortium made up of public, school, and university libraries, the group's mission will dictate which resources to pursue on the members' behalf. If that same library also belongs to a consortium of college libraries with a similar population size and research level, it may expect an entirely different selection of resource deals. In essence, the consortial market diversifies naturally. When the interests of library consortia do intersect, there is certainly a possibility of competition. While some view this competition as healthy and important to keeping consortia working diligently for the best possible deals, others see it as counterproductive: "If the member can shop, it results in the vendor creating a more common and less advantageous offer across consortia," explained Tom Sanville, former executive director of the Ohio Library and Information Network (OhioLink) and now with LYRASIS, a library member organization created by the merger of several former OCLC regional service providers, including SOLINET, PALINET, and NELINET. "I think it's harder for any negotiator to arrange a significantly better or the best possible deal."

To be sure that consortia are not creating a secondary market on which vendors can play groups against each other, both libraries and consortia need to have a good idea of what each group brings to the table and attempt to create partnerships where possible. Big multiconsortia deals, while sometimes too complex for their ultimate value, offer an example of this interconsortium cooperation. Cynthia Clennon, director of electronic resources for the Consortium of Academic and Research Libraries in Illinois (CARLI), provided an example: CARLI purchases memberships to the Missouri Library Network Corporation, giving each CARLI library the ability to participate in any deals negotiated by the Network. McBride gave another example of this sort, noting that sometimes it works to LYRASIS's advantage to be able to bring more people via other, smaller consortia, such as the Network of Alabama Academic Libraries, to the negotiating table. "It does allow you to leverage more if you have multiple consortia in a deal," McBride added.

Levels of membership are key to providing libraries, vendors, and consortia with the opportunity to band together expediently, without long-term commitments. Greg Doyle, electronic resources program manager for the Orbis Cascade Alliance, represents 37 academic libraries in Oregon, Washington, and Idaho, but his prospective buying power also extends to a nonmember program of 50 to 60 libraries, each of which can participate in any given deal for a fee, if the vendor agrees. This arrangement provides the vendor with a larger audience for the product, the consortium with a larger pool of possible participants, and the libraries with opportunities they might otherwise miss out on because of their inability to join the Alliance. The variety of ways in which libraries can participate in consortial deals gives flexibility to the librarians, which can be critical in producing the best possible mix of budget-conscious acquisition practices and user-needed resources.

While librarians are keen to work together, it is critical that a consortium have transparent policies and unobstructed communication channels, as well as a clearly articulated mission. Mission statements force a group to determine why and if it is beneficial to come together. A loose affiliation of institutions with a fuzzy goal and no clear mission does not translate into a strong united front and makes it difficult, if not impossible, for the person doing the negotiating to broker a good deal. Poor internal communication among the board of directors or the membership at large can absolutely kill consortial negotiation. Likewise, poor infrastructure for billing and other business functions erodes librarians' and vendors' confidence in a given consortium.

Networks-vs.-Consortia Is Still Up for Debate

Many consortia directors and members have traditionally drawn a stark contrast between a network and a consortium. McBride stated in early 2009, "At one time, I would have agreed with that.

However, I think that what you are going to see in the profession over the next 12 months or less is that networks as we know them are fading away." The distinction between consortia and networks is often based on differences in funding and cost recovery. Any nonprofit group of libraries, whether a consortium or a network, must recoup its costs, and this is done in a number of different ways. The group can recoup via membership fees as well as other types of surcharges, commissions from vendors or publishers, or administrative fees.

The network system, according to McBride, was built in the 1980s on the premise of primarily supplying OCLC services and acting as a cooperative of sorts. In 2008 and 2009, the OCLC regional network system went through significant changes. The previous regional service provider model evolved so that regionals no longer provide the same sorts of OCLC services they once did. The end result is that the regionals have to reinvent themselves and negotiate with OCLC to agree on a different kind of mutually beneficial relationship. Some smaller statewide networks may cease to exist entirely while the larger ones try to create new services and opportunities.

"I have begun to start using the word *consortium* for [LYRASIS] because I think that we will in fact become a very large consortium of consortia rather than a network. The network services, as we have all thought of them, are going to change. [LYRASIS will] still be a partner with OCLC; it will just be a different type of partnership. The difference in my mind has always been the OCLC services, but I think that you will see [LYRASIS] become a true consortium," McBride said in early 2009. The metamorphosis of the regional networks began in earnest in March 2009 as OCLC announced changes that led to standardized pricing across the OCLC regional networks. The prospect of lower revenues from the provision of OCLC services forced the networks to consider alternative models for survival. This change in relationship put the networks in the awkward position of needing to redefine themselves. One approach to survival was to band together. The consortium of consortia, or megaconsortium, of which McBride spoke is rapidly becoming a reality in many cases. In early 2009, SOLINET had already absorbed some Indiana libraries and was on the verge of a merger with PALINET to form LYRASIS. This April 2009 merger resulted in a megaconsortium, and LYRASIS grew again with the inclusion of NELINET in October 2009. Operating at such a large scale has its challenges, but sometimes bigger is better. McBride noted that these megaconsortia will be well-equipped to handle large national deals, such as the one SOLINET brokered with LexisNexis in 1998.

While some were merging, other networks were disappearing altogether. The change to OCLC's new compensation model has forced "141 Nebraska libraries in the statewide consortium NEBASE libraries to BCR (Bibliographical Center for Research) for their OCLC products and services."[2] The regional networks also now appear to focus more on activities that make them more like other consortia, such as providing training, consulting, coopera-tive borrowing, and digital collection initiatives, in order to remain vital to their community members. Big or small, the consortium-versus-network distinction is currently in flux and will remain so for the foreseeable future.

Are You Experienced?

There's nothing to prevent a consortial negotiation from going awry if the one doing the negotiation is inexperienced. Just as collection development and electronic resources librarians struggle with negotiating deals with vendors, so do consortial negotiators, only the stakes are much higher. This is what makes the careful hiring of consortia personnel so vital for any consortium, making negotia-tion skills and experience a top job requirement for the position, possibly more so than for the collection development or electronic resource librarian, who often has many other duties to perform. In fact, a number of the consortia representatives interviewed for this chapter come from backgrounds that involved working in sales for vendors or publishers or negotiating agreements in the worlds of business and higher-education administration. While acting as a single voice for a large number of libraries requires knowledge of the wants and needs of those libraries, it also requires a degree of negotiating expertise that many librarians may lack.

Familiarity with practices and priorities on both sides of the fence is a common trait among many seasoned consortia personnel. McBride noted that he has been working in libraries for almost 30 years in a variety of positions. He first encountered negotiation as an automation librarian in several public libraries but really honed his negotiation skills while working with libraries all over the world as senior vice president of sales for Gale.

The level of specialization that a consortium representative cultivates can benefit librarians and vendors in a number of ways. Understanding the other side's needs and concerns is critical to a successful negotiation. A negotiator working on behalf of a consortium can make maintaining relationships with all sorts of information professionals and their companies a top priority. As Doyle explained, "One of the most important parts of my job is getting that relationship with the vendor. They trust us, and they trust that I am going to be straight with them and that I am going to do all the things I tell them I am going to do and that is backed up with results."

Understanding the product lines and passing that information along to consortium members is another added benefit. The consortial negotiator not only saves the member librarians from having to do the actual negotiation but can also facilitate the dissemination of information. In some cases, it creates a one-stop-shopping destination for libraries to evaluate and choose resources in a custom database environment. Clennon describes the CARLI member experience: "You get a login and a password and you log in for your institution. You see all the products we offer and prices, click the boxes for the deals you want, it totals ... and you're done. It's amazing, and I think libraries really like the idea that they can go in, look at all that's available, pick out their resources, and be finished."

Vendors benefit from this centralized contact as well, leaving their sales representatives available strictly to educate the libraries about the products without having to undergo the negotiation process with each one. Vendors also appreciate the significant savings that single invoicing can bring. "The invoicing and collecting of payment is quite expensive for a vendor. If [the vendor] can cut that down to only one, it really does add to the discount," McBride said. With tight budgets for both vendors and libraries, any opportunity to get more bang for the negotiation buck is appreciated.

Consortia also benefit the negotiation process by providing user statistics at renewal time. While the consortial negotiators interviewed said that they did not use user statistics except when purchasing a resource through a pool of money held by the consortium itself, the advent of electronic resource management systems has given statistics a larger role to play in consortial deals. Current participants in a deal can share their statistics with similar institutions that are considering coming in on a deal, while consortial negotiators can use the aggregate to renegotiate a deal, particularly when pricing is determined by full-time equivalent (FTE) or simultaneous users. "If we see that a cost per use of a particular resource is out of line with a peer resource, we definitely talk to the vendor about it and use it to cap increases," Austin said. "If we find that a resource is not being used as much as its peer resources, that information can be used to encourage the vendor to provide marketing and training. We use cost analysis for statistics as one factor in determining [whether] we continue to subscribe to a resource, and we definitely let the vendor know that." Additionally, those involved with the initiative known as Counting Online Usage of Networked Electronic Resources (www.projectcounter.org) have worked with international library consortia to include reports specifically for consortial usage statistics.

One of the most important skills a negotiator can have is the ability and confidence to walk away when a deal is no good. Because any given consortial deal is just one of many ways that a library might obtain a resource, a consortial negotiator has the freedom to say no when a deal does not meet the standards for benefiting the consortium and its members. Without the pressure of immediate end users and/or programs to support, consortial negotiators may feel less pressure to accept a particular deal and more cognizant of other opportunities that might serve those institutions that wanted a deal to happen.

For example, one of the criteria that a deal must meet for acceptance by the Greater Western Library Alliance (GWLA) is that at least 20 percent of the membership must participate. McKee feels free to hold strictly to this important standard, while at the same time wanting to come through for all GWLA's member libraries. "There are many times that we get less than 20 percent. At that point, I tell the publisher that we can't do it as a GWLA deal, but there are four libraries who are very interested, and if you would like to extend the pricing to them, that would be great, and I think 99 percent of the time" the publisher does so. "The libraries still get the content and the discount, only they have to deal with the licensing and invoicing." Consortial negotiators have the skills and stomach for driving a hard bargain, which can leave librarians free to work on other tasks, safe in the knowledge that their interests are well-represented.

Choose Your Friends Carefully

For librarians, deciding which consortium to join can sometimes be the most difficult part of the consortium experience. Ultimately, the key to a successful consortium is a set of libraries that share a common set of goals. As Armstrong explained, "I think there are a couple of things that really drive success. One is that there is a common, agreed-upon set of goals. We all know what we are setting out to do, and we all know when we have achieved those goals. … Trust is also a big deal. If [a consortium is] going to ask libraries to do things, sometimes give up autonomy and time, for the greater good," then libraries have to be able to trust the consortium to help fulfill their mission.

With these shared goals in mind, librarians often find themselves joining partnerships brought together by a few basic demo-
graphic criteria: size, location, and research level and interests.
Each unifying factor may have its own advantages and disadvantages. Bringing groups of large libraries or small libraries together
can certainly assist in pricing allocations based on FTE. However,
by determining common research level or interests, the group can
focus on the particular resources most important to their users.
Location-oriented consortia can be the most community-minded,
as they may be the only consortia that are cost-effective for smaller
libraries to join. In the end, the goal is to succeed, and librarians
may need to kiss a few frogs before finding the right mix of princely
consortia. To find these ideal relationships, Anderson advises looking for "consortia that are able to negotiate on behalf of a significant segment of a vendor's market—whether in terms of
geography, library type, or audience."

One concern and possible misconception can make it difficult
for libraries to choose the best possible partnerships, namely, the
impression that the larger the consortium, the greater the bargaining power. Corinne Lebrun, former executive director of the
Alliance for Innovation in Science and Technology Information
(AISTI), pointed out that the size of a group may work against its
ability to function effectively. "Your workload is going to increase
exponentially and what happens is [that] things tend to slow down
to a glacial pace when an organization is too large." Whether this
glacial pace will infect the dealings of LYRASIS or other megaconsortia remains to be seen. To be sure, the larger the consortium, the
greater the pressure for efficient and transparent communication
channels. As with any large organization, consortia run the risk of
evolving into bureaucracies. The last thing an acquisitions librarian wants is to be bounced around among four customer service
representatives and still have no resolution for an issue. The
money saved by joining a consortium to purchase a given product
or service can quickly be spent in personnel time.

Concentrate on the Needs of the Many

Librarians who have had users breathing down their necks for access to a particular journal or database understand why librarians can sometimes have a need for speed. Sadly, consortial deals don't always move as quickly as librarians or their users would like. Working through the decision-making process for choosing resources within libraries and then tackling the bureaucracy for approving any license terms or expenditures can prove difficult within a single institution. When multiplied by all the interested members of a consortium, the time frame for acquiring new resources can be very discouraging. Doyle pointed out that the timeline can sometimes be a deal breaker: "When I talk with vendors who want a central license agreement, I will make sure they understand the likely timeline, and if they are ready to let the libraries' subscription or access to materials start while we do the license, then we can move forward, but if they have to have a signed license before anyone does anything, then we are probably not going to be able to do business."

Consortial deals can also leave librarians feeling as though they have lost a level of flexibility in their budgets for resources that, particularly during lean years, can seem like a deal breaker as well. "The major disadvantage is that the cost of improved effectiveness and efficiency is decreased flexibility," Sanville remarked. "To achieve the benefits of group licenses, we must be able to sustain these in both thick and thin times and regardless of individual short-term budget issues." The needs of the consortium and its members can sometimes unduly influence libraries to maintain resources that they otherwise might not continue based on resource merit alone.

Some of the difficulties associated with consortial negotiations have resulted in a few vendors who will not negotiate with consortia at all. One challenge to traditional vendor corporate structure is the use of regional sales representatives. With consortia that span many geographical areas, multiple regional sales representatives can find themselves all negotiating the same deal, leaving the consortium in a confusing situation. McKee, as the program officer for a consortium that spans an area from Hawaii to Illinois, finds this problem particularly difficult. "In some of the really big publishers, I work with four different sales representatives. I will copy the other representatives, but I make it clear that there has to be only one that I am working with."

A Consortial Cross Section

- AISTI (www.aisti.org) is a nonprofit association of university and research laboratory libraries and information centers "dedicated to providing librarians and researchers with a unique forum for sharing cutting-edge ideas, implementing innovative solutions, and combining resources for research tool development and information sharing."

- The University of California libraries rely on the California Digital Library (www.cdlib.org) to provide support for their services in a variety of ways, including offering access to a wide variety of vendor and content provider opportunities.

- The CIC (www.cic.net) is made up of the Midwest's Big Ten universities plus the University of Chicago and supports a wide variety of collaborative projects, including the Center for Library Initiatives, which handles resource negotiation.

- In addition to supporting a shared catalog, a library delivery system, and a book digitization initiative, CARLI (www.carli.illinois.edu) brings some major bargaining power to the table, with 151 member institutions that together serve "over 93 percent of Illinois higher education students, faculty and staff."

- GWLA (www.gwla.org) is a selective consortium of 32 research libraries and supports many services, including digital libraries, cooperative collection development, and shared electronic resources.

- OhioLink (www.ohiolink.edu) represents 88 Ohio libraries and, among its many accomplishments, offers more than 140 electronic research databases.

- The Orbis Cascade Alliance (www.orbiscascade.org) serves 36 libraries in Oregon and Washington. The alliance was initially formed to build a union catalog and borrowing system but later added an electronic resources group-purchase program, among other services.

- LYRASIS (www.lyrasis.org) is a regional member organization created by the merger of several former OCLC regional service providers, including SOLINET, PALINET, and NELINET.

- UNILINC (www.unilinc.edu.au) is an Australian consortium that offers consultancy and advisory services, accreditation advice, and the opportunity to participate in database discounts.

- Representing the University of Missouri libraries and other academic institutions in the state of Missouri, University of Missouri Library Systems (digital.library. umsystem.edu) primarily provides digitizing and electronic resource acquisition.

- Many other states also have consortia of different constituencies, such as the Network of Alabama Academic Libraries (www.ache.state.al.us/NAAL). This network has a full-time director, but other state or regional consortia may rely on membership for administrative tasks.

For more consortia in your area and around the world, visit the International Coalition of Library Consortia (www.library.yale.edu/consortia).

Too Many Cooks Are in the Kitchen

Negotiating an agreement between more than two parties can exponentially increase the amount of difficulty in obtaining a good deal. Negotiating licenses in an age of consortia and collaboration requires a true commitment to transparent communication and decision making. The ways in which consortia determine how much participating institutions pay to participate in a deal are as varied as the consortia themselves. Wade describes part of the problem: "On the face of it, the amount paid should reflect the level of use. However, use-based pricing may be seen as discouraging use or creating budget uncertainty for the library. A flat fee based on FTE gives budget certainty but reflects potential use rather than actual likely use. It also disadvantages small, specialized libraries with small budgets, but also very small userbases." To provide the most flexibility for pricing, most consortia must maintain a variety of allocation formulas to ensure that, regardless of how the allocation is determined, all the libraries involved reap the benefits. "We have been playing with some models in the CIC—a whole matrix of factors. Some of the things we have been looking at are collection budget size, FTE, and research intensity," Armstrong noted.

All the formulas and data necessary to execute different allocation formulas are predicated on the library's ability to actually pay the invoice, which, in down-market times, can prove frightening and difficult. Ensuring that license agreements have opt-out clauses in times of extreme budget crises is essential for both consortial and nonconsortial deals. However, the penalties associated with exercising these clauses can be devastating in a consortial environment. When vendors have thresholds for the level of discount that a group may receive, the exit of one or more partners can affect the bottom line for everyone involved. "Some publishers will create deals [in which] they say if an institution cancels a title, and it is the only institution that holds that title, then everyone else is cut off from that title," McKee stated. "This has happened a couple of times, but we can usually get another institution to step up and subscribe to the canceled title so that the content will remain available for the rest of the participating members." While the goodwill of fellow consortium members is undoubtedly strong, financial hardship can drive libraries to tough choices. And just as all members reap the benefits of increased funding, the budget deficits of one institution can have ripple effects throughout the whole organization. An example of just such a tidal wave of economic trouble is the Open Letter to Licensed Content Providers (www.cdlib.org/news/docs/UC_Libraries_Open_Letter_to_Vendors. pdf), which the California Digital Library sent to vendors. The letter articulates that California libraries need to work with vendors for creative solutions to get through the state's and the country's economic crisis as unscathed as possible.

There are many levels of negotiation within a consortial deal: the negotiation between the consortium and the vendor, as well as the negotiation among the consortium members themselves. Competing priorities and competing personalities can affect any negotiation, especially a difficult one. (Chapter 4 discusses one such difficult scenario of consortium negotiation.)

Consortia large and small are coming together in new partnerships. An Association of Research Libraries (ARL) press release from November 2011 announced that "On November 18, 2011, ARL and LYRASIS signed an agreement designating LYRASIS as an agent to negotiate licences for online content on behalf of interested ARL member libraries. This is the culmination of an effort the began in 2010 to identify a strategy for ARL to influence the marketplace regarding licensing rights, technical specifications, and business terms to meet the needs of research libraries."[3]

There are no easy answers when it comes to resource acquisition. When it comes to deciding what constitutes the best pricing or the most desirable method of access for a resource, the answer will differ for each librarian negotiating a deal. This is what makes the consortial model such an unlikely winner in this game. And yet, libraries continually find new and important avenues in which existing consortia, as well as brand new partnerships, allow them to accomplish things that they never could have done as individual institutions. Will consortial purchasing and licensing of resources solve all the pricing and access problems that information professionals currently face? Probably not, but with the help of experienced and savvy negotiators at the helm of these organizations, librarians, vendors, and publishers can continue to find creative solutions from which all involved can benefit.

Endnotes

1. Rona Wade, "The Very Model of a Modern Library Consortium," *Library Consortium Management* 1, no. 1/2 (1999): 5.

2. Norman Oder, "Nebraska's OCLC Network Dissolves, Libraries Move to BCR," *Library Journal* (April 22, 2009), accessed July 22, 2011, www.libraryjournal.com/article/CA6653492.html.

3. "ARL and LYRASIS Sign Agreement for Licensing Initiative (press release)," November 29, 2011, accessed December 2, 2011, www.arl.org/news/pr/LYRASIS-29nov11.shtml.

Chapter 4

Negotiating in Times of Economic Stress

Negotiating for products and services can be a tricky business in the best of times. Information professionals and vendors alike might make a knee-jerk assumption that in the worst of times, such as the economic downturn that crystallized in 2008, negotiation would become even more difficult. However, such an assumption is not necessarily accurate. Times of economic stress can actually provide increased opportunities for negotiation. However, a constricting economy always requires special consideration when negotiating or renegotiating contracts for products and services.

The literature is flooded with articles about the troubled economy. Mary Ellen Bates noted in her March 2009 *Searcher* article, "Living Large in Lean Times," "It's getting so that I am afraid to open the morning paper. I can always seem to count on at least one headline with bad news about the economy."[1] Hear, hear, Ms. Bates. The media have hyped our economic meltdown to the hilt, making it difficult not to become paralyzed with fear. While the press release about the Springer–Elsevier–Wiley merger was a 2009 April Fools' Day joke (scholarlykitchen.sspnet.org/2009/04/01/mergers-create-uber-publisher), the reality of increased vendor and publisher mergers and content transfers among publishers is no laughing matter. Economic horrors are very real; the South Carolina General Assembly's reduction of funding by 90 percent for the PASCAL group's Statewide Electronic Library programming (www.pascalsc.org/content/view/173/1) is just one example.

To offer a broader picture of the impact of the economic recession on public libraries in particular, *Library Journal*, in partnership with Mandy Knapp and Laura Soloman, launched

LosingLibraries.org to track "the myriad cuts and changes affecting public libraries around the country."[2] According to the site's creators, it is meant not just to provide a depressing look at the economy and libraries but rather to galvanize concerned librarians and citizens to take action. This kind of advocacy tool can be critical in times of economic stress, particularly when negotiating with funding agencies. As outcomes-based assessment becomes more popular, it is no longer enough to play the "happy-happy, feel-good" card when lobbying for money or support. Libraries need to show meaningful data (quantitative and qualitative) about how the library is a great return on investment: Patrons use proprietary eresources such as Hoover's Online or the Small Business Reference Center from EBSCO or other business databases to stimulate local business growth; public libraries heavily subsidize the school media centers and lead to higher test scores; public and academic libraries offer job hunters eresources such as Gale's Career Library and Ferguson's Career Guidance Center from Facts on File; among many other examples. (More in-depth discussion of negotiating with funding agencies is found in Chapter 5.)

In collection development practices, evidence-based decision making is rapidly gaining ground. The use of materials is driving collection decisions as never before, and librarians can employ this sort of use data to prove their value to funding sources and possibly negotiate for a bigger piece of a shrinking pie. Nor is such use data limited to usage statistics. A richer and more meaningful picture of use can be drawn by triangulating usage statistics, bibliometrics, and user-community feedback via surveys or focus groups. Use-based and user-driven collecting models can make libraries more vital and more *used* than ever before.

Just as the need for advocacy tools and meaningful-outcome data is not decreasing, publisher consolidation, mergers, divestments, and acquisition show no sign of slowing, and this affects the librarian's ability to negotiate for digital content and services. It took 2 years, but Reed Elsevier finally divested its U.S. trade publications. Marydee Ojala, editor of *ONLINE* magazine, explains the implications for information professionals: Many trade publications' sites "provided data and special features beyond what appeared in print. … Similarly, backfiles of the printed publications, as they appear in traditional library aggregators such as Dialog, Dow Jones Factiva, EBSCO, LexisNexis, and ProQuest, are usually electronic analogues to print and do not contain any additional information that appeared on the web." This is not true of all publications. Moreover, discontinued titles that have new owners may get embroiled in licensing issues between the new owners and the aggregators as to whether they will rejoin the aggregators' content.[3] This sort of licensing issue is clearly beyond the librarian's control, but certainly anyone involved in negotiating with an aggregator over price should be up-to-date about any gaps or missing content that might result in a lower price.

Another example is that publisher A may choose to expand its scope and begin to publish online journals on behalf of small societies or small publishers. This is not a new model: Highwire Press, Ingenta, Scitation, and others have hosted online journals for smaller societies and publishers for years. Remember that the major publisher has a card in its negotiation pocket if it is selling its own content as well as the small society content. The publisher can put together a big deal of all available ejournals, its own and those of the societies, and insist that it cannot do anything about the price set by the societies on whose behalf it publishes. We find this scenario with indexes and databases as well—a library can subscribe to the American Psychological Association's PsycINFO from a variety of vendors, such as EBSCO and ProQuest, to name just two. Let's say EBSCO insists in its negotiation with the library that it does not set the price for PsycINFO; the American Psychological Association does. While this may very well be true, it behooves the savvy negotiator to understand all the links in the supply chain in order to paint as broad an economic picture as possible. When a core resource such as PsycINFO is available from more than one vendor, get price quotes from each and ask why the markup is higher at vendor A than at vendor B. When content is available from only one source, make sure the society is setting the price and, if so, haggle over the additional charges levied by the publisher.

Advocate through relevant constituents (e.g., faculty members on society boards) to help societies lower their prices. Regardless of the tactic, understand the economic situation at hand and take appropriate action.

Broadly, the economic landscape during a recession is far from the land of milk and honey. Librarians must make an effort to track who owns what now and who just jettisoned what to whom. Likewise, vendors must make an effort to understand the culture, politics, and funding sources of a library.

When asked if she had experienced this sort of economic downturn over the course of her career in the information industry, Jane Burke, former vice president of Serials Solutions, emphasized that we need to guard against becoming too frightened by media hype. While there is no doubt that the salad days are over and serious times call for serious people, seriousness does not necessarily mean we have to follow a Chicken Little policy of panic.

In the preceding chapters, we have explored negotiation as it relates to information professionals, offering advice from library leaders and vendors as well as an examination of the intersection between consortia and negotiation. In this chapter, we explore how these tough economic times—or TET, as Roy Tennant, senior program officer for OCLC Research, says the folks at OCLC are calling it[4]—affect the information professional's ability to negotiate for products and services.

The Glass Is Half-Full ...

When budgets become tight, the instinct is often to batten down the hatches and hold tight to what one has. Tight budgets, however, can actually empower librarians to determine—internally and externally—just what the critical products and services are and perhaps make some long-needed changes. For example, the "dis-integration" of the integrated library system (ILS), as well as the general unsuitability of the ILS to manage electronic products and services, has become a hot topic. Librarians are often in the undesirable position of maintaining a fleet of products to manage their print and electronic collections—the ILS, the electronic resource management system, the link resolver, federated search tools, next-generation discovery tools, and more. When a budget is slashed by 5 percent, 10 percent, 20 percent, or more, this multi-tool scheme morphs from undesirable to unfeasible. Thus, what was once unthinkable—jettisoning parts of the traditional ILS—becomes thinkable, and the library has made an evolutionary jump forward.

In essence, the librarian determines the library's core mission and negotiates the acquisition of the technology needed to meet that mission. Is it more important to facilitate linking among disparate eresources via the link resolver or to check in and claim print serials? Is it possible to relegate some acquisitions work to a centralized purchasing office—such as those that exist on many college campuses—and thus free staff time and budget line items for other purposes? If the ILS cannot be pared down, can the library afford the $50,000 for the software upgrade, or should the librarians suspend that upgrade until the budget recovers? There are no simple answers to any of these questions, but TET forces us to negotiate with ourselves about what it means to offer 21st-century library service. Moreover, TET often calls for greater cooperation via friendly negotiation with vendors, publishers, and other content providers.

Let's not forget that such "friendly" negotiation needs to occur among the vendors, publishers, and aggregators as well. For example, if libraries simply cannot bear the cost of an aggregated database or cannot justify the duplication among various aggregated products, then perhaps it is time for the aggregator to renegotiate its own contracts with publishers. Aggregators may have agreed to pay a certain publisher high royalties for content in flush times. However, in a weak economy, all players along the content supply chain can take the opportunity to revisit previous agreements and be realistic about whether the market can continue to bear such costs. In the same vein, publishers can take this opportunity to seriously evaluate their title lists to determine the value and use offered by each title. If a title is 3 years behind schedule and the primary userbase has still not begun screaming, then maybe it's time to let that journal die a peaceful, quiet death. Sue Medina, former director of the Network of Alabama Academic Libraries, noted that a constricting economy may require a constricted title list.

Everyone along the supply chain must make an effort to understand the challenges each constituency faces. For example, let's look at one possible scenario. In difficult times, more and more libraries cut subscriptions directly from the publisher. In an effort to make up these revenues, the publisher decides to put its content out for bid to aggregators, promising that the winner will have exclusivity. If the publisher content is viewed as valuable enough, the cost for it in this kind of bidding war may skyrocket. The aggregator must then attempt to pass on its new costs to guess whom? You got it: the library. While this is an oversimplified example, exclusivity agreements are very real, and if the vagaries of the supply chain remain opaque, then we can all feel like hamsters running on a wheel. The furor over exclusivity agreements reached a fever pitch when EBSCO announced in early 2010 that it had garnered exclusive rights to some content. This example is discussed in Chapter 6.

Use Role Reversal and Creative Solutions

Floods of articles about the gravity of the economic downturn inundate the media, along with articles detailing how to use the recession to one's advantage. In a March 2009 *Wired* article, Cliff Kuang asked the burning question, "Can I use the recession as a bargaining chip?" In particular, Kuang recommended trying some price negotiation with the cable and phone companies, saying "The recession has actually increased your leverage. By articulating their worst fear (losing customers), you can w[r]angle huge savings."[5] A March 14, 2009, *New York Times* article went so far as to recommend negotiating one's medical bills: "When money is tight, everything is negotiable—including your health care bills."[6]

In the previous chapters, library leaders, vendors, and those involved with consortia have repeatedly noted that, when it comes to negotiating for products and services, librarians often have more power than they perceive. This certainly holds true in times of economic stress. Can we, as Kuang suggests, use this recession to our advantage? The answer is yes, but yes with a serious caveat: Tread lightly. The economy will eventually improve, and burning bridges may not constitute a wise investment for the future. Work with a vendor to come to a creative solution to your mutual economic troubles, but don't be rigid. It's a small world, after all, and it's going to keep on turning.

Depending on how dire the economic situation and the loss of revenue for content providers, they may be willing to entertain more than just price slashing. For example, perhaps the purchase of a specialized digitized product is on the table between a content provider and a flagship university, in particular a product of particular interest to African-American studies. In addition to negotiating cost, the content provider may be willing to expand access beyond the flagship institution, to include additional participants, such as the historically black colleges and universities in the state, at no additional charge. Creative partnerships can emerge for those who search them out.

Possibilities for creative solutions exist at the consortial level as well. Perhaps a state-subsidized virtual library program, which in years past has provided eresources to all the citizens of a given state, has had its budget slashed and is unable to offer these eresources. The entity responsible for managing the virtual library—perhaps a committee of librarians from around the state—can re-evaluate its role and begin advising individual libraries about re-negotiating contracts for specific eresources. Thus, eresources are customized based on library needs rather than a one-size-fits-all approach. Or a consortium can re-envision programs to include greater education about quality, free eresources, such as institutional repositories.

Free and Good Enough
Sound Better and Better

In her "Review of the Year 2009 and Trends Watch—Part 1" blog posting (newsbreaks.infotoday.com/Spotlight/Review-of-the-Year--and-Trends-WatchPart--60372.asp), Paula Hane devoted a section to the "good enough revolution," citing a *Wired* magazine feature article that coined the term (www.wired.com/gadgets/miscellaneous/magazine/17-09/ff_goodenough?currentPage=all). Hane noted that whether we like it or not, "the trend is here." Perhaps "free" and "good enough" often go hand in hand for librarians.

With free content available via Google Books, the Open Content Alliance, and more, perhaps money spent on these sorts of monographs or products that index these monographs would be better spent elsewhere. Likewise, is it fiscally responsible to purchase Books in Print electronically if your librarians can make do with Amazon.com, WorldCat.org, or other similar bibliographic-rich sites? Products such as Associations Unlimited, which index all sorts of associations, may be the first on the cancellation list when it is possible to find much of this information on freely available association websites, even if not all the information is there and it is not as easy to access.

In response to a question about the success of midyear contract renegotiation, Denise Davis, director of the American Library Association Office for Research and Statistics, said, "Publishers have gotten better at being willing to revisit an agreement." Burke echoed this statement, saying that overall, vendors and publishers have become more amenable to negotiating contractual terms and obligations, as we all have become more experienced with leasing and purchasing electronic resources and tools. Indeed, coming to a middle ground is the essence of creating a win–win situation. For example, if a library needs price reductions in ILS or electronic resource management tools, then perhaps a vendor would be willing to accept a lower price in exchange for the library's agreement to become a beta tester or a genuinely committed reference. Likewise, if the vendor is unwilling or unable to budge on price, then the library might push for more favorable terms and conditions.

Ultimately, Medina emphasized that librarians need not be afraid or timid about negotiating for lower prices and more favorable terms and conditions, regardless of the economy. The first rule of negotiation remains valid regardless of a particular economic situation: Do your homework. For example, the perception that all vendors, publishers, and content providers have wide profit margins is false. These margins are leaner than often perceived. Just as publishers cannot reasonably expect libraries to pay $1,600 per issue for a high-impact medical journal, libraries cannot expect publishers to absorb all cost cuts in perpetuity. Knowing the company on the other side of the table is critical. If the profit margin is lean, where can the publisher be flexible? In the payment plan? In the suspension of an inflation rider in an agreement? All of this is negotiable. Remember, in the final analysis, vendors and publishers want our business now and in the future.

The Glass Is Half-Empty (or Shattered Altogether)

While opportunities do exist for renegotiation of programming, products, and services during TET, conditions remain far from rosy. The simple fact remains that in some cases, no amount of negotiation or renegotiation will prevent the loss of services and products. Or, to rephrase with a colorful mixed aphorism, "If the frog's wallet is empty, then there's no use for him to hop to the bar for a beer." Larra Clark, project manager, and Denise Davis, director, ALA Office for Research and Statistics, offered a detailed and informative analysis of the economy as it relates to libraries in the January 2009 *Library Technology Report.*[7]

In conversation, Davis noted that one of the greatest challenges facing libraries in TET is that many librarians do not negotiate agreements for products, particularly electronic resources. Typically, the state library or another entity conducts the negotiation on the librarians' behalf, and the individual libraries and their constituencies benefit. This is the heart of cooperative purchasing: The ideal is an expert in the centralized office, such as at the state library level, who works within a given procurement system in order to negotiate the best possible terms and prices. The sources and services are then either paid centrally, as in the case of many state virtual library programs, or the individual libraries pay from their own budgets.

The Digital Download on the Recession

Perhaps in quantum physics one can do more with less, but beyond the laboratory, it is far from realistic. If the money isn't available, something is on the chopping block: hours, staff, digital collections, services, and more. This is the time to throw down the gauntlet and exploit every possible avenue the internet has to offer. The internet is arguably the greatest instrument of democracy the world has ever seen, so use it to mobilize your supporters— many of whom may be far beyond your ZIP code.

Case in point: When the library school at Louisiana State University (LSU) was threatened with possible closure, a group of concerned students rallied the troops. These students created a Facebook page so that "friends" could join. They created a public wiki that offered information about how to contact the relevant administrators in charge of the decision to close or not to close. The wiki also tracked all of the emails sent to those administrators, collected any links to stories in online media about the school's possible closure, offered meaningful data about libraries in general and about the library school itself, and more. In essence, they created a grass-roots system that resulted in support far beyond the borders of campus or of Louisiana. Librarians, library schools, and others picked up the thread and shared the story on listservs, personal Facebook pages, and school websites, among other places. Emails from supporters far and wide flooded administrators' email accounts to the point that the LSU board of supervisors had to create a separate email account to handle the traffic. These students also created an online petition that allowed anyone, anywhere, and at any time—the three hallmarks of the internet—to sign.

Efforts such as those undertaken by LSU students, along with mashups such as www.LosingLibraries.org, can prevent, or at least limit, the eradication of programs, collections, and services. As of September 2011, a merger among general departments was initiated, and the library school dean reassured students that such a merger would create no noticeable changes. More information is available at savelsuslis.wikispaces.com/The+Merger--September+ 2011.

In the case of centrally paid programs, when coffers are full, libraries in the cooperative purchasing program have access to generous amounts of information. Unfortunately, when coffers begin to empty and are not replenished, situations such as the Partnership Among South Carolina's Academic Libraries' (PASCAL) funding crisis emerge. Ideally, then, the expert negotiators in the centralized office step in and attempt to continue the purchasing program at some reasonable level, perhaps renegotiating purchasing agreements or mobilizing a grass-roots movement to influence the state legislature or other funding agencies. Medina noted, however, that such lobbying efforts should not be only reactive but proactive as well.

Whether the party doing the negotiating is a state agency or other centralized program or an individual library, the initial response to a current or projected budget cut is twofold. First, the librarian must review the original agreement and determine the contractual obligations. Once the contractual obligations have been clearly determined and considered, then the librarian approaches the vendor to ascertain what—if anything—can be done. Davis emphasized that any good contract has an out clause, and lack of available funding is a typical out. The worst-case scenario is that the central agency or individual library exercises this option, and in the case of electronic or other materials, the content ceases to be available to members. In the unfortunate event that subscriptions are canceled, the previous negotiation of perpetual access rights becomes critical.

If the content has been centrally provided and that centrally funded program is no longer supported, either in part or in whole, the ripple effect can be enormous. In other words, if the centrally funded resources have become a core part of the collection and services and then suddenly those resources vanish, dramatic negotiation at the individual library level necessarily takes place. In other words, libraries are told, "If you want it [this year], you are going to have to pay for it yourself," Medina stated when asked about the slashing of cooperative program budgets. "It's going to be a fundamental rewrite of the individual library's content and collection development plan as a result of losing centrally paid databases." If librarians become casual about the state electronic libraries, they risk losing that content. According to Medina, "We cannot stop being vigilant every single day to make sure we keep those central entities in front of the legislature." Nor can we forget that a significant population often benefits from these programs—public universities and colleges, public libraries, K–12 school libraries—in other words, people who can call themselves members of a particular community. This makes for a tremendous audience for these programs and therefore a large potential base of individuals to lobby on behalf of the programs.

Of course, even the most successful lobbying program in the world cannot prevent budget cuts. If the state simply does not have the money, then cuts to content present themselves. Because the state virtual libraries serve such a wide population—public, school, and academic libraries—decisions about what content to cut can be fraught with politics. If the content of a state's virtual library is determined by committee, then each constituency needs to have a voice. It's easy to slip into "I have to protect me and mine" mode when times get lean. To prevent this sort of negotiation, decision makers need to have all relevant information in front of them when determining cancellations. For example, it can be tempting to cut citation-only databases in favor of those resources that provide full text. Seems like a no brainer, right? Not always.

Let's take the WorldCat database from OCLC. This database is available in a number of different ways: by subscription on the FirstSearch platform or freely available at www.worldcat.org. If it's freely available, then why would a library pay for a FirstSearch subscription? OCLC requires a subscription to WorldCat via FirstSearch in order for a library's holdings to appear on the freely available version. Thus, if a library cancels its subscription, its holdings are no longer visible to the world via www.worldcat.org directly or via Google or Google Books, Yahoo!, or any of the other partnerships OCLC has forged in order to display library holdings on the free web. If the state virtual library committee determining cuts to content was not aware of the FirstSearch WorldCat requirement, then a switch to a citation-only database has a much wider impact than perceived at first glance.

The collection, print or electronic, is the first area to take a hit during difficult economic times. Based on evidence gathered in a 2003–2006 study of funding issues in public libraries,[8] Davis described the way in which libraries prioritized cuts: "Where they cut first is in collections because they can. It is the most flexible of their expenditure categories. Salaries are fixed, and many libraries have union shops, so they just can't fire people. Any kind of negotiating on letting staff go is delayed to the next fiscal year." Davis went on to explain that other expenditure categories, such as utilities, are often not negotiable: "They simply have to pay their electric bill."

When asked about the magnitude of the economic downturn, Davis said, "All bets are off … They are off for publishers, and they are off for libraries." Evidence of the elasticity of contractual agreements exists beyond the library world. A March 31, 2009 *New York Times* article plainly declares in its lead: "Contracts everywhere are under assault."[9]

Bye-Bye Big Deal?

The big deal can represent a significant commitment of a library's collection budget to a single content source. The temptation to see this expenditure as sacrosanct is exactly why the big deal can be so powerful. Librarians feel committed to the package and, unlike a list of journals purchased individually, often don't seem able to cut this budget item. But as the 2003 big deal retreat taught us, these deals are not unbreakable. Unlike in 2003, vendors and publishers may be more interested in morphing the big deal into a more flexible package, allowing for continued subscriptions at a reduced level to accommodate cuts, but also taking into account the need to create more flexible title lists with individual title cancellation powers.

During tough economic times, a big deal can hold a vice-like grip on a budget that is simply no longer feasible. How do you begin to back away from a big deal? Review the original agreement and be aware of what powers, if any, librarians have to reduce the aggregate cost. If the purchase was made consortially, as many big deals are, many reviews of this kind may involve bringing together fellow consortium members. A global economic crisis may give this situation a silver lining as all boats sink in an ebbing tide. Unlike when individual institutions experience a budget crisis, a global crisis can motivate all partners to renegotiate the deal. In the past, publishers may have been reluctant to allow a big deal to be broken and reworked, but facing the total cancellation of a package by a whole consortium of libraries, publishers may seize an opportunity to work on relationship building rather than revenue growth. Chapter 7 considers big deal negotiations in more depth.

We're All in This Together

A number of library organizations, vendors, publishers, and others have issued official statements addressing the economy. Perhaps most notable is the International Coalition of Library Consortia (ICOLC), simply because of its size, scale, and the number of dollars it represents. The ICOLC statement, released January 19, 2009, is "intended to help publishers and other content providers from whom we license information resources … understand better how the current unique financial crisis affects the worldwide information community." The statement also aims "to suggest a range of approaches that we believe are in the mutual best interest of libraries and the providers of information services." The ICOLC added a preamble to the statement in June 2010 in order to update vendors on the state of affairs and added a section expressing its opposition to agreements. Such statements from ICOLC have been very effective in the past in leading the way for significant change. For example, ICOLC's stance on usage statistics, first released in 1998 and revised several times since (www.library.yale. edu/consortia/webstats06.htm), helped pave the way for content providers to adopt standards of the Counting Online Usage of NeTworked Electronic Resources (COUNTER) project (www.project counter.org), "an agreed international set of standards and protocols governing the recording and exchange of online usage data." Such adoption and standardization of usage data allowed libraries to have reliable metrics for eresource collection development decisions.

Flexibility and receptivity to creative solutions that allow for minimal reduction in content are key points in the ICOLC economic statement. It also appeals for more flexibility in opt-out and reduction clauses and renewal cycles—which, if actually adopted by publishers, would affect the viability of the big deal, among other issues. (The big deal is explained in more detail in Chapter 7. Briefly, it is "an online aggregation of journals that publishers offer as a ... one-size-fits-all package."[10] The statement also notes that price will be the first and foremost factor and that purchasers will be willing to trade new features and functionality for price breaks. This approach might allow publishers and libraries to facilitate a win–win situation. Publishers offer a lower price but absorb the price cut by temporarily reducing their development costs. In terms of flexibility, the statement encourages content providers to offer more customized options for subscriptions: Look at usage patterns and set prices accordingly; create core content packages (e.g., computer science ebooks), and base the price on relevant possible constituents and usage, among other variables. While creating core content packages is useful, libraries should also be permitted to purchase one-off titles, perhaps from a variety of vendors in a variety of models. Perhaps a large conglomerate publisher can offer its one-off etitles on its own platform for one-time purchase while also allowing libraries the option of subscribing to the etitle via an ebook aggregator.

The ICOLC statement concludes on a positive note, indicating that economic crisis might have a silver lining in serving as a catalyst for change in the global scholarly publishing community. This sort of optimism is an important tactic to use in negotiations because it shows a willingness to work toward mutually beneficial solutions rather than simply bemoaning that "publishers continue to gouge us." Other organizations, such as the Association of Research Libraries, have followed ICOLC's lead and issued statements of their own:

- International Coalition of Library Consortia Statement on the Global Economic Crisis and Its Impact on Consortial

Licenses, January 19, 2009, www.library.yale.edu/
consortia/icolc-econcrisis-0109.htm; preamble and
reissued statement added June 14, 2010, www.library.yale.
edu/consortia/icolc-econcrisis-0610.htm

- Association of Research Libraries Statement to Scholarly
  Publishers on the Global Economic Crisis, February 19,
  2009, www.arl.org/bm~doc/economic-statement-
  2009.pdf

These pronouncements from librarian-endorsed groups put the
content-provider community on notice, and some publishers have
already responded. However, it remains to be seen whether such
statements will effect true change in future renewal cycles.

Library organizations are not the only ones creating statements
and making announcements. Vendors and publishers are also recognizing the unique economic situation. JSTOR/ITHAKA, in its
March 2009 newsletter, noted that the Association of Research
Libraries statement is a "call to arms" and reported that its core
principles have been expressly guided by the academic community. EBSCO released a statement to its customers on March 10,
2009, stating, "When you experience pain, we experience pain."
EBSCO went on to offer to do an "overlap analysis" in order to
identify duplication of content. LexisNexis announced that its discussions with SOLINET (now LYRASIS, www.lyrasis.org) about
funding concerns had led it to forego the previously announced
2.5 percent annual rate increase on all LexisNexis Academic and
Library Solutions web products for the subscription year starting
July 1, 2009.[11] JSTOR, EBSCO, and LexisNexis are by no means
alone. Nature Publishing Group announced in March 2009 via correspondence with customers that its policies met "many of the rec-
ommendations outlined in recent statements from the library
community, including a flexible 'a la carte' site license model, sta-
bilized pricing over three years, local currency pricing, and considered decisions around product launches."[12]

Other issues for negotiation still remain. Two of the most challenging are the transfer of titles among different publishers and the

possibility that some publishers, particularly niche content providers, will not weather an economic dust bowl. The buying and selling of titles among publishers has concerned librarians for some time. The Transfer Code of Practice (www.uksg.org/transfer) offers guidelines for publishers to ensure that libraries have consistent access to titles transferred between publishers or when publishers merge. For a library faced with extreme budget cuts and cancellations, perpetual access clauses become even more important: Does the new owner honor the agreement, particularly for perpetual access, negotiated with the previous owner, or is a renegotiation in order? Will the previous owner notify the library before the transfer so that the library can retrieve its subscriptions and host them locally? The possible utter demise of some publishers points again to the importance of negotiating clauses for archiving initiatives such as Lots of Copies Keep Stuff Safe and Portico. For more discussion about these and other economic issues, see other ICOLC statements about preferred practices for selection and purchase of electronic information (www.library.yale.edu/consortia/statementsanddocuments.html).

Is the Sky Falling?

It remains to be seen whether we as a library community will devolve into *Lord of the Flies* or into a vision worthy of Dr. Pangloss, the über-optimist of Voltaire's *Candide*, famous for his favorite saying that "everything is for the best in this, the best of all possible worlds." Chances are that some publishers and some libraries will be more flexible than others. Some individual, publicly funded libraries will lobby state governments for funds of their own, fearful that dollars given to centralized state virtual libraries will be dollars taken away from their individual budgets. Some publishers will refuse to negotiate or budge on prices, terms, and conditions. The wisest among us, however, will recognize that the economy will rebound and we will still need to work with one another. The wisest among us will look on the constricting economy as an opportunity to re-evaluate, renegotiate, and re-envision our services.

Perpetual Access and Publisher and Content-Provider Volatility

Examples of libraries losing access to content because of publisher and content-provider consolidations and discontinued partnerships are plentiful. Decisions made yesterday or today about perpetual access clauses in contracts can affect future access for patrons. For example, SAGE Publications ceased its partnership with Cambridge Scientific Abstracts (CSA) and is no longer offering its journals through CSA. Via CSA, customers could purchase subject collections (e.g., political science) of journals and receive access to current content as well as a deep backfile. When SAGE announced it was ceasing its partnership, deep backfile access ceased as well. However, SAGE is happy to sell a backfile for a fee.

A happier example is the purchase of NetLibrary from OCLC by EBSCO in 2002 "to protect libraries' investments in eBook content purchases." EBSCO moved the NetLibrary content to the EBSCOhost platform, but unlike the SAGE–CSA example, "All NetLibrary eBooks purchased by libraries will be placed in a dark archive—the OCLC eBook Archive—at least through March 2013" (www.oclc.org/news/releases/2010/201015.htm). The platform transition causes issues for library workflow (new MARC records, etc.), but at least for now, the content is safe.

These examples remind us to carefully evaluate the need for and inclusion of perpetual access clauses in contracts.

The California Digital Library epitomizes this approach. In its "Open Letter to Licensed Content Providers," released May 26, 2009, the authors do not mince words, but approach the recession with the right attitude: "While we will not be able to spare every product, we will pursue every possible creative option to maintain access to resources important to the UC [University of California] mission."[13] The authors go on to note that this tack may include less centralized purchasing and more customized options for individual campuses, which is akin the ICOLC call for flexibility. The very existence of a recession means cutbacks, so something will have to go, but depending on the stakeholders' commitment to fruitful negotiation and flexibility, we won't throw the baby out with the bathwater.

Endnotes

1. Mary Ellen Bates, "Living Large in Lean Times," *Searcher* 17, no. 3 (2009): 22–27.

2. Norman Oder, "ALA 2010: Library Journal Helps Launch LosingLibraries.org," *Library Journal*, June 25, 2010, accessed July 25, 2011, www.libraryjournal.com/lj/community/ala/885525-264/ala_2010_library_journal_helps.html.csp.

3. Marydee Ojala, "Reed Elsevier (Finally) Divests U.S. Trade Pubs: Facts and Fallout for Information Professionals," *NewsBreaks*, May 27, 2010, accessed July 25, 2011, newsbreaks.infotoday.com/NewsBreaks/Reed-Elsevier-Finally-Divests-US-Trade-Pubs-Facts-and-Fallout-for-Information-Professionals-67457.asp.

4. Roy Tennant, "Metasearch Options," slide show presented at the Association for Library Collections & Technical Services (ALCTS) Symposium, American Library Association (ALA) Midwinter Meeting 2009; Breaking Down the Silos: Planning for Discovery Tools for Library 2.0, Denver, Colorado, January 22, 2009, accessed August 8, 2011, wikis.ala.org/midwinter2009/index.php/ALCTS.

5. Cliff Kuang, "Burning Question: Can Recession Be a Bargaining Chip?" *Wired*, March 23, 2009, accessed July 25, 2011, www.wired.com/culture/culturereviews/magazine/17-04/st_burningquestion.

6. Lesley Alderman, "Bargaining Down the Medical Bills," *New York Times*, March 14, 2009, accessed July 25, 2011, www.nytimes.com/2009/03/14/health/14patient.html?emc=eta1.

7. Larra Clark and Denise Davis, "The State of Library Technology Funding in Today's Economy," *Library Technology Reports* 45, no. 1 (January 2009). Clark and Davis include findings from "Libraries Connect Communities: Public Library Funding & Technology Access Study 2007–2008." Davis also conducted and released a study, "Funding Issues in U.S. Public Libraries, Fiscal Years 2003–2006," www.ala.org/research/sites/ala.org.research/files/conent/library stats/public/fundingissuesinuspls.pdf.

8. "Funding and Technology Access Study," accessed December 3, 2011, www.ala.org/ala/research/initiatives/plftas.

9. Mary Williams Walsh and Jonathan Glater, "Contracts Now Seen as Being Rewritable," *New York Times*, March 31, 2009, accessed July 25, 2011, www.nytimes.com/2009/03/31/business/economy/31contracts.html?_r=1&emc=eta.

10. Kenneth Frazier, "The Librarians' Dilemma: Contemplating the Costs of the 'Big Deal,'" *D-Lib Magazine* 7, no. 3 (March 2001), accessed December 3, 2011, www.dlib.org/dlib/march01/frazier/03frazier.html.

11. "Executive Notes," *JSTORNews* 13, no. 1 (March 2009), accessed July 25, 2011, news.jstor.org/jstornews/2009/03/march_2009_no_13_issue_1_execu.html; "SOLINET Successfully Negotiates Zero Price Increase and a Flat Renewal With LexisNexis on Behalf of ICOLC," SOLINET press release, February 11, 2009, accessed July 25, 2011, www.lyrasis.org/News/SOLINET%20and%20PALINET%20Archives/SOLINET%20Press%20Releases/~/media/Files/Lyrasis/News/Press%20Releases/2009/LexisNexis%20Academic%20Fee%20Waiver%20Release.ashx.

12. Correspondence as a nature customer.

13. University of California, "Open Letter to Licensed Content Providers," May 26, 2009, accessed December 3, 2011, www.cdlib.org/news/docs/UC_Libraries_Open_Letter_to_Vendors.pdf.

Chapter 5

Negotiating With Funding Sources and User Communities

A recurring theme in this book is the great advantage one has when negotiating from strength. This advantage is a universal truth, but it is not always apparent from where such strength might come. In simplest terms, a great deal of strength comes from true confidence born of effective preparation. This is hardly new advice. The classical Roman poet Virgil said "Fortune favors the bold" more than 2,000 years ago. The great 19th-century scientist Louis Pasteur restated Virgil's advice as "Fortune favors the prepared mind."

Here is another tidbit of advice from the great comedian W. C. Fields: "You can't cheat an honest man." Combine Fields's honesty with Virgil's boldness and Pasteur's preparation, and you have the makings of a powerful negotiator.

It doesn't alter Fields's observation to change the word "honest" to "ethical." The same principle applies to negotiations in which each party is essentially an ethical player, though guided by different agendas. After all, your local city council, for example, needs to distribute funding equitably to police, fire, and other agencies, as well as to the public library, and keep the voters happy at the same time. Council members, in most cases, operate from sterling motives, but their agendas don't always place the library's needs first. How can we ensure that our institution receives its fair share of limited resources? First, we must be fully prepared to enter into the negotiation process. You might remember that the first chapter of this book discussed Shapiro and Jankowski's seven elements of effective preparation:

- Identify pertinent precedents.

- Identify alternatives.

- Clarify interests.

- Identify deadlines.

- Define strengths and weaknesses.

- Identify your ultimate goal (the best possible outcome).

- Recruit a team.[1]

The amount and quality of preparation one can muster will help determine one's negotiation strategies. The more thoroughly prepared a negotiator is, the greater freedom he or she has to employ multiple strategies. Extrapolating from Shapiro and Jankowski, it is possible to outline a strategy for an effective budget proposal, starting with the basic premise of understanding your own institution's needs and, just as important, understanding its place within the context of your community. This is not an easy step, but it is essential. As in your student days, you must do your homework. This is the only way to understand what is being negotiated.

In the case of budget allocations, do not get caught in the trap of thinking your part in budget negotiation is only about your institution. Rather, it is about how the community should best allocate its resources. The wise public library director will know the needs and resources of his or her own library and will, to the greatest extent possible, know the needs and resources of the community as a whole and those of competing agencies. Keeping abreast of general community needs involves such strategies as paying close attention to local news media, serving on public committees or commissions, attending open meetings such as the PTA, and keeping lines of communication open between yourself and the movers and shakers. It is also most helpful to know what your competitors are up to. Find out, for example, the police department's needs, resources, and wishes. Make note of the successful budgetary negotiation techniques that department has employed in past years. Do this with each major competitor for a piece of the budgetary pie.

The bottom line is that you should know your community's current economic, social, and cultural status. Map out, in detail, how the library currently enhances, and will improve, your community in each of these areas.

Immersing yourself into the life force of your community should remind you that it is impossible to move mountains without the help of others. Burn this into your brain: *Enlist the support of multiple constituencies.* Library board members are a natural resource here, but don't overlook teachers, the PTA, the chamber of commerce, and other centers of community power. Become a true friend to local media. A well-placed editorial or news story can work wonders come budget time. Reporters and editors are far more likely to support your efforts if they perceive the library as a cooperative, friendly, and useful institution. Use the information you have gathered and generated, bolstered by the support you have mustered, to craft your strategy for negotiating budget allocations.

Remember to toot your own horn! If you don't tell the story of how your summer reading program enhanced the lives of families throughout your community, who will? And while you're tooting that horn, remember to tie specific successes to specific community needs. That summer reading program, for example, most likely helps boost test scores in the public schools. It also promotes literacy and learning, which generally translate into fewer delinquents and a lower crime rate. All these things make your community a more desirable location for businesses looking for a new home. If you approach negotiations this way, it is not a great stretch to suggest that allocating money to the library is akin to allocating money to the police department, the city schools, and the chamber of commerce. Be creative and dynamic here, but make sure not to overstate your case. Fortunately, effective libraries actually do enhance their communities in many ways.

Once you have your facts in place, have constructed your argument, and are otherwise ready to make your pitch, there is one thing left to do: Practice, practice, practice. If possible, do so in a room similar to the one where you will make your presentation.

Know when to pause for effect. Know when and how to make an appropriate gesture. Be prepared, be bold, and be honest. Make Virgil, Pasteur, and Fields proud.

Sometimes, strength is inherent to an institution. A prime example is the cultural high ground that libraries have long held and that translates into a type of capital that gives them strength within their communities and pays multiple dividends. Workable budget allocations, successful bond issues, and all manner of blessings flow in large part from this inherent strength. It is worth noting, however, that this cultural high ground is almost entirely a matter of public perception. It is obvious that such perception can be squandered by malfeasance or poor policymaking. Insensitivity to the public's needs or the library's role in fulfilling those needs can just as easily cause great harm to a library's reputation. Even a shining reputation can be tarnished, and such tarnish bleeds away negotiating strength.

Never Take Goodwill for Granted

They are rare, thank goodness, so we think of them as horror stories: sad tales of squandered goodwill that threaten the high ground libraries have long held in our culture. This high ground is one of our most valuable assets and a potent tool when the time comes to make a case for our share of scarce resources. Some of these horror stories are serious, as in the case of the Lexington, Kentucky, public library. This institution in the heart of bluegrass country got a black eye in 2009 when stories appeared in the city's newspaper of the director's allegedly questionable purchase of gifts, meals, and other expensive amenities on the taxpayers' tab. The embarrassing outcome was Lexington's mayor requiring library board members to attend workshops on the proper use of public funds. Other instances are perhaps less dire, as with the blogger who became offended when an art display at a New York library included fanciful mug shots of members of the George W. Bush administration, meant to look as though the politicians had been arrested and booked on charges stemming from their actions while in office. As dissimilar as these cases may be, each has a similar, unfortunate outcome: a potential loss of confidence in the library. The order of magnitude is clearly different, but neither situation makes life any easier for those whose job it is to make the library prosper.

Why mention these uncommon situations? Because it is important to keep in mind the strong positive regard in which most libraries are held and the ease with which a reputation can be tarnished. A tarnished reputation does not help at the negotiating table.

Like it or not, the public eye is always on libraries. Two related areas of public librarianship that occasionally draw attention, and sometimes crowds, are collection development and circulation policy. And it is here that negotiation with user groups can be, by turns, inspiring and sticky. Take for example the controversy that bubbled up in late 2009 at Connecticut's Cheshire Public Library. The library found itself in a tug of war between a group of citizens who did not want the library to purchase a true crime book exploring the murder of a local family and a group of people upset by what they viewed as censorship.

This case provides an excellent example of media being a player in a positive outcome for the library. While the controversy raged, Chris Powell, managing editor of the nearby *Manchester Journal-Inquirer*, urged calm and reason from both camps, in essence championing the neutral stance on information cherished by the library profession. To those opposed to adding the book to the library's collection, Powell suggested that they could better honor the victims by supporting tough laws on career criminals. To those who complained that the library's willingness to consider not adding the book to the collection was tantamount to censorship, he offered that "crying 'censorship' whenever there is controversy" is an extreme position that demeans the library.

But media support of itself was not enough to win the day. Keeping in mind that "fortune favors the prepared mind," it is clear that a lack of preparation in this case could have been disastrous to the library's reputation. The library was caught in the middle of a fight between opposing factions, and it is difficult to see how it might reasonably "win" any other way than by basing its decision on a close and enlightened reading of its own bedrock roadmap of preparation: its collection development policies. That, in fact, is what happened. Library board members were eventually called upon to make a final judgment, and their interpretation of existing policy resulted in a 5–1 vote in favor of keeping the book in circulation. Library director Ramona Harten, however, continued to receive angry letters from citizens who disagreed with the vote.[2]

The case drew attention within the professional sphere. A June 2010 blog post by Anna Katterjohn on *Library Journal*'s website lauded the outcome and Harten's advice to other librarians who might find themselves in a similar position. "She stressed the importance of having a clear, publicly available selection policy that delineates a final arbiter who decides what will stay in the collection so challenges cannot be rehashed indefinitely—a major time-suck and productivity killer for the library and board." American Library Association (ALA) Intellectual Freedom Manual editor and contributing author Candice Morgan, who became involved in the case, "recommended keeping information on how the library deals with complaints and how to file them on the library's website."[3]

The complexities associated with collecting certain print materials can grow even greater with digital products and services. Adding digital content calls for reimagining the intersections among libraries, their vendors, and their constituencies. When that digital content is available on the internet, unavoidable questions are "Who gets to use it?" and "Who pays the tab?"

As a hypothetical, let's say that a library director in southern California is a huge fan of noir master Raymond Chandler and, knowing that there are many, many others like her in the world, decides her library should build a digital library of Chandlerania for use by anyone who wishes to access it. Is it fair to ask the taxpayers of her city or county to pay for this? Perhaps it is, because they will have unfettered access as well. That is a case that the director could easily, and probably successfully, make. If the director is even more ambitious, she might construct a report citing Chandler's worldwide popularity, as evidenced by broad and sustained book sales, film adaptations, and scholarly interpretations, and use this as the basis of a grant proposal in support of building the collection.

And how might she construct such a report so that it is the most effective negotiation tool it can be? First, she should adhere to Shapiro and Jankowski's essential preparation steps, using them as the basis on which to research and outline her report. As to the report itself, its sole purpose is to convince its audience that the project is appropriate and that its benefits outweigh its costs. She can do this by applying fundamental elements of persuasive rhetoric. That is, the report should have a defensible point, often referred to as a *thesis*, backed up by strong evidence. Such evidence should both highlight the proposal's benefits and anticipate any objections or doubts about its worthiness. We will assume it is obvious why one would highlight the benefits associated with the proposal, but perhaps some will question the sanity of anticipating objections. The answer is that by anticipating objections, the director can address and nullify them before someone who opposes the project voices them and they become a problem. The concluding section should flow logically from the evidence and point to tangible benefits to be derived from the project. Preparing this document serves at least two purposes. First, it allows the library director to get the situation, in all of its pertinent details, straight. Second, the report serves as the foundation for all future negotiations on this topic. It demonstrates the director's professionalism and the strength of the case.

By making situations such as this feasible, the internet has become a game changer for librarians. We must embrace this change and draw strength from it. A given library's user community can be much larger than its own ZIP code. Barbara Quint reminded us in a 2010 column that "we need to see ourselves as serving the world and not just narrow clienteles."[4]

What Can You Do When Things Get Complicated?

What was once stable, in the sense that printed materials exist in the most stable format available and present generally predictable challenges and benefits, becomes more dynamic, even potentially explosive, in the digital realm. The most familiar example of this reality involves the provision of internet services. Most libraries see providing internet access as a basic service, and the majority of the public seems to agree. Beyond the niceties of research for children's school projects or an adult casually surfing the net for a meatloaf recipe for the evening's dinner, there are important social issues at stake. For example, the debate is far from settled on what is appropriate for minors to access on the web. Teens and adults, too, need adequate information literacy skills to make the internet experience a useful one. Librarians understand that innocent reliance on untrustworthy sources can undercut one's intellectual life.

The vagaries of internet use provide ample areas for negotiation with user groups. Usually, these users will have benign or positive issues at the core of their interactions. Some may question time limits on terminal use. Others may have questions or suggestions for librarian-created links pages or concerns over what constitutes appropriate patron use of social media sites such as Facebook or Myspace in the library. In most of these cases, librarians will argue from a position of strength if they take Harten's advice and proceed from an understanding of clear, well-reasoned, board-approved policies.

One element such policies should contain is an unambiguous statement that the library does not function as a substitute parent for minors. The concept of some educational institutions functioning *in loco parentis* is familiar to almost everyone who has attended a primary or secondary school. The concept generally means that during school hours, students must obey teachers and school administrators as though these people were their parents. If students misbehave, the school has the institutional authority (some might say the duty) to discipline them. Such discipline should be bounded by legally approved policies and state law, of course, but depending on the locale, it could range from detention to expulsion, with a variety of other disciplinary tools thrown in for good measure. In other words, when a child messes up in school, the school can lay down the law.

Librarians must understand that they do not and should not have similar powers. This understanding should be explicitly stated in the library's legal, board-approved policy. The policy should apply broadly to the library environment and explicitly include the access and use of all resources—print, digital, you name it—the library offers. In making the case for this policy to confused or disgruntled community members, the wise librarian will rely on the library's core policies and the profession's foundational documents, especially the ALA's "Library Bill of Rights" (staging.ala.org/ala/aboutala/offices/oif/statementspols/statementsif/librarybillofrights.pdf) and more specifically "Free Access to Libraries by Minors: An Interpretation of the Library Bill of Rights" (staging.ala.org/ala/aboutala/offices/oif/statements pols/statementsif/interpretations/freeaccesslibraries.cfm), available to ALA members. These documents do not carry the force of law, of course, and librarians should in no way imply that they do. Nor should these documents be used as a stick to beat the other side in rigid defense of one's position. Remember, negotiation is about give and take. We must understand how much we can give and how much we cannot. A better way to view these documents is as a way to help patrons understand why policies are as they are. As a side note, these documents can also help library board members unfamiliar with intellectual freedom concepts to understand why a policy might need to be implemented, revised, or rescinded. They help the savvy librarian negotiate from strength.

The Library Bill of Rights

The ALA affirms that all libraries are forums for information and ideas and that the following basic policies should guide their services.

I. Books and other library resources should be provided for the interest, information, and enlightenment of all people of the community the library serves. Materials should not be excluded because of the origin, background, or views of those contributing to their creation.

II. Libraries should provide materials and information presenting all points of view on current and historical issues. Materials should not be proscribed or removed because of partisan or doctrinal disapproval.

III. Libraries should challenge censorship in the fulfillment of their responsibility to provide information and enlightenment.

IV. Libraries should cooperate with all persons and groups concerned with resisting abridgment of free expression and free access to ideas.

V. A person's right to use a library should not be denied or abridged because of origin, age, background, or views.

VI. Libraries which make exhibit spaces and meeting rooms available to the public they serve should make such facilities available on an equitable basis, regardless of the beliefs or affiliations of individuals or groups requesting their use.

Adopted June 18, 1948, by the ALA Council; amended February 2, 1961; amended June 28, 1967; amended January 23, 1980; inclusion of "age" reaffirmed January 24, 1996. From staging.ala.org/ala/aboutala/offices/oif/statementspols/statementsif/librarybillrights.cfm.

Sometimes negotiations become too complicated for typical strategies. This is especially true when complaints are brought by outside pressure groups. A high-profile case from around the turn of the millennium involved a feud between media personality Laura Schlessinger and the ALA. "Dr. Laura," as Schlessinger is generally known, used her substantial media resources to dramatically accuse ALA of purveying smut. Her complaint apparently originated from learning that the sex education book *Go Ask Alice* received a starred review in the July 1998 issue of *Library Journal.* Schlessinger began a loud, though largely unsuccessful, campaign against public libraries. A cornerstone of this campaign was opposition to unrestricted internet usage for minors, but she went further, urging her audience members to work to eliminate their local library's public funding. Though libraries across the U.S. did not disappear, Schlessinger is credited as a catalyst in Toys-R-Us's 1999 decision to abandon a substantial grant to the Fund for America's Libraries aimed at providing children's reading rooms in public libraries around the U.S. Schlessinger's use of mass media and rhetorical techniques amounted to a certain level of strength in "negotiating" her audience's attitudes and perceptions.[5]

How Can You Deal With Budget Crises?

Remember that trust breeds support, and supportive user communities can be a library's best advocates when the library must deal with troublesome issues, including budget crises. Indeed, mobilized library supporters can help a library director negotiate from a position of strength. For example, in the mid-1990s, the Sunflower County Library, a small library system headquartered in the impoverished Mississippi Delta, was faced with an ongoing budget crisis. The county board of supervisors voted to fund the library with no increase over the previous fiscal year, and the money in that previous year had hardly sufficed to allow the library to provide proper service to its patrons. A new director took charge of the library that year and decided on an aggressive, public strategy on the library's behalf. The plan was to fight the battle for next year's budget in the media. The director formed a close relationship with the local newspaper and made inroads into radio and television outlets as well. Every time a story was published or broadcast about the library, the director did his best to make sure it included the fact that there was no money in the current budget to purchase any books. He made a point not to insult the county board of supervisors, but he wasn't shy in reminding readers, listeners, viewers—and voters—that the supervisors had it in their power to increase the budget in the upcoming year so that new books could grace the library's shelves.

The most attention-grabbing event in the process came when the manager of a local radio station offered to host a "radiothon" to raise money for new books. While the few hours the station spent urging listeners to pledge did not raise a fortune, it was highly effective in other ways. The library hosted the event on the main service floor of its headquarters, with radio personalities requesting donations and library staff answering phones and taking money from supporters who came to the library to see what all the buzz was about. This fundraiser became the centerpiece of a final media blitz that beautifully highlighted the library's financial woes. The blitz included newspaper stories and on-the-scene television news reports from multiple stations, all focused on the radiothon and the community spirit that inspired it. When it came time for the next budget to be set, the library received an increase in its allotment. In subsequent news reports, the director was effusive in his praise of the supervisors and enthusiastic about what the increased funding would mean to the people of the county. In this way, an unfortunate problem turned into a win–win situation for the library and the board of supervisors. Media coverage made the budget into a high-profile issue, and both sides could honestly point to a positive outcome when asked about the library budget crunch.

Without question, the press, and its power to motivate the citizenry, can be a powerful tool for libraries in need of giving funding sources a little extra motivation, and it can be used effectively in support of libraries of all sizes. In September 2009, the Free Library of Philadelphia (FLP) appeared to be in a death spiral. Major news outlets around the U.S. and the world reported that, because of major financial shortfalls, the FLP would close all locations as of October 2. Reports were unclear on whether plans called for the library to eventually re-open, but ABC News, for one, reported on the other services in the city scheduled for termination shortly after the library got the ax. Officials said there was just no money to keep things running. The smart money would surely have been on the library door remaining shut indefinitely.

Advice From an Expert: Rebecca Mitchell, Part I

Thoughts on Funding Sources

Librarians are one group of professionals who take very little and offer much. With the downturn in the economy, patrons are flocking to their public libraries in record numbers for free or inexpensive access to entertainment and information to satisfy their curiosity and educational needs. We encourage our public libraries during this fiscal year to "beat their drums" for the services they provide to their communities. Look at the partnerships you maintain with schools, civic organizations, local government and its various departments, Head-Start, United Way organizations, and on and on. These partnerships provide libraries with a strong argument for funding at the local, state, and federal levels. How many other agencies do you know that truly reach from the cradle to the grave? Seek every opportunity to put your library and its programs in front of the community.

Since 2002, Rebecca Mitchell has been the director of the Alabama Public Library Service, which promotes and supports equitable access to library and information resources and services to enable all Alabamians to satisfy their educational, working, cultural, and leisure-time interests.

But the smart money would have been wrong. The library got an 11th-hour reprieve after thousands of anguished supporters, motivated by the library's media campaign, lobbied the Pennsylvania State Senate on its behalf. The Senate passed Resolution 1828 just a day before the closings were to commence, supplying funding to the library and allowing it to continue the mission it has followed since it became one of the first public libraries in the U.S., a direct successor to Benjamin Franklin's 18th-century Philadelphia Library Company. While no one can say for certain what will happen in the future, as of this writing, the FLP's doors remain open.

Be Successful at Lobbying

An unqualified success story arising from a confluence of grass-roots support, interagency cooperation, vision, and determination is the Alabama Virtual Library (AVL). This remarkable venture, mainly comprising online databases containing articles from magazines, journals, and newspapers, describes itself on its website (www.avl.lib.al.us/about) as providing "all students, teachers, and citizens of the State of Alabama with online access to essential library and information resources." The AVL's goal is to provide a high-quality baseline of information sources for all Alabamians, thus holistically improving education in the state. Although all libraries have the potential to help bridge the gap between the information haves and have-nots, the AVL was conceived as a way to greatly enhance that potential.

Created in the mid-1990s as a way to stem the tide of sometimes rowdy high school students crowding into public and academic libraries to use electronic library resources for homework assignments, it was and remains the mission of the AVL to provide a broad range of high-quality databases to the people of Alabama via public schools, colleges, universities, and libraries. It was a bold undertaking, essentially without precedent. The state of Georgia's virtual library, Galileo, was the first such statewide initiative to be up and running, but according to former AVL administrator Sue Medina, Galileo's concept was based on Alabama's planning documents. Now many, if not most, states have implemented similar projects.

What can the AVL teach us about negotiation? Plenty.

As we have seen throughout this book, arguing from a position of strength is always a plus, but it isn't always clear how to gain this strength. No matter how much of a no-brainer the AVL must have seemed to its instigators, without significant clout it would probably have been difficult to convince election-conscious politicians to provide the substantial monies necessary for the network to launch. After it became clear that the state's academic libraries, the K–12 media centers, and the public libraries (via the State Library) agreed on the AVL concept, the primary negotiation strategy for gaining funding was twofold: Drum up solid, passionate support from the citizenry and deliver that support to the state legislature via tens of thousands of postcards, either sent directly by the people or taken in bulk by Medina and other players who haunted the halls of the legislature building, talking up the project endlessly to their elected officials. The plan worked to the tune of a $3 million appropriation, and the AVL was on its way.

This is a prime example of negotiating from strength. The weight carried by the various library agencies alone would have been much smaller without the unambiguous support of voters. It is also a lesson in the value of interdependency. Without the tireless lobbying from the prime movers, the will of the voters would have been neither mobilized nor heard.

The lesson to be learned from these examples is that the people's voice can be a strong and powerful tool in negotiations. This lesson applies to large undertakings, such as the AVL, as well as to challenges faced by the smallest public library. The library must engage the community and make sure its members understand the challenges, dire and otherwise, that stand in the way of the library's full potential. In the case of both the tiny Mississippi Delta library system and the mighty FLP, news reports provided plenty of motivation for the citizenry to organize an impassioned campaign in support of libraries.

Interact With Users and Funding Sources

Of course, except for what news organizations choose to cover from library board, city council, and county government meetings, most negotiations will not take place in the media. To succeed in direct, face-to-face negotiation, you must have a plan, a command of pertinent facts, the ability to think on your feet, and, ideally, the capacity to work toward equitable solutions for all involved. If you've read this far in the book, you already know the basic elements of successful negotiation. We will spend some time now looking at how these elements have been applied to some real-world problems.

For this chapter, we picked the brains of three highly skilled and seasoned librarians who rose through the ranks from public library directors to become the heads of state libraries in Alabama, Kentucky, and New York, respectively, and one veteran community journalist who has seen, time and again, the delicate and sometimes brutal dance that is budget negotiation between public library directors and their funding agencies. The state librarians' experience as public library directors ranges from small-town institutions, such as the public library in Gadsden, Alabama, to the very large—the Boston Public Library (BPL), for example. As we have seen repeatedly on our negotiation journey, because successful negotiators tend to follow similar strategies, it will likely come as no surprise that their thoughts on the art of negotiation dovetail, though tempered by experiences unique to each of them. In simplest form, these thoughts coalesce around the following general admonitions: Be prepared, be honest, be a good listener, be sympathetic, be empathetic, know what you wish to accomplish, but remain flexible. All of these attributes bring strength to your side of the table.

While public library directors who would be effective negotiators must possess solid communication skills, the cultural capital possessed by their institutions can go a long way toward helping them succeed in many situations. Plainly stated, public libraries generally benefit from the positive regard with which most are held in their respective communities. This goodwill can provide powerful leverage when it comes time for budget negotiations. Occasional mistakes aside, public libraries tend to be high on everyone's hit parade, and a smart director will highlight the positives to anyone who will listen. For example, libraries deliver goods and services aplenty in the form of books, DVDs, CDs, databases, newspapers, magazines, and practically any other format you might care to mention. And let's not forget the librarians who slave over hot reference desks, build collections, and generally make the places where they work, work. Public libraries are a goldmine for genealogists, a place where youngsters can go for gleeful story hours and engrossing summer reading programs, a safe and convenient after-school hangout for teens, a front in the fight for literacy, and a haven for the community to come together to relax, learn, and be entertained. And they are so much more. A good public library is a source of pride for its community and a tangible sign that the people there value culture and learning. It also shows that very likely the community knows a thing or two about showing its best side to the world at large. For example, experts in community asset mapping include public libraries in their list of institutions that communities should look at when taking stock of the positive aspects of the place.[6] Yes, a savvy director can and should point to all of these strengths whenever the opportunity arises.

However, just because the public appreciates the services libraries provide, the public may not necessarily rally around the library when it comes time to fund the next fiscal year's budget. Part of the reason is that people tend to believe that libraries are on sound financial footing. As the Sunflower County and FLP examples illustrate, though, if the people know that a library is in trouble, they will often come charging in like the cavalry. A 2006 report from the Americans for Libraries Council brought the news that "While Americans give their public libraries an A more often than any other community service asked about (45% give libraries an A) and a large majority of the public (71%) says their local library uses public money well, few Americans are aware of the increasingly tenuous financial picture faced by many libraries."[7] The overwhelming majority of respondents agreed that if a public library closed because of lack of funding, it would be a great loss to the community.

While the basic functions of public libraries mirror that of their academic cousins—information collection, storage, organization, retrieval, and dissemination—the arenas in which negotiation takes place tend to differ. Whereas academic libraries tend to engage in negotiation primarily with individuals or entities of a professional nature—vendors, scholars, and so forth—and are somewhat insulated from public scrutiny, or even interest, by being housed within institutions of higher learning, public libraries are on the front lines of their communities. And practically anyone in the community, from church leaders to PTA parents, elementary schoolchildren, the illiterate, the homeless and their advocates, the mayor and members of the city council, are potential partners or adversaries in negotiation opportunities. And the day-to-day negotiation duties of frontline librarians and staff pale in comparison to those routinely held by members of the administration. Directors routinely find themselves in negotiations, formal or not, with library board members, elected officials, staff members, vendors, the public, the media, local schools, business leaders—you name it.

So what's a public library director who wants to succeed in negotiating with so many different constituencies, friends, "frenemies," and occasional adversaries to do? As in all negotiating situations, the keys are knowledge, clarity of purpose, strategy, and a command of effective communication skills. This raises the question of what knowledge base a director who wants to succeed in negotiations might require. There are the bread-and-butter elements, such as state library laws, the particulars of the library's policies, and the details of any contractual agreements with vendors or anyone else with whom the library may do business. These elements also include an understanding of how things run officially and how things happen in real life. It is the real-life part of the equation that can be hardest to learn, but it is always an important element for successful negotiation. Wayne Onkst, state librarian and commissioner for the Kentucky Department for Libraries and Archives, suggests that the biggest obstacle to successful negotiation is unenlightened self-interest, without any regard for the needs of those on the other side of the issue. And what breeds success? "I think it is being able to see both sides of the issue and finding common ground on which to create a resolution. Also, creativity that brings solutions that allow both parties to reach goals."

Onkst learned the value of figuring out both the official and real-world strategies for success soon after taking over the Commonwealth's top library job. Called on to negotiate a contentious grant award process that had gone awry, he struggled mightily to find a way for all of the principals to achieve their goals. He says that he learned a great deal from the process, but his new knowledge came at a price:

> The process of resolution was very ugly and left lasting scars with which I have had to deal. While I could clearly see the goals of all the parties, I had great difficulty finding a path that resolved the situation to the satisfaction of anyone. At that point I had very limited knowledge of how state government worked. And as this situation had not occurred previously, there wasn't much of a precedent to follow. Looking back, there were several paths that I could have taken to obtain a successful resolution. This situation was a great learning experience for me. As a result I developed a good support system for making future decisions. I have learned how the system works. I do a much better job of anticipating issues and trying to avoid similar situations. Also important, I try to talk to parties before potential situations arise.

Get to Know Your Constituency

Just as important in the long run as learning the official and unofficial techniques and strategies for working through a negotiation, but far less cut and dried, is knowledge of the people. It has long been accepted that librarians who wish to build effective, useful collections—digital, print, or otherwise—need to understand for whom they are building the collections and for what purposes these collections will be used. The same principle is involved in being a successful negotiator for the people. Learn who they are, learn what they need, determine the ways in which the library can help meet those needs in the most effective, ethical, and economical ways possible. As former president of the New York Public Library Paul LeClerc told a *New York Times* reporter who interviewed him on the occasion of LeClerc's retirement, "Find out what people want and give it to them."[8] On a national level, "Long Overdue: A Fresh Look at Public and Leadership Attitudes About Librarians in the 21st Century," a report prepared by Public Agenda with the support of the Bill and Melinda Gates Foundation and the Americans for Libraries Council, identified four actions public libraries might emphasize in order to place themselves in a position of strength: 1) provide stronger services for teens, 2) help address illiteracy and poor reading skills among adults, 3) provide ready access to information about government services, including making public documents and forms readily available, and 4) provide access to computers for all patrons.[9] A public library director wishing to maximize community goodwill would be wise to consider how to frame one or more of these issues for local media in relation to the library's service area, as well as identifying other pressing local issues the library might reasonably address. Making life better for patrons involves knowing what the patrons need and knowing how to get them to support the library in meeting those needs.

Establish Effective Communication With Funding Sources

As previous examples have illustrated, making a strong, clear case in the local press is a great way to build support. From nontraditional ideas such as Sunflower County's radiothon to news stories and editorials that alert citizens to a broad range of library issues, the media help people know what the library is doing and what it needs. Public support flows from public understanding. Curtis Robinson, a longtime community journalist who has, among many other things, covered municipal and county budget discussions for more than 30 years in a half-dozen states, urges librarians to address specific issues when petitioning for a budget allocation:

> You have to make it about results—you're not buying 1,000 new books; you're providing hundreds of children with the chance to read books they won't get at home. You have to be specific, engaging those who will benefit from the money you're asking for. Too many times, you see people with perfectly valid and really vital ideas, but they cloak those ideas in terms of the trade. You have to stress who benefits, and you have to show how that will happen. And I'd strongly suggest just the hint of a downside—what happens if that budget doesn't get approved? Who will not receive the services or materials being considered, or will there be cutbacks? It's competitive out there, and there are trends—in the last budget cycle, anyone who could tie budgets to jobs was in good shape, but a few years ago it was all homeland security. And I'd suggest looking at nontraditional grant proposals; for example, a lot of non-appropriated funding lately is coming through the Community Development Block Grant system, which is locally allotted, and then customize your appeal to those decision makers.

Robinson offers similar advice to the heads of other departments or organizations dependent on public funding, though he recognizes a huge difference in the ability of librarians, compared with police and fire chiefs, to engage their audiences:

Those areas have built-in megaphones, groups that identify the "end users" and lobby on their behalf; even their unions work differently because they are more specific—most library workers suffer from being part of a "bigger picture." For safety services, the "down side" is implied at every step—don't fund us, and you will be robbed and your house will burn down. So for a library advocate, it becomes even more critical to engage your community—and it really is a question of engaging the library's community. Then you have to go a step further—lots of people outside the library's immediate community realize its importance. I once saw a county economic development director deliver a moving speech about how he takes every single prospect past the library—these are people bringing jobs to the community—and he could not imagine explaining that it wasn't open on Wednesdays. He made it clear that the library was part of a vital community and part of why people choose to live and work in that community.

Robinson also suggests that, were he a library director, he would make certain that positive information about the library was included in relocation packages for local realtors. This, he says, would help to build a negotiation point.

Know the Three Basic Classes
of External Negotiations

Broadly speaking, there are three classes of external negotiations in which public libraries regularly engage: those mandated by law, which include governing bodies and funding agencies; those presented by custom, which include vendors, the media, and commerce and civic leaders; and those made necessary by service, which include library staff members and all potential patrons, sometimes including individuals who live outside the library's established and funded service area. Those libraries that elect to apply for grants or other supplemental funding add still more external negotiation opportunities into the mix. Effective negotiation with elements in each of these classes will be conducted on the basis of specific protocols, but the same principles broadly apply: Know your objectives; be clear and effective in your oral, written, and nonverbal communication; and be prepared for give and take within acceptable limits.[10]

Onkst suggests how to apply these principles in a professional situation: "Of course the first requirement is having a good plan for the future and knowing where your library is going—which should enable you to know what you hope to get out of any negotiations, along with what is absolutely necessary (or you can live with) when the negotiations are completed. I think it is equally important to know what the parties across the table need to come out with. If you can put yourself in the other parties' place and try to see the situation from their viewpoint, then you will have a better chance of success."

Onkst stresses the value of seeking ways in which both sides walk away from the table with some sort of positive result:

> I think an appropriate attitude is trying to find a way that both parties can win. More than likely, no one will get everything they want, but looking for unique ways to get both parties as close to their goals as possible will result in successful negotiations most of the time. If you can demonstrate this attitude, I think the trust you will create will also be helpful. Obviously communication is a required skill, along with empathy for the other party. Being able to focus on the major issues and looking for ways "out of the box" to achieve different goals is very helpful.

Underlying all this is a baseline skill that Rebecca Mitchell, director of the Alabama Public Library Service, lists as the most important characteristic of a successful negotiator. That skill is having, and exercising, genuine receptivity to the needs of the other party: "First and foremost, be a listener," she advises. "There's a good reason why we have two ears and one mouth." Mitchell stresses that this is the first key to successful negotiation, "whether it's your funding source or an irate patron at the desk or a staff member with whom you're not communicating well. Listen to what they're saying. Be slow to respond. Don't do an immediate flash back."

Mitchell advocates the age-old advice of taking a moment or two to consider unpleasant comments or situations before responding. She admits that, being human, "If you hit the right spot at the wrong time, I will flash, and I usually regret it tremendously. I'll give a quick answer" that "probably would have been better if I had taken a minute or two," let things sink in, and responded calmly. Once the heated moment has passed, Mitchell recommends calm, direct language. "Be extremely honest, while being tactful, but don't evade. Definitely don't lie, because you can't remember what the lie was after you've built upon it." When the negotiation involves a staff member or colleague, Mitchell suggests that good practice takes "into account where the person you're working with is coming from, as well as where you're coming from," in order to "be sure that you're on the same page. As a public library director, you're going to hit this on a daily basis. The only way you might not … is if you're the director of a one-staff-member library and you're the staff. Otherwise, if you've got one employee or a hundred employees, you have the potential every day of having to negotiate." Mitchell identifies the biggest hurdle facing a would-be negotiator as "rigidity: the feeling that 'how dare a junior person on my staff try to tell me how to do my job or have an idea that might make my job easier?' It's that false ego that's really easy to get into when you're in a role of leadership."

A rigid position from either side of the table can cause negotiations to reach a point from which it is impossible to move forward. If the other side refuses to budge, Mitchell advises library directors to do what they feel is best for the library and move on. "You've got to feel comfortable in making a decision and sticking with it," she said. Prior to her service as director of the Alabama Public Library Service, Mitchell directed the Gadsden Public Library, a midsize institution in a smallish Alabama town. One memory stands out of a failed negotiation with which she nevertheless feels comfortable, she says, as it was done in good faith and taken as far it could reasonably go. The incident involved a patron who was angry over access to local newspapers. The patron wanted a new newspaper every morning, but the library was at the mercy of mail delivery. As almost anyone who has worked in a public library knows, newspapers sometimes seem to arrive on a whimsical schedule. Some days they don't come at all; other days, three editions might arrive. The irate patron did not know or care about the vicissitudes of the U.S. Postal Service and made his displeasure painfully clear. Mitchell explained that the problem was out of her control, but this did nothing to calm the patron. "After about 15 minutes, it was obvious I was not going to make him happy. I finally just said, 'I've explained to you our procedure; I'm sorry you're unhappy, but there's not a thing I can do about it, and if you'll excuse me, I have to go back and handle some things I do have control over.' Don't be afraid to end it, but try to end it as politely as possible. Good manners will go a tremendous way in helping to defuse a situation."

Mitchell touched on the added dimension of dealing with others from a position of real power and the importance of being fair to all parties, both in action and in appearance.

> This can be difficult when dealing with institutions of greatly varying needs. Because as state librarians, we have to make powerful elected officials—the governor, the legislature— comfortable with what we do. We have to give them a sense that we're trustworthy, that we do care about their constituents, regardless of whether they represent a community that may have 10,000 people in the county or whether it has 400,000 people in the county, that there is no favoritism based on the strength of the population. Then we have to deal with the public

librarians themselves to make them understand that we
understand where they're coming from, and we've got
to treat everybody as fairly as possible. It's like raising
children. Sometimes—having been a child, having
raised children, and now having grandchildren—I know
there are times when the needs of one child make you
give a little more attention to that child over another.
Same thing with libraries.

Not surprisingly, many of the same elements Mitchell lists as
necessary for good negotiation are echoed by her colleague, former BPL president and current New York State librarian Bernard
Margolis. Margolis led the BPL for roughly 11 years, from 1997
through early 2008. Taking a broad view of the topic, he notes that
"almost all of life is negotiation of one sort or another." Among the
qualities he attributes to a successful negotiator are an ability and
willingness to listen to the other side and the skills to clearly communicate one's own points. Beyond this, Margolis stresses the
human—even humane—elements that play a part in successful
and ethical negotiation practices. "Clearly you have to have some
degree of empathy and, at times, sympathy as well. You have to be
able to establish rapport and trust."

As to how rapport and trust might be nurtured, Margolis notes
that librarians have a built-in level of trust with the general public.
"We are, as a professional group, and as an institution, fairly well
respected, and I think that there is some implicit trust already that
surrounds the concept of library and librarian." However, when it
comes down to achieving the best negotiated outcome for a library
and its constituents, Margolis stresses the need to pay attention to
the details. His advice goes beyond the details of the deal to the
level of self-presentation. "You need to, in terms of your own character, and your own public behaviors, and your own demeanor, do
those things that a negotiator would want to do to establish trust."
Margolis's advice on establishing trust includes attention to everything from dress—"don't wear a green suit"—to tone of voice,
polite greetings, shaking hands, deciding where to sit, offering a

beverage, and so forth. "The trappings of the actual process are, I think, when done well, all designed to create a sense of comfort and a sense of trust on the part of the parties that are engaged."

Advice From an Expert: Rebecca Mitchell, Part II

Balancing Competing Interests

By way of an example of balancing competing needs and interests, Mitchell cited the case of the public library at Bayou La Batre, a casualty of Hurricane Katrina in 2005:

> There was no library service in that part of Mobile County. I couldn't do for everybody in the state—they didn't need it, for one thing—what I was doing to get Bayou La Batre back up. I had to take money and pump it into their community to provide rent, ... computers, ... shelving, ... [and] books so that they could get back up and serve the community. There were other libraries with needs in the state, but that one was so severe that it wasn't a matter of favoring it; it was a matter of need. So state librarians have this balancing act.

> In dealing with large or multiple constituencies, Mitchell advises looking at the big picture. The question to ask is, "How can I serve? not, How am I going to make all these people happy?"

Margolis also believes it is imperative that librarians understand the underlying values for which the negotiation is taking place. "What you do is critically important, whether you are negotiating with a donor for a gift, whether you are negotiating with a political structure for a budget increase or a budget allocation, or whether you are negotiating with an irate parent unhappy about rules for internet filtering. You need to have clearly in your mind the principles underlying the institution that you are representing in the negotiation."

The Digital Download on Negotiating With Donors

Book plates, named reading rooms or areas, and other traditional donor activities remain relevant, but the digital age offers a wider variety of opportunities for donor involvement. Many proprietary databases offer branding that allows a library to indicate who bought a given eresource. For example, if a potential donor has a special interest in historical newspapers, vendors such as Accessible Archives, Readex, and ProQuest, to name just a few, offer digitized historical newspaper collections. The landing page for products within these vendor lines can be customized locally to say "Brought to you by Mr. and Mrs. Smith."

Another example might be a donor interested in genealogy. In addition to the individual accounts available from Ancestry.com, a library edition is available from ProQuest. Like the newspaper example above, the landing page could tell authorized visitors who purchased this eresource for their community.

Many libraries already do this sort of locally customized branding, putting their institution's name somewhere on the landing page. This allows patrons who access these resources to understand that a particular eresource is not available on the free web but is instead brought to them by their local library. Libraries as a whole are interested in surfacing their content through the free web via Google, WorldCat.org, and more. If patrons come to the library-provided content via Google or Google Scholar (courtesy of the OpenURL), then the local library wants the patron to understand that although the indexing via Google may be free, the accompanying full text is not.

The negotiation Margolis counts as his most successful came in his days at the helm of BPL. He had been with the library a short time when a Boston philanthropist invited Margolis to the philanthropist's home for a breakfast meeting. The BPL Foundation had tried for years, with limited success, to enlist the man's financial support, so when the call came, Margolis was happy to take the meeting. As it turned out, the philanthropist had a proposition in mind. "He wanted to chat with me because he had amassed a huge collection of very rare maps: maps of North America, ... of New England, ... of Boston—a multimillion-dollar collection. And he was in the process of deciding where it should go. Not that he was tired of it, not that he was going to stop collecting, but he was making his plans—a very thoughtful man." The Library of Congress, Harvard, and the Massachusetts Institute of Technology had expressed interest in obtaining the collection, but it was clear that the potential donor was interested in housing his collection at the public library. It was at this point that Margolis employed a basic tenant of ethical negotiation: honesty.

Margolis admitted that BPL would love to have the collection but was in no position to accept it. "The library," Margolis said, "is a mess." He told the donor that BPL was underfunded and undersupported and physically incapable of housing the maps. Grab any good offer from a major institution, Margolis said. But Margolis knew the map collection could be a major boon to the library, so he took the conversation forward. "I said, 'You need to give me probably 5 years at least to get the library fixed up, back on track, back to its position of prominence before I could, in good conscience, say to you that I could be a good steward of your collection.' Well, needless to say, the negotiation had begun. He wanted to tell me that his stuff was available. I wanted to tell him that I wasn't prepared right then but I would be prepared. And I sort of invited him to the table to help me bring the [BPL] back to life." During the next 9 years, the donor invested about $2.5 million in the library, as well as paying for some major exhibitions and map materials. In the end, the donor made a $10 million gift to the library—twice what Margolis had proposed—and created a map center. "And we negotiated basically every step of the way," Margolis said.

Margolis's strategy was to keep the process moving forward by maintaining positive, open communication while always engaging in good-faith efforts:

> We invested in architects to do some architectural planning. We did some publications. We created a website. We named the map center even before we had a major gift, real major gift. We named the map center in this man's name—in his honor. With it being clear that in doing that, there was no quid pro quo—that we were not naming it as a part of a negotiation to get his collection or any money. So we did almost classic negotiation to the point where it was appropriate for him to say, "Okay, I wanted it at the library anyway, you know that. And not only will you get the collection, but here's $10 million to support it."

This case serves as a reminder, though, that libraries do not function in a vacuum. Regardless of what type of library is under discussion, it exists as part of a larger economy, and other powerful players in this larger economy can and do have significant impact on the library's negotiations and outcomes. A situation that ultimately led to one of Margolis's proudest achievements became mired in political infighting with a Boston mayor who, Margolis says, believed that "if you get outside resources, then the city can spend less." The resources for which Margolis entered into negotiation—a major art collection and concomitant funding—were substantial, "and so we needed, very carefully, for the mayor to understand that a gift of this sort did not let the city off the hook for having some obligation to feed and nurture a collection like this, even if money came with it."

Advice From an Expert: Elizabeth Aversa

Thoughts on Management

I look at negotiation as a part of all the planning that we do as managers. When we plan, for example, to make an offer to a job candidate, we are wise to plan the negotiation in advance of the conversation or before writing the offer. We need to have in mind just how far we can go in the offer—be it salary, starting date, perks and benefits, the start-up package—in other words, the "whole deal." To plan our negotiation, we have to know what our objective is: Do we want to hire this person immediately or several months out? Are we willing to pay top dollar, or is it worth it to satisfy the job seeker while possibly irritating the staff already in place? What are the costs and benefits of different solutions for which we'll negotiate? This is the key.

The same is true if we are dealing with a budget agency or funding authority. What can we afford to do without and, if we take less in our budget, can we make the dollar shortfall up in some other way? Providing lesser services, for instance, could be a solution. Again, the manager should consider the costs and benefits of making a particular offer. But the primary question is always, what is the objective that I need to meet?

At the same time, one needs to listen to the other party's point of view—and be flexible in thinking about the objectives of the negotiation. In library negotiations, what do we want to accomplish for the user when we negotiate with a vendor? What are the long- and short-term goals? Can we accomplish something that will eventually benefit the user by taking a pass on an immediate benefit?

Besides seeing to it that we know where we're trying to go with a given negotiation, another point I'd emphasize is that the manager also needs to know when the negotiating will end. What is the bottom line or the "final offer"? A manager should have a clear idea of this in advance of the opening offer or opening conversation.

These are the kinds of considerations that managers have to make in negotiating (and navigating) everyday business. I believe the basic principles—plan it, be flexible, and have a "last offer" in mind—are negotiating tips that serve us regardless of what and with whom we are negotiating. And last but not least, remember that the negotiations will end well if both parties win something in the deal!

Elizabeth Aversa is a professor with the School of Library and Information Studies (SLIS) at the University of Alabama (UA). From 2003 through 2011, she was director of SLIS at UA, and she has also served as director of the School of Information Sciences, University of Tennessee, Knoxville, and as dean of the School of Library and Information Science, The Catholic University of America, Washington, D.C.

And it is an object lesson that even a skilled negotiator with far-reaching accomplishments can sometimes fall victim to powerful enemies. After years of unpleasant association with Boston's mayor, Margolis's contract was not renewed on its 2007 expiration. Turning lemons into lemonade, Margolis made the move to the even larger stage of the New York State Library, where he continues to promote ethical and human negotiation practices. He offers this advice to those wishing to sharpen their skills: "No. 1, practice. No. 2, you need to observe others who you think do it well. No. 3, you need to observe good and bad negotiations. And, while I don't wish that on anybody in terms of observing the bad, I think that is one way we sort of learn and get some perspective."

In Chapter 1, we introduced the parable of the orange to illustrate the idea that you should talk, actively listen, and research the situation at hand in order not to miss the opportunity for a win–win bargain or at least a better alternative. Negotiations can be win–win if both sides perceive mutual benefit in a proposed solution. In any negotiation scenario, it is possible that one side wants the meat of the orange and the other wants the rind. The message of this story is that in a perfect world, each side would be able to negotiate exactly its desired outcome while helping the other side achieve its goal. And while none of us lives in a perfect world—how often, really, does the other side want nothing but the rind?—there are almost always ways in which both sides can come away with things they want. This is especially true when each side stands to benefit from the other's success. And this is nowhere more true than in cases of library negotiations with funding sources and user communities. After all, user groups certainly benefit from a strong, responsive library, and funding sources can point with pride to a library they helped to meet the public's needs.

Onkst advises to "watch people who are great negotiators. Talk with them and gain insights. Reading good articles and books on the topic [is] always helpful."[11] Onkst also reminds us that "experience is the best teacher." But none of us need to reinvent the wheel. The experiences of others can be as useful as the bloodied lip we earn at the negotiating table. The ability to succeed in negotiation is directly related to how you prepare yourself before you ever begin negotiations.

Endnotes

1. Ronald Shapiro and Mark A. Jankowski, *The Power of Nice: How to Negotiate So Everyone Wins—Especially You!* (New York: Wiley, 1998), 97–99, 110, 193.

2. Chris Powell, "Library Controversy Isn't About Censorship," *Connecticut Post Online*, October 30, 2009, accessed August 10, 2011, www.allbusiness.com/society-social-assistance-lifestyle/censorship/13361709-1.html.

3. Anna Katterjohn, "ALA 2010: Learning With Cheshire Public Library," June 27, 2010, accessed December 3, 2011, reviews.libraryjournal.com/2010/06/uncategorized/ala-2010-learning-with-cheshire-public-library.

4. Barbara Quint, "Searcher's Voice: Long Thoughts, Big Dreams," *Searcher* 18, no. 6 (July/August 2010), accessed July 19, 2011, www.infotoday.com/searcher/jul10/voice.shtml.

5. "Go Ask Alice? Not If Dr. Laura Can Help It," *School Library Journal*, June 1, 1999, accessed November 25, 2011, www.schoollibraryjournal.com/article/CA153261.html.

6. John Kretzmann and John McKnight, *Building Communities From the Inside Out: A Path Toward Finding and Mobilizing a Community's Assets* (Evanston, IL: The Asset-Based Community Development Institute, Institute for Policy Research, Northwestern University; Chicago, IL: Distributed by ACTA Publications, c1993).

7. Public Agenda, *Long Overdue: A Fresh Look at Public and Leadership Attitudes About LIBRARIES in the 21st Century* (New York: Public Agenda, 2006), accessed December 3, 2011, www.publicagenda.org/files/pdf/Long_Overdue.pdf.

8. Patricia Cohen, "Library Leader in Era of Change to Step Down," *New York Times*, November 18, 2009, accessed December 3, 2011, www.nytimes.com/2009/11/19/books/19library.html.

9. Public Agenda, *Long Overdue.*

10. All quotes and paraphrases attributed to Curtis Robinson are from an email interview conducted on September 8, 2009.

11. Unless otherwise noted, all quotes and paraphrases attributed to Onkst, Mitchell, and Margolis are from telephone interviews conducted in August 2009.

Chapter 6

Playing Hardball: When to Get Tough and When to Walk Away

While mutually beneficial negotiation is the gold standard among ethical professionals, sometimes it becomes necessary to vanquish an opponent. Classic advice to those in such a position comes to us by way of the 17th-century Japanese warrior Miyamoto Musashi. Between the ages of 18 and 29, the great *ronin*, or masterless samurai, is said to have fought 60 accomplished swordsmen to the death. Musashi then retired from the world and spent the last decades of his life dwelling in a cave, writing a book that today is recognized worldwide as a classic treatise on prevailing in combat, *A Book of Five Rings*. Musashi's book is more than just a roadmap to effective swordplay; it is a timeless guide to tactical success in most any competitive endeavor.

As evidence of the business world's embrace of Musashi's ideas, we refer to Donald G. Krause's gloss, *The Book of Five Rings for Executives*. Krause says of *A Book of Five Rings* that it "trains you to use a competitive sword which is capable of winning in all phases of business." He takes pains to differentiate between tactics and strategy, the twin pillars that support any successful enterprise. It is primarily tactics that concern both him and Musashi, and Krause succinctly explains the rationale behind adapting Musashi's tactical expertise to contemporary business dealings:

> Tactics are different from strategy. Strategy is a longer-term concept, while tactics are more immediate. Strategy is, to a great extent, academic and theoretical; tactics are practical. Businesses and executives can survive and

> prosper without expressed strategies. But, if businesses do not apply effective tactics on a daily basis, they will not survive for very long. No amount of planning for the next campaign does any good if you and your forces are destroyed in the current one. This does not mean that long-term strategy is not important, particularly as a context for tactics. However, the outcome of most competitive interactions in business life eventually boils down to which person uses the better tactics in the present situation.[1]

Krause discusses Musashi's ideas about the attributes of a strong tactician. In a nutshell, Musashi urges the warrior to approach conflict with "ordered flexibility," which provides a context from which to choose the appropriate action at the appropriate time. The warrior, or in this case the negotiator, must be prepared to strike with necessary resources and a full understanding of the environment, a proper attitude, concentration, and timing.

Krause argues that ordered flexibility is the most important of these principles, the one from which the others flow. Within this deceptively simple concept lies the essence of the martial spirit: "It embodies preparation, observation, poise, timing, and readiness to act. That is, in this position, the warrior is prepared to do whatever is necessary given the actual situation. He is grounded in the reality of the moment, observant and poised. Yet he can easily respond to changing circumstances. He does not make up his mind to act until the appropriate time; then when he does act, he moves decisively."[2]

In a duel between samurai, that decisive move is intended to kill the opponent quickly and efficiently. There is no thought of personal victory or defeat, of life or death, only of the appropriate action for that moment. That action is the mortal attack. The contemporary negotiator forced into a hardball situation would do well to emulate the samurai in all of this except the actual death blow. Destroying the opponent's position suffices. Krause provides a number of trenchant examples illustrating real-world applications of Musashi's ideas in situations ranging from Starbucks's brilliant business plan to Robert E. Lee's defeat in the American Civil War. Suffice it to say that Starbucks emulated Musashi's ideas and General Lee did not.

Though it is less intuitive that librarians will find themselves in situations requiring the cool, killing attitude of the samurai, the tactics laid out in *Five Rings* apply to almost any situation requiring tough negotiations. Let's face it; the phrase *ordered flexibility* could be a succinct job description throughout much of library land. And the concepts it contains—those of preparation, observation, poise, timing, and readiness to act decisively—translate well into hardball negotiation.

Lest we get too caught up in the macho connotations of samurai warriors and in-your-face-buddy confrontations, it is important to remember that hardball does not always equal violent or even heated debate. Careful, ethical preparation, while attending to the principles of ordered flexibility, can provide a basis for an unbeatable argument, even against powerful adversaries. When you make that kind of case, you are playing hardball.

In the world of libraries, hardball negotiation frequently concerns money. We need it, someone else has it, and both sides want very much to protect their own interests. This is apparent year in, year out when budget negotiations commence for the upcoming fiscal year. That is why preparation is vital. Wise administrators know not only their own institution's financial situation but learn what they can about the funding agencies' assets and liabilities, as well as the assets and liabilities of competing agencies. For example, a public library director who goes before the city council with a budget request can make a far stronger case if the director knows the city's financial condition and the financial condition of the police and fire departments, public works, and so forth. If the director can argue convincingly that a sound financial footing in one or more of the competing agencies could mean that agency doesn't need a budget increase this year, and that those funds should instead go to the library in order help reduce illiteracy, poverty, ignorance, and crime, it becomes easier to justify a budget increase for the library. Knowledge is power, and it can translate into money.

Other attributes of ordered flexibility come into play here as well. Observation? That's crucial. Our wise administrator observes a variety of nuanced situations, from the personalities of important officials and businesspersons to the condition of city streets and the general attitudes of the public. The more the administrator observes, processes, and transmutes into evidence for the funding argument, the better. Poise? Poise demonstrates confidence. It tells the folks on the other side of the table that you are in command of your facts, you know why your case is important, and you have mastered effective communication. A poised librarian is often a successful librarian in any situation. Of course, all parts of an effective argument must be timed to their best effect. Proper timing prevents solid points from being dismissed or lost in the shuffle. It allows for the gasp of recognition when just the right thing is said at just the right time. It is akin to what Mark Twain meant when he said, "The difference between the right word and the almost right word is the difference between lightning and a lightning bug." All of this coalesces in decisive action, the effective and irresistible move to turn a request into a reality.

If a librarian attends to all of these elements when preparing for any sort of negotiation, from budget concerns to patron complaints, a successful outcome is much more likely. The example of the Free Library of Philadelphia has been described in an earlier chapter, so only a summary is provided here. Faced with closing its doors for good after more than a century of service, the administration went on the offense. In addition to the inevitable back-channel machinations and official pronouncements at public meetings, administrators brought together massive public support through a brilliant public relations campaign waged in the local media. The public became outraged, and that outrage boiled over into a massive letter-writing campaign that library officials credited with turning the political tide in their favor.[3]

Using the media to one's advantage can be helpful in negotiating for digital content and services. Librarians often rely on one another for the scoop on companies, products, and services. This reliance can come in the form of publications in magazines such as the *Charleston Review* or in *Against the Grain*. Or librarians may present on certain topics at conferences and symposia. This is particularly effective if a negotiator has any sort of publication or presentation record. A remark akin to "I was thinking of writing an article about the differences between EBSCO and ProQuest's discovery system … " can be quite successful when used during negotiation.

Another informal example is personal communication. For example, a library might be considering purchasing an electronic resource management system. The library decides to compare products from three companies. As part of the comparison process, librarians on the decision committee call librarians at peer institutions and ask about their experiences with products A, B, and C. Reminding companies that we do this sort of sharing can be a powerful tactic if introduced at the right time.

Unfortunately, the trenchant negotiator playing hardball is not part of the standard librarian or information professional's persona. That can be to our detriment when dealing with an adversary who uses our service-oriented nature against us. After all, we are trained to give people what they want, and everyone knows that about us.

Certainly, if you are the type of person who likes to barter and negotiate in your personal life—if paying full price for anything goes against the grain—then difficult negotiation scenarios may prove less daunting. However, for both the natural negotiator and those who happily pay sticker price, the specific maneuvers and skills associated with playing hardball can be cultivated and learned. Most negotiations are respectful affairs, and many are nonevents. The contract sails through with changes accepted on both sides without question. The potential employee asks for salary X, the employer counteroffers reasonable salary Y, and the employee accepts. Some negotiations, however, require more finesse, and some can be downright painful. In such cases, Musashi has much to teach us.

Negotiating Salaries

Negotiating for salaries is a delicate issue and one that many of us find distasteful. Many librarians entered the profession because of a desire to serve the public and therefore may expect the low salaries that can accompany service professions. Moreover, librarianship is without a doubt a "pink collar" profession, and historically women have been paid less than men. While many would argue with this statement, it remains true that women are generally not encouraged in our society (at least in the U.S.) to be aggressive, which translates in the professional world as being less than forceful when it comes to salary negotiation. This is no excuse, however, for refusing to negotiate your salary.

In an *AALL Spectrum* article from September/October 2004, Elizabeth G. Adelman summarizes a session given by Leigh S. Estabrook at the 2004 American Association of Law Librarians Annual Meeting (www.aallnet.org/products/pub_sp0409/pub_sp0409_Salaries.pdf). In the session, Estabrook gave six rules for salary negotiation. All six are worth reading and considering, but Rule 6 is especially pertinent: "If you get everything you ask for during negotiations, you did not ask for enough." Make a list prior to the negotiation and be sure to include some items that are highly unlikely. This way, the employer feels that you compromised and you feel as if you received enough of your desirables to warrant a "yes" to employment.

One industry veteran shared the following scenario of a negotiation between a librarian employed by a publisher and an aggregator wishing to include the publisher's content in its products. In the mid-1990s, in the early days of digitization, publisher A had accepted a one-page aggregator contract as is, no questions asked. Publisher A hired a new librarian, and the librarian closely read the contract and realized that while the business terms were sufficient, other parts of the contract were too simplistic and did not address all the necessary terms and conditions. She contacted the appropriate representative at the aggregator, and the two agreed to meet and work through the issues together. In the meantime, upper management at the aggregator arranged a surprise meeting at a conference with both the aggregator's representative and the librarian in attendance, in essence disregarding their agreement to meet.

With this action, the upper management at the aggregator was taking advantage of the environment, acting from a position of strength, and using surprise to unsettle the librarian and diminish the librarian's power. All of this, it would seem, was in preparation for a deathblow to the librarian's case. If that was the intent, then the unannounced meeting was the decisive, appropriate action at the appropriate time. Trade the surprise meeting for a sword, and the librarian is cut in two, end of story. Musashi would be proud. As it happened, the death blow was not delivered. Rather, the upper management at the aggregator backed down from the meeting after learning that a good working relationship already existed between the two parties. But the aggressive action of calling the meeting seriously damaged, for a time, the trust that had been carefully built between them. Now, you may be thinking, Musashi's pride would turn to scorn. You are sure that he would make it clear that when one strikes an opponent, the only positive outcome is to vanquish that opponent. In serious conflict, leaving the opponent wounded but able to respond is never a good idea. And that would be one way to look at things. Another way would be to declare that the aggregator, realizing the reality of the situation at hand, employed ordered flexibility by calling off the meeting and letting the original negotiators proceed. Trust was restored; in time, a mutually satisfactory conclusion was reached. As this was the desired outcome, Musashi would certainly approve.

The preceding scenario offers several teaching points. One has been discussed in previous chapters but cannot be stressed enough: Every contract needs to be read and understood by both parties. In this example, the complexity of the deal between the publisher and the aggregator necessitated a more detailed contract. Especially in the early days of digitization and electronic journal publishing, publishers, libraries, and the like had any number of individuals within the organization signing contracts and agreeing to terms and conditions. Companies were more likely to have lawyers reviewing contracts, but lawyers may or may not understand the intricate world of electronic publishing and library-publisher relationships. In the preceding example, previous personnel at the publisher did not fully understand the nature of electronic content and thus assumed the one-page contract was sufficient.

Experience Is an Expensive Teacher

In the library world, those responsible for selecting content, such as reference or collection librarians, may have signed contracts without understanding common legal terminology. Libraries had to quickly rein in this practice and assign the task of carefully reading and negotiating contracts to qualified individuals. Depending on the size of the organization, this task might fall to the director, the associate director, or perhaps an electronic resources librarian. (Issues of workflow and duty assignment are discussed in greater detail in Chapter 8.) However, during difficult negotiation, having the most experienced and skilled negotiator becomes crucial. As noted at the beginning of this chapter, difficult negotiations often offer the most teachable moments, but experience can also be the most expensive teacher. Charging information professionals with negotiating big-ticket items without giving the professionals the necessary skills is akin to throwing a child into a lake to teach the child to swim. That being said, it is still important to include novices in the processes involved in difficult negotiations. Excluding the next generation from the give-and-take involved in any important negotiation denies novices the opportunity to become skilled negotiators in their own right. Furthermore, new electronic resource librarians can negotiate their presence at the table with the publisher CEOs and the library deans, if only as bystanders.

For example, learning when a handshake is appropriate and when it is not is one of those real-world skills that can be learned from observing the pros. Agreeing to something on a handshake is proper for certain situations but by no means for every step in the negotiation process. In the earlier scenario, the publisher's librarian and the aggregator's representative had agreed by a "handshake" to sit down at a future date to work through the details of a better contract. They were not agreeing to the terms and conditions on a handshake. In difficult negotiations, it becomes ever more important to get terms in writing. Industry veterans interviewed for this book—from library directors and deans to publishers and consortia directors—all repeated again and again as a mantra: "Get it in writing." The famous remark attributed to Sam Goldwyn remains a classic: "An oral contract isn't worth the paper it's written on."

One example emerges from a potential employee and employer negotiating terms of hiring. The potential employee was pleased with all of the negotiated terms. The salary and the moving expenses, along with other elements, duly appeared in the offer letter. The employee accepted the position and began happily. During the negotiation, the new librarian had also requested 2 days of vacation during the first month of employment, even though the vacation time would not have been earned by then. The employer agreed, but unfortunately, this item was omitted from the offer letter. On the first day on the job, the new employee reminded the employer of this agreement, but the employer would not honor it, saying that vacation could not be taken before it was earned. While it is easy to blame the employer for "getting the best" of the new employee, it is far more likely that the employer simply forgot the original agreement. Moreover, since it was not in the offer letter, other employees wanting vacation without yet earning it could cause the employer grief. The notion of getting terms in writing protects everyone involved in any negotiation.

What the new librarian lost was fairly small—a couple days of vacation—but much more can be at stake. Chapter 4 refers several times to the importance of negotiating perpetual access. It is particularly important to get such perpetual access in writing in the contract. Instead of a few days of lost vacation, your library could lose hundreds of thousands of dollars of content. Lots of Copies Keep Stuff Safe (lockss.stanford.edu/lockss/Home) and Portico (www.portico.org) are the two best-known initiatives to assist librarians and publishers alike in dealing with the complicated issues of perpetual access. Librarians negotiating contracts should familiarize themselves with both options.

Even amenable changes to terms and conditions, particularly regarding midyear contractual changes or changes for which the company does not require a new amendment or contract, should be written down. For example, in discussing an upcoming renewal of a business database, the head of a business library requests the vendor's customer service representative to allow remote access, something previously prohibited. The rep checks with the higher-ups and indicates in a phone call that this change is acceptable. Before the library adds said business database's URL to the proxy server or other remote access authentication schema, however, the library must get the new terms in writing, if only in an email. If the vendor is not willing to write it down or remove the original clause prohibiting remote access, then red flags should start waving for the librarian.

Removing an original clause from a contract or simply remaining silent on a given provision is invaluable. Remaining silent is a common tactic that often resolves any number of disputes. Perhaps a state institution that cannot legally agree to an external state governing law will agree to remain silent on this issue, weighing the risk that litigation is unlikely and the product at hand too important to walk away from the table. Perhaps a publisher will agree to remain silent on interlibrary loan rather than spelling out all the tedious details of interlibrary loan for its electronic content. A large part of any negotiation is weighing the risk of a future problem against the time and money spent writing and revising contracts. Is it important for a library to insist that a contract explicitly state that walk-in users be allowed access to its licensed electronic resources? Perhaps it is, depending on the institution's status as a private or public library and its mission statement as a whole.

When one is reviewing a license with unacceptable terms, one tactic is to transfer the assessment of risk to the other party. In other words, the librarian can simply strike out the unacceptable terms and return the contract. Perhaps the vendor's or publisher's lawyers will determine that the risk is acceptable and not put up a fuss—it may simply be easier for them to cash your check than to fret over unlikely breaches of contract. If a fuss does ensue over a clause, then unless you have a legal background, risk assessment is something best done with a lawyer. Lawyers are more familiar with this process and can advise about the realistic chances of litigation versus the hours, days, and even months of time it can take to wrangle over a given clause.

Ineffective Communication Is a Barrier to Effective Negotiation

Trusting, getting it in writing, and remaining silent are three elements that become ever more important in a difficult negotiation. Another useful tactic is, "My boss won't approve that." Most of us have experienced it either personally or vicariously through television or the movies: buying a car and having the salesperson disappear to check a price with the boss. Upper administrators are often too busy to deal with each and every negotiation. While it is important to deal with the person who can make the ultimate decision on price and other matters, it is not always practical to do so. An organization's workflow and staffing model can create a situation in which lower-level personnel begin the process but may not have the final word.

For example, if signatory authority, which is the legal right to sign contracts on an organization's behalf, does not reside within the library, a librarian is often caught in the middle. (However, if you are expected to sign legal documents, make sure that is clearly specified in your job description. Again, get it in writing.) The legal or purchasing office is simply too overwhelmed or too understaffed to handle the volume of contracts generated by the library. Many academic libraries spend 50 percent or more of their collections budgets on electronic resources. The mean for libraries in

2007–2008 was 51.45 percent of the library materials budget being spent on electronic materials, with some institutions as high as 88.5 percent.[4] This growing number of eresources means that more manpower is needed to deal with all that goes along with their acquisitions. While initiatives such as the Shared Electronic Resource Understanding (see Chapter 7) are gaining ground, the vast majority of eresources still require licenses. The math speaks for itself: Even the largest institutions are not likely to have a lawyer or purchasing agent on hand to negotiate each and every eresource contract. Depending on the institution, it may not be wise to out-source all negotiation to a unit external to the library. Regardless of the distribution of duty, when negotiation becomes sticky and one gets stuck in the middle, internal communication must reign supreme. The last thing anyone wants in a negotiation is to say one thing and then have the other party call the boss, only to hear something entirely different. Trust and credibility can disappear in the space of a phone call. When a negotiation transforms from the norm to the unusual, it behooves the non-administrator to know when to call in the boss. Likewise, wise administrators give their employees a clear understanding of when and where the employee's authority begins and ends.

All those in the business of negotiating for products and services must do a delicate dance up and down the ladder of authority. It is the job and raison d'être of a salesperson to sell products. It is the role of the acquisitions librarian to buy those products. Is it worth the time of the wise director or dean to get involved and negotiate a $1,000 price tag instead of $1,500? Perhaps it would be a wiser use of time and money to grant the acquisitions librarian the authority to negotiate or accept all prices or terms within a given range. Is it important the buyer communicate with the seller who can make the final decision on price? It is, but a wise company will, like the library director or university administrator, grant its employees the authority to accept terms and prices within a given range. If the price extends beyond that range, then it is fitting that future negotiation be handled by upper management or administration. Again, clear and consistent internal communication and policy can create a cost/benefit analysis that makes funding sources smile. If librarians or information professionals find themselves in a position without a clear policy, they must create and/or negotiate it with those who reside further up the food chain.

Advice From an Expert:
Anne E. McKee

How to Negotiate Fairly and Honestly
(Without Imploding Like AIG)

In late 2008, unchecked corporate greed corrupted and brought the world's economy to the brink of utter devastation. Perhaps it is time to dust off, educate, and re-employ the well-meaning phrase "ethical business tactics." While relatively few libraries, publishers, content providers, and so forth have ever shown the avarice that some of the business sector has demonstrated, there is no doubt that there are many gray areas in content negotiations all along the information chain.

The first step to ethical negotiations is one of those "head-slapping" moments. Simply put, all involved parties need to understand that both sides can and should learn from each other! With the onset of electronic content and the long, involved negotiations and contracts that go with it, librarians have had to reach outside their comfort zones and learn contract legalese. Electronic content has forced libraries to re-examine and employ better business practices—courses not usually taught in library science graduate courses. Accordingly, the commercial side has recognized (like never before) that content and products cannot be developed—much less sold—in a vacuum. They now actively seek librarians' opinions and advice on what products are needed in the library marketplace.

Frank, open, honest, and ethical negotiations are vital to acquiring a needed resource or service. Both sides simply need to consider and employ the Golden Rule. Libraries should remember that the commercial side offers needed content or services but must generate a profit to maintain these services or information. An ethical dilemma occurs in the librarian's eyes when the profit is perceived as being excessive. Certainly in the case of public libraries, publishers must realize that libraries view themselves as information providers to the disenfranchised. Academic libraries serve faculty and students in the name of education, as well as researchers whose primary motivation is often nonprofit-based. Frank discussions and mutual rapport are paramount to ethical, long-term business relationships.

Unsavory business practices on both sides need to be exterminated once and for all. Ask any librarian or commercial representative, and one will hear examples of unethical behavior rearing its ugly head. "Suggestions" of new computer software or hardware or donations to the institution's annual fund are not unheard of during negotiations. As a matter of fact, the commercial side has some very unsavory nicknames for librarians who welcome or even expect these offers. The commercial side may attempt to get a decision awarding business to a competitor overturned, sometimes even to the point of contacting the decision-maker's supervisor or persuading some sympathetic alumni to become involved.

With business ethics much more under the microscope these days than in the past few decades, these unsavory (albeit never very widely used) practices or expectations may die a much-needed death. Library science graduate students, publishers, and vendors alike should be encouraged to attend seminars on ethical negotiations. Library associations and commercial professional organizations should be encouraged to offer courses on maintaining integrity while negotiating for business. Perhaps the creation of a certification process on ethical negotiations should be explored.

In conclusion, a library and the commercial representative should emphatically agree that a positive, frank, and ethical relationship has been formed by the time negotiations are concluded. If mutual rapport and trust have been established on both sides, then integrity can triumph over hypocrisy, and neither party would consider the other a creature from the dark side. Surely, this would make the Gods of Ethics sigh in satisfaction!

Anne E. McKee is the program officer for resource sharing at the Greater Western Library Alliance (www.gwla.org), a regional consortium of leading research libraries located in the central and western United States. She has spoken and written frequently on the topic of negotiation and ethics in libraries.

Beware of Culture Clash

Sometimes there is a literal culture clash, particularly when one is negotiating with vendors or publishers from countries other than the U.S. For example, a researcher at a large state university negotiated for laboratory supplies from a French company. The researcher went through the appropriate channels in the university purchasing and contract offices, and all seemed well until he got the bill. The French company had added tax to the order. The researcher had simply assumed the university's tax-exempt status would apply, but in reality, this status exempted the university only from state sales and federal excise taxes. The university purchasing office got involved again and negotiated that, because of the university's existing tax-exempt status, no tax would be added.

More often, however, the culture clash has less to do with geography. Many negotiations go awry because of a lack of understanding of the different cultures within which libraries, content providers, publishers, aggregators, and other relevant parties exist. Previous chapters discuss the importance of conducting research about the other party. Appendix A offers information about how to conduct such research.

For example, an academic librarian may become immediately distrustful of a salesperson who insists on calling the faculty directly, trying to convince faculty members that a product is indispensable. Sometimes this sort of direct marketing is simply the result of a salesperson's or company's misunderstanding of the culture of a particular organization. The eager salesperson might think, "Why not market directly and have the end user request my product?" Indeed, more and more vendors are renting booths at meetings of professional associations, such as the American Historical Association or the American Psychological Association. A very fine line separates informing end users about a product so that they will ask the library to purchase it, on one hand, and attempting to railroad the library into buying a product, on the other. It would be lovely to think that all such practices are the result of cultural ignorance. They are not. Information samurai Barbara Quint makes a vigorous case for librarian vigilance:

> Sometimes vendors attempt to acquire their own leverage, for example, by marketing directly to your clients or your managers. Stop that fast! Let them know, in no uncertain terms, that any attempt to backdoor your own institution had better work 100 percent because if they don't kill you, you will certainly kill them. A vendor who attempts to push you out of the loop is not just an opponent but an enemy. Against such vendors, you fight hard, with no holds barred. You burn them with other clients. You bad-mouth them at Special Libraries Association meetings. You write and complain to *Searcher* magazine and other trade press. You dance on their grave. Vigorous, open assault on "enemy" vendor practices assures that other vendors will think twice before trying the same. If you have any Goody Two-shoes qualms about such open warfare, just consider. Why don't they want you in the loop? What do they plan to sell the suckers after you are gone? How good will their products stay, with no one around to watch them?[5]

Quint is dead right. We are not exchanging calling cards over cakes and tea with Emily Post or Miss Manners. Sincerity, respect, and truthfulness—all these things and more are critical elements of a successful negotiation, especially a difficult one. However, negotiating for products and services on behalf of our users is a hard-nosed business deal. It is not personal; it is business. Consider with whom we are dealing. When negotiating with a vendor, we usually interact with individuals who have a minimum of a bachelor of science degree in marketing, business, or a similar field. Upper-level managers may even have a master's degree in business administration. These individuals are motivated by considerations (job security, bonuses, commissions, etc.) that are different from those of information professionals. They operate on a completely different reward system. To treat a negotiation with a vendor as less than a business deal is to deprive it of the respect it deserves.

Understand Exclusivity Agreements

Speaking of business deals, much furor was raised when EBSCO announced its exclusivity agreements with several new publishers in January 2010. Quint and others weighed in. For a sampling, see the following:

- newsbreaks.infotoday.com/NewsBreaks/EBSCO-Exclusives-Trigger-Turmoil-60836.asp

- www.libraryjournal.com/article/CA6716120.html

- www.gale.cengage.com/fairaccess/index.htm

- www.ebscohost.com/special/temp01-2010/EP-Response-to-Gale.pdf

Amid all the letters, rebuttals, opinions, conference presentations, and analyses, it was difficult for rank-and-file librarians charged with evaluating and purchasing eresources to separate the wheat from the chaff. *But that is part of the job.*

Obviously, exclusive access to content via one publisher can be challenging, especially in terms of negotiation. A monopoly on content can drastically increase prices, but such content monopolies are nothing new. In the July/August 2001 issue of *Searcher* magazine, Larry Krumenaker examined the issue of unique and exclusive titles with the same players who would be enmeshed in the exclusivity flap nearly a decade later: EBSCO, ProQuest, and Gale.[6] Analyzing all the components of exclusivity agreements part by part allows librarians to determine what is at stake. This is all part of doing one's homework prior to negotiating for any digital content. The librarian should ask the following questions:

- What content is now exclusive?

- When will it become exclusive?

- When do the exclusivity agreements expire?

- Will the content be pulled from other aggregators?

- If so, when?

- Is this content core to the mission of the library?

- What is the price this year for this content? Next year?

- Is it truly exclusive, or is it available in a different form elsewhere? In other words, are there alternatives to offer this content to patrons?

- Can the library work with other libraries, even those with different missions, to provide access to this content?

The Digital Download on Exclusivity Agreements

Let's examine one of the questions a librarian must consider when dealing with a vendor who purports to have exclusive content: Is it truly exclusive, or is it available in a different form elsewhere? In other words, are there alternatives for offering this content to patrons?

Popular titles (e.g., *TIME* or *People*) make some or all of their content available for free on the web because much of their revenue comes from advertisements. If aggregator A claims exclusivity, then perhaps aggregator B indexes the content and links to its free full-text counterpart on the web. This free content may be less stable or may not offer as many value-added features, but it may meet the needs of a library's patrons.

If the titles are truly exclusive, alternatives such as document delivery or interlibrary loan may suffice, although they are less convenient for users. Open and honest communication with the stakeholders about exclusivity and its myriad ramifications is paramount if the librarian is to be an effective negotiator and an effective patron advocate.

Before any discussion of the institution's philosophical stance on exclusivity, librarians must consider the day-to-day impact on the user. Is it possible to cancel the subscription? Perhaps, after careful consideration of the preceding questions, among others pertinent to a local library or particular situation, cancellation is feasible.

The International Coalition of Library Consortia, Association of Research Libraries (ARL), and other associations and organizations may issue statements and lobby against exclusivity, but if the local library does not have the support of its constituents to cancel an eresource, then discussions of ethics may become moot. This is not to say the local library should throw up its hands and surrender. Education of the users is paramount, and while a library may need to subscribe for the near term, perhaps its librarians can launch an aggressive user education campaign.

Does Gender Play a Role in Negotiation?

Librarianship is known as a pink-collar profession. According to the 2010 *Statistical Abstract of the United States*, in 2010, 82.8 percent of librarians were women. This statistic varies little from year to year; in 1983, the number was 87.3 percent, and in 1993, 88.3 percent.[7] Does gender play a role in how we negotiate? Are women more cooperative? Carol M. Rose wrote in the *Harvard Journal of Law & Public Policy*, "It seemed that women's actual taste for cooperation—if such a taste exists—is much less important than something else: people think women are likely to be cooperative types." If indeed women are more cooperative or perceived as more cooperative, women could conceivably "get less" in a bargain than their male counterparts could.

Rose goes on to note that being cooperative is not a bad thing, and actually, it is what allows the world to work. In fact, a taste for cooperation "is just disadvantageous to have when you are dealing with others who do not have it, or do not have as much of it, or do not have it towards you. In such instances, a taste for cooperation can lead to a losing strategy: if you behave too cooperatively, you will wind up with the short end of the stick."[8] It is important in a difficult negotiation to determine, to the extent possible, whether you are dealing with someone who is going to cooperate very little, if at all. This necessitates a shift in one's negotiation strategy in order not to give away too much. Perhaps the resolve to walk away needs to be ironclad in these situations, when no amount of cooperation is going to achieve a desirable result. It must be stressed, however, that if possible, when dealing with a difficult person, the better approach would be to call that person's boss and demand someone more cooperative at the negotiation table. Moreover, if indeed society perceives women as more cooperative and most librarians are women, we may be fighting an uphill battle. To be fair, there is the disparity between the percentage of men in the profession and the percentage of men in upper administration—upper administrators are often the ones conducting the most difficult negotiations for content from vendors and publishers. Yet, Marta Mestrovic Deyrup explains in a 2004 *College & Research Libraries* article, "women comprise 52.1 percent of all top administrators [in libraries] and serve as the majority on ARL's board of directors."[9] The fact remains that most of us are women, and we negotiate in any number of ways every day. Does gender play a role in this aspect of the job? If so, to what extent? It's worth considering.

Give and Receive R-E-S-P-E-C-T

Also worth considering is the perception of librarians as a whole. In conversations with frontline librarians, library administrators, retired information professionals, consortial directors, and more, one company emerged as consistently difficult, both in attitude and cooperation. Lore and preconceived notions—on both sides of the fence—can doom any negotiation before it begins. In an ideal world, we would all set aside these preconceived notions in an effort to "just get along." In the real world, just recognizing the problem and approaching it without emotion may be the best for which we can hope. If negotiators are rude and uncooperative, simply walk them to the door and indicate that you would be delighted to discuss the situation at a future date when they are willing to be reasonable. Then pick up the phone and ask their boss whether they will be more professional in the future or whether you should start dealing with someone else. Rudeness itself can be a strategy, and in the rare situation, it is in fact the boss who dictates the approach. If this is the case, then it is time to muster the troops. For example, get relevant faculty members involved and have them call the vendor and demand professionalism. With rare exceptions, you can always find alternatives, and abandoning negotiation remains an option.

Advice From an Expert:
Bernard Margolis

The Necessity of Playing Hardball

Let me talk about philosophy for a minute. I once sat with a man who was the marketing manager for a major publishing company, and he'd been very successful. And he told a story about an experiment with buying goods, such as jewelry, from the street vendors in the New York City parks. There were two groups [of buyers]. Group 1 deprecated the goods in an effort to reduce price. Group 2 praised the quality of the goods in an effort to reduce price. For example, a member of Group 1 might say, "The beads on this necklace are cracked. How much do you want for it?" The vendor responds, "$20." Group 1 member replies, "Well, it's so inferior, I'll give you $10." By contrast, a member of Group 2 might say, "Oh, these beads are beautiful. Look how well-proportioned. How much are they?" The vendor responds, "$20." Group 2 member replies, "Oh, I would love to have them … but I only have $5 with me today."

These scenarios were repeated again and again with multiple vendors, and every time, the people who praised and built up the goods got better prices than those who deprecated the goods. I share this story because it represents how I negotiate. Don't try to be powerful or forceful in a way that undermines or demeans the products and services. Always try to do the opposite. And this holds true for almost every kind of negotiation that I can imagine—whether it's a negotiation that is focused on economics, a negotiation on attracting an employee, or a negotiation for a different policy or procedure. Don't demean their perspectives. Don't demean their products and services.

If presented with a high-powered, hardball situation, I would simply say, "I don't think we're on the right track to be successful here, so let's revisit this. Let's come back to it again."

Bernard A. Margolis began serving as New York State Librarian and assistant commissioner for libraries in January 2009. He feels that imposing limits and making those limits transparent are critical components of the respectful negotiation. He also emphasizes that respect itself is the most important component of any negotiation.

Walking away requires the support of internal personnel and external constituencies, so communication among those groups is crucial. Check with a faculty member or researcher to find out whether you could dispense with publisher X's "indispensable" title. Determine whether the publisher or content provider is willing to risk the bad publicity you are willing to distribute. Demand transparency in pricing schema. If the vendor's negotiator continues to offer opaque explanations of pricing, ask the same questions over and over again until you receive a satisfactory answer. In terms of pricing, one library administrator warned against pricing schemes that take into account an institution's budget. A car dealership does not offer a price based on my personal income but rather on the quality of the car. Likewise, an institution's budget is irrelevant to any discussion of price—price can be determined by any number of other variables, including but not limited to the quality of the product and the size of the potential userbase.

As the samurai know, remaining respectful and jettisoning timidity are by no means mutually exclusive. By respecting ourselves, our profession, and our mutual goals, we collaborate to meet difficult challenges directly and successfully. One such example is the Big Deal Contract Project (www.econ.ucsb.edu/~tedb/Journals/ BundleContracts.html), launched by Ted Bergstrom, Paul Courant, and R. Preston McAfee in an effort to publish the big deal contracts between publishers and academic libraries. Using state open-record laws, the project forces the disclosure of contracts, regardless of confidentiality clauses. Confidentiality clauses can hinder the ability of information professionals to research a given product or service; thus, deals can vary wildly from institution to institution and consortium to consortium. The ARL has also issued a statement urging its members to reject confidentiality clauses and nondisclosure agreements (www.arl.org/bm~doc/rli-264-non disclosure.pdf). Not everyone takes issue with confidentiality clauses, however. One retired corporate librarian who spent years negotiating agreements noted that confidentiality clauses are the norm in other business arenas, and she simply felt it was "good faith" not to discuss a particular agreement.

Before we don armor and prepare for heavy battle, it is important to remember that most negotiations are amicable, and rare is the person who is truly and uncompromisingly uncooperative. Negotiation is about mutual gain. There is a difference between walking away from a given deal and suggesting that both parties revisit the deal when either one or both can be more reasonable and cooperative.

Endnotes

1. Donald G. Krause and Miyamoto Musashi, *The Book of Five Rings for Executives* (London: Nicholas Brealey, 1998), 6.

2. Ibid., 6.

3. Corey Doctorow, "Philadelphia Free Library System Saved," *Boing Boing*, September 21, 2009, accessed July 27, 2011, boingboing.net/ 2009/09/21/philadelphia-free-li-1.html.

4. These statistics can be found at the Association of Research Libraries, www.arl.org/stats/annualsurveys/arlstats/arlstats08.shtml and the Association for College and Research Libraries, www.ala.org/ala/mgrps/divs/acrl/publications/trends/2008/index.cfm.

5. Barbara Quint, "Six Rules of Engagement: Negotiating Deals with Vendors," *Bottom Line* 10, no. 1 (1997): 4–10.

6. Larry Krumenaker, "A Tempest in a Librarian's Teapot: EBSCO, ProQuest, Gale Exclusive and Unique Titles," *Searcher* 9, no. 7 (July/August 2001), accessed July 27, 2011, www.infotoday.com/searcher/jul01/krumenaker.htm.

7. These statistics can be found at www.census.gov/compendia/statab; 1983, 1993: Table 637; 2010: Table 616.

8. Carol M. Rose, "Bargaining & Gender," *Harvard Journal of Law & Public Policy* 18, no. 2 (1995): 547–555.

9. Marta Mestrovic Deyrup, "Is the Revolution Over? Gender, Economic and Professional Parity in Academic Library Leadership Positions," *College & Research Libraries* 65, no. 3 (2004): 242–250.

Chapter 7

Negotiating in the Era of Publisher Consolidation and the Big Deal

The importance of understanding any and all outside factors that might affect a negotiation cannot be understated. This includes understanding the options if a deal cannot be reached with a current provider. When negotiating for a new integrated library system or choosing a subscription agent for both print and electronic subscriptions, never forget that there are other products or providers of the same service. However, when negotiating for the acquisition of a particular journal or collection of journals, the ability to find a comparable product can be much more difficult, if not impossible. There is a sense, particularly in the science, technology, and medical field, that each periodical is a monopoly.

In a 2002 article in the *Journal of Economic Methodology*, Henk W. Plasmeijer described how this situation works in the publisher's favor: "Everyone seems to agree that an (almost) obligatory transfer of copyrights from the author to the owner of the journal is the foundation of the publishers' market power. Obviously, since a scientific article is a unique product for which in scientific communications no substitute exists, the transfer puts the publisher in the position of a monopolist."[1] How does one negotiate in a monopolized market? And what does negotiating in a monopolized market have to do with the much-lauded and much-maligned big deal pricing model? Let's advance our thimble past "Go," collect our $200, and find out.

What Is the Big Deal?

Discussion of the big deal is rampant in library literature, but on the whole, rumors of the big deal's death have been exaggerated. At the North American Serials Interest Group 2008 annual conference, Gary Ives defined the *big deal* as a deal that "provides access to all titles in a publisher's package, one that is accessible at all campuses, one whose pricing is based on [a] historic print subscription base, and one that may be offered as a multi-year agreement with negotiated price caps for each year of the agreement."[2] Chances are that any acquisitions librarian has heard the Ronco-esque pitch "For just a couple hundred dollars more than what you are already spending on subscriptions, you could get access to thousands more titles. ... " Just like the ShamWow infomercials, it is a tough pitch to resist. Increasing consolidation within journal publishing and consortial purchasing of journals has kept the big deal pricing model a popular one for many institutions.

Research on the big deal tends to provide evidence of its value—at least for some. A 2008 study by Cecilia Botero, Steven Carrico, and Michele R. Tennant in *Library Resources and Technical Services* demonstrated definitively that "despite a growing percentage of materials budget being spent on online bundled packages, the Big Deal at the UF [University of Florida] Libraries is a Good Deal if measured by overall use and by price per full-text downloads." While the University of Florida's Health Science Center Libraries saw a $12-per-article savings on big deal titles compared with document delivery, there is an inherent danger if libraries become increasingly reliant on big deals for access. Botero, et al., noted, "The team discovered very few titles received independent of the Big Deals that were both underused and expensive, concluding that canceling these titles would save little in the materials budget."[3] If budgets become tight, there will be a few individual titles that could be canceled to bring costs down, leaving libraries in the enviable position of needing to cannibalize other parts of the budget in order to support the costs of the library's big deals.

In "good" budget times, it is difficult to argue against the value. Consortia, in particular, can exploit these deals since they represent many subscriptions from individual libraries. Loretta Ebert, research library director at the New York State Library, noted that collaborative collection development is a definite advantage of the consortially negotiated big deal. From a negotiation perspective, this advantage is both empowering and terrifying. The idea that collection development librarians would have to consider not only the budget, collection, faculty, and students of their own institution, but also the budget, collection, faculty, and students of the institutions with which they are allied seems a Herculean data-crunching effort at renewal time.

On the other hand, this kind of collaboration can provide an opportunity to go into negotiations with greater leverage, as well as a contingency position in tough budget times: If one library has to cancel a title, another library can pick it up and still maintain access for all members. According to Ebert, it is not that consortia and the libraries within them do not want to see the reform of scholarly communication. Instead, as she puts it, "Our collective goal is to choose from among the best possible current options and at the same time provide our collective group of scholars and researchers, regardless of their home institutions, access to the best current research collections available to them."[4]

Not everyone is swayed by this measurement of the value of the big deal. When one library picks up a title that another library is forced to cancel, issues of territoriality can emerge. For example, faculty and administrators at one institution might not support spending their dollars on maintaining a title no one at their institution necessarily needs. One conjures images of betrayal and self-sufficiency in the film *O Brother, Where Art Thou*, set during the Great Depression: "They got this depression on. I got to do for me and mine."

Kenneth Frazier, director of the University of Wisconsin-Madison General Library System, is one of the biggest opponents of the big deal model. Frazier recognizes that while the cost might be persuasive initially, the big deal is not sustainable over time, and it doesn't set librarians and publishers on a path that will reform the scholarly communication and publishing industry: "Without reform of scholarly communication, there is no end to the cutting in sight. ... Librarians should be asking whose needs are being served by the Big Deal and whose needs are being sacrificed."[5] In late 2003 and early 2004, it seemed as though the big deal was in big trouble. Cornell University Libraries led a mini-revolt against the commercial journal publishing community with a faculty senate resolution that shunned the big deal and called for title-by-title selection due to the stress that bundled pricing plans were exerting on already-stagnant library budgets.

Harvard University Libraries and the California Digital Library announced similar plans, and it seemed that the revolution had begun. Ross Atkinson, associate university librarian for collections at Cornell, described the vicious cycle that big deals can create: "While some institutions had refused from the outset to buy into the bundled option, very few, if any, large institutions had actually started the plan and then stopped it, as we (and several other institutions this year) have now done. It's as if there had been a general assumption until this year that it was somehow impossible to do that—which is obviously not the case."[6]

Cornell and company's rejection of the big deal pricing model was big news. Even formidable consortia such as the Triangle Research Libraries Network (TRLN) have found themselves at the mercy of the big deal and in need of relief. In a 2005 presentation at the 28th U.K. Serials Group conference and subsequent article in *Serials*, Nancy J. Gibbs, head of the acquisitions department at Duke University, described how the four institutions that make up TRLN (Duke, University of North Carolina, North Carolina State University, and North Carolina Central University) undertook a careful but swift retreat from two big deals that it had entered into collaboratively. The retreat was called in the face of the "increasing costs of journal titles, the inability to cancel journal titles in order to subscribe to new titles and, of course, the inevitable reason: declining or static budgets."[7] Sound familiar? Like many of the other universities in big-deal trouble at this time, TRLN tried to negotiate with the publishers to meet users' needs and decrease expenditures to meet budget restraints.

However, negotiations continued to falter because of one of TRLN's stated licensing principles. Gibbs explained, "Librarians needed to be able to manage their collections and respond to changing budget situations."[8] Through much communication with users and university administrations and examination of usage stats and research program needs, the TRLN libraries were able to remake their Elsevier and Blackwell subscription lists. Moreover, they reaped the benefit of increased understanding from faculty and administrations about the need for budget increases and scholarly communication reform.

What do these libraries tell us about how to handle the current budget crisis that most if not all libraries are facing? Is the world economic crisis of 2008, 2009, and beyond going to be the straw that breaks the big deal's back? Has the perpetually inelastic scholarly journal market finally found its bounce? Maybe, but there's a method behind the big deal madness, and it has to do with the ever-shrinking academic publishing market.

The Digital Download on the Big Deal

Let's face it—without the internet, there would be no big deal. Sure, periodical titles have always been "bundled." Usually much-beloved, high-impact-factor titles are bundled with spin-offs and less-well-known titles that serve the same population of researchers. This practice allows the publisher to charge more without leaving buyers feeling as if they have been had, even if they would not have purchased the tag-along titles if given a choice. But the big deal goes well beyond a trio of titles that always travel together; it extends to thousands of titles joined at the hip, neck, knee, and foot, at least as far as your license is concerned, since 1995.

In the early days of the internet, ancestors of the open access (OA) movement gave publishers the bright idea to take the bundling of journals to new heights. In the late 1990s, librarians were suffering from a "serials pricing crisis," and the internet represented a possible tool in taking back control of their budgets. Librarians envisioned a world where collections of electronic-only, low-cost or no-cost journals—or OA journals—would be introduced into the marketplace and create some much-needed competition for existing print journals, especially those with prices spiraling out of control. Some of these OA journals caught on with their target audiences, but many had no chance of supplanting the status and reputation of their scholarly, print grandfathers. However, it turns out that you can teach old journals new tricks.

Commercial and academic publishers alike may not have seen much potential in these new upstart journals, but they did see a gold mine in their delivery methods. The term *desktop publishing* had never meant so much to so many. Publishers saw the potential of using the web to draw academics into their collections of journals within various fields. It had all the convenience of the new electronic-only journals, as well as all the prestige of the print counterparts. What's more, little things such as IP address authentication made it possible to bundle and offer much larger collections of journals to users without the costs associated with the same approach with print journals. Thus, a Frankenstein monster was born. But before you run off for your pitchfork and torch, take heart. This chapter and the next discuss how one can negotiate for a better big deal or back away from it altogether.

Publisher Consolidation—What's Next?

Publisher consolidation creates less competition in the marketplace while building monstrous collaborations. One of the reasons that the big deal can be so seductive is the sheer size of some of the journal collections that publishers now carry. In addition to publisher consolidation through mergers and acquisitions, the buying and selling of individual titles from publisher to publisher and the hosting of titles from nonprofit societies by commercial publishers have led to a greater number of journal titles being held by a smaller number of publishers (see sidebar on page 150). The internet has made the situation more complex as publisher deals can vary, and access rights change dramatically when titles are sold. The hosting of journals from nonprofit societies by commercial vendors is another practice that has increased because of the popularity of ejournals and can make what may have once been a simple negotiation between libraries and professional societies much more complex.

Not unlike the newspaper and television industry, academic publishing has seen great consolidation during the past 30 years. In the preface to the sixth edition of his book *The Media Monopoly*, Ben H. Bagdikian explained why consolidation is a cause for great concern. "For the first time in U.S. history, the country's most widespread news, commentary, and daily entertainment are controlled by six firms that are among the world's largest corporations, two of them foreign. ... There are pernicious consequences. While excessive bigness itself is cause for economic anxieties, the worst problems are political and social. The country's largest media giants have achieved alarming success in writing the media laws and regulations in favor of their own corporations and against the interests of the general public."[9] Substitute *academic community* for *general public* and you have the idea.

The consolidation of publishers in the academic publishing world makes for bigger and more inflexible bundles, should the publishers decide that's the way they want to go. Publisher consolidation has a real effect on the overall academic publishing market as well. When one examines the academic journal market, the inelastic nature of journal prices is the most striking characteristic.

Top Commercial Journal Publishers and Selected Imprints, Brands, and Subsidiaries

- Informa includes Datamonitor and Taylor & Francis (which includes Routledge and Haworth).

- John Wiley & Sons includes Current Protocols, Interscience, Jossey-Bass, and Wiley-Blackwell.

- McGraw-Hill Companies include J.D. Power and Associates, McGraw-Hill Education, Platts, and Standard & Poor's.

- Pearson includes Financial Times Group, Pearson Digital Learning, Pearson Education, and Penguin Group.

- Reed Elsevier includes Elsevier, LexisNexis Group, Academic Press, and Mosby.

- Springer Science+Business Media includes BioMed Central, InfoChem, and Springer-VDI-Verlag.

- Thomson Reuters Corporation includes Reuters, Thomson Elite, Thomson Scientific (which includes ISI Web of Knowledge), Thomson Tax & Accounting, and Thomson West.

- Wolters Kluwer includes Aspen Publishers, CCH Incorporated, Facts and Comparisons, Kluwer Academic Publishers, Lippincott Williams & Wilkins, and Ovid Technologies.

Sources: Corporate information from Mergent Online, www.mergentonline.com; Hoovers Company Records via ProQuest, proquest.umi.com; and company annual reports

The amount and frequency of price increases for commercially published academic journals are well-documented.[10] There are competing arguments as to how these prices have been able to grow without some kind of market push back. One argument contends that the academic publishing market has become a monopoly and requires reorganization under antitrust laws. This is a tough case to make, but a persuasive one nonetheless. On behalf of the Information Access Alliance, Thomas M. Susman and David J. Carter wrote about the standard that the Department of Justice and the Federal Trade Commission use to determine whether a merger would constitute a monopoly. This antitrust analysis involves looking at the "nature and extent of the markets in which the merging firms operate" and "the overlap among the merging parties in these markets." However, this standard for a monopoly implies that one academic journal is interchangeable with another, and as Susman and Carter describe it, "Since academic journals are the source of original research, each journal is in reality a poor substitute for any other in the same field."[11]

This approach also does not take into account that library selection processes for journals are very different from the selection processes for many other consumer goods. For libraries, journals from different disciplines can compete for scarce funds, and rather than purchasing a single journal as one would purchase a single car or couch, libraries attempt to collect as many journals as they can to support their users' research. The solution that Susman and Carter recommend is for merger analysis to define a market based on "broad portfolios of journals, rather than on narrow content-based comparisons that fail to take into account the competition for library dollars among journals with little content overlap."[12]

Publisher consolidation can have a final chilling effect on the ultimate goal of libraries—wide access to varieties of research and information—because of the publisher's role as buyer or acquirer of research. Albert A. Foer, president of the American Antitrust Institute, spoke on this issue at the 2004 American Library Association annual meeting in Orlando, Florida: "Writers need a reasonable range of publication choices when they decide what to write about, how to format their writing, and how to distribute their work. The publishers exercise huge influence not only on these factors but also on a writer's decision of what content and format to pursue. A reduction in the number of choices for the writer, at least when the remaining number of competing publishers is becoming small, can be expected to shift the balance of power that shapes bargaining between writer and publisher."[13] In the light of reports in 2009 of Elsevier being paid by Merck to publish a "journal" that consisted solely of abstracts and excerpts from articles with favorable data on Merck pharmaceuticals, the idea that a publisher would decide what's published rather than editors and editorial boards makes for an even more dire situation than previously perceived.

Sections 1 and 2 of the Sherman Antitrust Act provide standards to judge whether a company is participating in noncompetitive or exclusionary activities. In a 2004 article in the *Antitrust Law Journal*, Aaron S. Edlin and Daniel L. Rubinfeld put forth two analyses of big deal bundling under the bright light of the Sherman Act. Section 1 of the act "bans contracts, combinations, and conspiracies that restrain competition." The possible violation that Edlin and Rubinfeld identify lies in the aggregate amount of library budgets that serials budgets have increasingly absorbed, to the exclusion of other publishers and vendors: "In this case, if we consider the serials budget for a given library, much of it could already be taken up by its Big Deal arrangement with one publisher or another. If a plaintiff showed that this was true, and was true of a large portion of libraries, and that serials purchases were not themselves highly price sensitive, then this could demonstrate that these deals in the aggregate foreclose too much of aggregate library budgets to competition by new small publisher entrants."[14]

Edlin and Rubinfeld also analyze whether the "bundling of a large publisher such as Elsevier constitute[s] monopoly maintenance under Section 2 of the Sherman Act." This would mean that current academic publishers have "raised price[s] above competitive levels" to make it difficult for others to enter the market and that these publishers have the ability to maintain that power aside from the regular growth of their company or the fact that their product is better than other products on the market or new entrants to the market. Edlin and Rubinfeld make the argument that even though per-journal cost in the big deal is low, the overall price is high and possibly high enough to be considered exclusionary toward competitors.[15] While the determination of whether big deal pricing would meet this standard would need to be determined by a court, research conducted by Theodore C. Bergstrom, Carl Bergstrom, and R. Preston McAfee would lead us to believe that a strong argument could be made that commercial publishers are pricing above competitive levels (see Table 7.1).[16]

Edlin and Rubinfeld recognize that the increased title access and improved 24/7 remote online access that make the big deal so seductive to libraries in the first place could provide the publishers with their best argument against charges of exclusionary activity.[17] In other words, the added benefit that online access provides justifies the pricing. In the end, a successful case against any of the large academic publishers is far from certain. When asked about whether an antitrust case had ever been brought against a publisher, Edlin commented, "To my knowledge there has not been a case against the major publishers. ... If libraries wanted to, they could sue the major publishers, but that might not be something libraries want to spend their time doing, and it would be a very hard case."

While Edlin and Rubinfeld provide a scenario in which publishers' activities have led to an unsustainable market for libraries, Henk W. Plasmeijer, in his 2002 article from the *Journal of Economic Methodology*, saw the defect in the system on the demand side of the market. Plasmeijer finds the arguments of both librarians (that publishers have a monopoly and therefore charge whatever they want) and publishers (that the costs associated with publishing have risen significantly and therefore require price increases on this order) unpersuasive. Citing the publish-or-perish model of academic productivity as the catalyst for the serials crisis, Plasmeijer sees the real problem as "an increase in the number of journals in combination with an elastic individual demand and an inelastic institutional demand. The anticipation of price increases changed the elasticity of institutional demand, which caused further price increases."[18]

But Plasmeijer doesn't see publish-or-perish as a problem. In fact, he is a fan of this market approach as the best way to motivate research. Instead of seeing research as a common good, a point of

Table 7.1   Price Differences Between Nonprofit and For-Profit Journal Prices by Discipline (Used with permission from Ted Bergstrom and Preston McAfee, "Summary Statistics," *Journal Cost-Effectiveness* 2006-8 BETA, www.mcafee.cc/Journal/Summary.pdf)

Discipline	Nonprofit Journals		For-profit Journals	
	Mean price per article	*Mean price per citation*	*Mean price per article*	*Mean price per citation*
All disciplines	$7.98	$12.73	$24.20	$39.55
Agriculture	$5.75	$9.54	$18.30	$24.48
Biology	$8.19	$8.13	$23.36	$22.59
Business	$10.00	$16.11	$35.19	$63.87
Chemistry	$6.37	$8.38	$24.92	$26.16
Comp. Science	$11.01	$14.79	$29.38	$57.52
Economics	$10.29	$18.25	$24.84	$52.57
Education	$8.30	$14.73	$25.34	$54.70
Engineering	$7.98	$22.25	$30.51	$66.49
Geology	$8.93	$12.22	$27.37	$31.25
History	$11.34	$32.98	$28.45	$93.64
Humanities	$8.60	$14.18	$26.19	$135.89
Law	$4.12	$6.47	$25.56	$92.10
Mathematics	$10.32	$16.16	$29.14	$58.07
Medicine	$5.61	$5.43	$17.17	$16.24
Physics	$9.94	$11.48	$32.88	$47.76
Psychology	$11.27	$8.38	$22.90	$25.35
Social sciences	$8.70	$24.44	$24.16	$70.96

view often embraced by many open access initiatives, Plasmeijer believes that libraries have insulated their user communities from the costs of information for too long and that this has caused what should be an elastic market to become inelastic, as libraries raid other parts of their budgets to try to maintain the journals they believe to be of the highest quality and the most importance to the programs they support—regardless of price. "Bluntly stated: the researcher is in the position to say that he must have an article for which he can pass the bill to the librarian or his department. The librarian has an incentive to defend the serials collection and to pay whatever it costs for a collection which is tailored to the needs of the research staff." Instead of having the tough negotiations with publishers, librarians will need to have the tough negotiations with users. Plasmeijer has some difficult, if not counterintuitive, ideas about how to make users aware of the price of the information they use. "The information is no longer free: the use of high-priced information costs time, effort, the nuisance of having to click away the pop-ups and, in the worst case, money. The researcher still does not have to pay the real price, for this would probably be a bridge too far in most institutions. However, experiments with relatively mild measures such as these may scare the most expensive publishers to death. Buyers who recognize cheaper alternatives always diminish their willingness to pay."[19]

The idea that one might be able to have more effective negotiations with publishers by having better negotiations with faculty first is not necessarily a new one, but to know the market economics behind the continuing high prices might make it easier to schedule that faculty meeting and even persuade faculty to see why you need to walk away from a big deal or a ridiculous price increase.

Does Big Deal + Budget Cut = Panic or Possibilities?

So what's a librarian to do? How can negotiation get us out of the confines of the big deal without requiring our users to take up their pitchforks and torches? While open access publishing and education efforts such as the Public Library of Science and the Scholarly Publishing and Academic Resources Coalition have gained steam with both librarians and the greater academic community, the current economic recession could provide the push off the cliff that the current scholarly communication model needs to loosen the stranglehold of commercial publishing on library budgets. When asked about what possible negotiation techniques would be effective in the publishing market he and Rubinfeld described, Edlin commented that the negotiation options are limited but powerful. "If they [libraries] can't afford them, then they can't buy them, but as long as it is possible, they will probably buy all the packages they can, which means that the main negotiating leverage that they have is to pretend to not have the money. To the extent that they don't have the money, that makes it easier for them." If the best leverage librarians have is to claim poverty, then the current economic situation makes for a pretty believable claim.

So if a library can't afford the big deal, it's back to list prices, right? Not necessarily. In fact the lessons of 2003–2004 demonstrate for us that it might even be in the publishers' best interest to be open to the desire of libraries for alternative methods of bundling titles for discounts and flexibility. In discussing the major cancellations that TRLN made when abandoning its big deals with Elsevier and Blackwell, Gibbs suggests that "vendors would have been better off giving us some leeway. We canceled much more than if we had been given a little 'wiggle' room."[20]

Even in the days of individual print subscriptions, librarians struggled with the fact that much of the content acquired through periodical subscriptions goes unused. Electronic bundled collections give librarians an opportunity to actually see the amount of usage, or lack thereof, for each title within a bundled deal, and while the overall cost-per-use may be persuasive, the number of titles with actual use can often be very disappointing. This fact becomes even more disheartening when coupled with the current economy and the need to cut electronic and periodical expenditures. But changes to these packages are discouraged and even penalized, as David Baker emphasized in his 2008 *Interlending and Document Supply* article. "A headline number of journal titles available tells the library manager nothing about how many are used and therefore their value for money, which links in very much with the desire to see changes in the models of purchasing journals which will see them become much more flexible, with the ability to choose and modify collections based on patterns of actual usage. The models at the moment protect against this, through limiting the number of titles that can be swapped and penalising cancellations."[21]

It is in the best interest of the publishers to be more flexible in their subscription models, and that kind of flexibility is the best chance for libraries to develop a more tenable subscription model. "Viable business models for the future need to be considered and market tested with users in the community for most effective planning, even though it will be some time before it is clear which models work well." Baker says, "These models will need to be owned by all those involved in the delivery chain, including the ability to provide frameworks to enable library professionals to balance and justify the costs involved." Possibilities on the table include moving to a transaction-oriented, pay-per-view model. While this model ensures maximum usefulness, much of the research on pay-per-view indicates that it may not be sustainable for every library, for every title, or over the long term. In fact, some research demonstrates that the real advantage of pay-per-view is that it leads to informed collection development decisions on which journals should be chosen for subscription.[22]

Another reason that pay-per-view may not be the best alternative to more-traditional subscription models is that it creates a great amount of budget uncertainty. Traditional subscription models, even with hefty yearly increases, provide much more budget predictability. Baker also suggests that the pay-per-view model comes with additional costs not present in subscription models. "Any usage-based model has high overheads in terms of monitoring usage; generating, handling and paying invoices; converting non-subscribed titles to subscribed titles etc. The overheads are real costs that need to be borne by both sides."[23] But is there a somewhere-in-between that mixes the flexibility of individual journal subscriptions with the pricing benefits of bundled ordering based on the number of titles subscribed? Of course there is, but first everyone needs to get to the table and agree on the need for a new model. Getting publishers to the table is not always easy, but the threats of big deal cancellations may be just the thing to catalyze the discussion.

An Interview With Derk Haank, CEO, Springer Science+Business Media

(reprinted from *Information Today*
28, no. 1, January 2011)

In a January 2011 interview with Richard Poynder, Derk Haank, CEO of Springer Science+Business Media, offered the following thoughts about the Big Deal:

Q: *Librarians have complained about a "serials crisis" for decades. Publishers responded by packaging large bundles of journals in electronic form: the so-called Big Deal. The Big Deal, however, has been widely criticized, and many believe its days are numbered. When I interviewed you in 2002 (when you were chairman of Elsevier Science), you said, "The Big Deal has had some bad press, but in principle there is nothing wrong with it." Is that still your view?*

A: Absolutely. The Big Deal is the best invention since sliced bread. I agree that there was once a serials pricing problem; I have never denied there was a problem. But it was the Big Deal that solved it.

Q: *How?*

A: It did two things. First, it corrected everything that went wrong in the serials crisis in one go: People were able to get back all the journals that they had had to cancel, and they gained access to even more journals in the process.

Second, electronic publishing reduces the overall costs of publishing, since distribution costs become virtually nil. We could never have offered the Big Deal in the paper world. So in inventing it, we publishers made absolutely perfect use of new technology in a way that benefited both ourselves and our customers.

Q: *Why then do librarians still mutter darkly about the Big Deal?*
A: It is all part of the process of negotiating with publishers. The truth is that it is in the interests of everyone—publishers and librarians—to keep the Big Deal going.

However, for publishers, it means having to control ourselves when it comes to price increases, and from what I can see, everybody is now doing that. If you look at the public reports of both Springer and our colleagues, you will see that price increases are very close to inflation now.

If the threat of big deal cancellations is not enough to put publishers in a negotiating frame of mind, then librarians can take a page from the economists of scholarly publishing, Bergstrom and Bergstrom, Edlin and Rubinfeld, and Plasmeijer, and recognize that the campaign for scholarly communication reform is all about changing hearts and minds. The publish-or-perish system of academia, the engine that drives scholarly publishing, can actually provide great benefit at the negotiating table. Usage statistics can demonstrate to publishers that the amount of use does not support high subscription prices for journal titles. Libraries need to address with publishers the pricing gap between their titles and those from other publishers. Confronting publishers with the unexplainable pricing gap between their titles and other titles gives libraries the opportunity to very logically say no. This is a two-front campaign, of course. This information needs to go to both publishers and faculty to address the alternatives for the acquisition of scholarly information.

User communities and librarians are often seduced by the big deal because, when it comes to journal collections, more is more. But the service-oriented nature of libraries can often work against the establishment of real market pressures on the demand for articles. As Edlin and Rubinfeld observe, "What makes a journal valuable is the simultaneous consensus of authors, reviewers, editors, libraries, readers, tenure committees and indexing services that the journal is of high quality."[24] In a normal market, the demand for a high-quality product can be affected by another product entering the market and being perceived to have equal or higher quality or the determination by the buyer that the price has outstripped the perceived quality. Librarians and tenure committees may have inadvertently made the introduction of new journals or the determination that a quality journal is too expensive more difficult than would occur in another market, but this journal price inflation is not an uncontrollable freight train leading to library and university bankruptcy. Through shrewd negotiations, with publishers and faculty, better faculty price education and recognition, an understanding of the unique economic market that underlies scholarly communication, and a willingness to walk away when the deal is no good, librarians might create the possibility for something better than the big deal—a fair deal.

Endnotes

1. Henk W. Plasmeijer, "Pricing the Serials Library: In Defence of a Market Economy," *Journal of Economic Methodology* 9, no. 3 (2002): 342.

2. Tina Feick, Gary Ives, and Jo McClamroch, "The Big E-Package Deals: Smoothing the Way Through Subscription Agents," *Serials Librarian* 50, no. 3/4 (2006): 268.

3. Cecilia Botero, Steven Carrico, and Michele R. Tennant, "Using Comparative Online Journal Usage Studies to Assess the Big Deal," *Library Resources & Technical Services* 52, no. 2 (2008): 66–67.

4. Loretta Ebert, "What's the Big Deal? 'Take 2' or, How to Make It Work for You … ," *Serials Librarian* 48, no. 1/2 (2005): 67–68.

5. Kenneth Frazier, "The Librarian's Dilemma: What's the Big Deal?" *Serials Librarian* 48, no. 1/2 (2005): 54.

6. Ellen Finnie Duranceau, "Cornell and the Future of the Big Deal: An Interview With Ross Atkinson," *Serials Review* 30, no. 2 (2004): 127.

7. Nancy J. Gibbs, "Walking Away From the 'Big Deal': Consequences and Achievements," *Serials* 18, no. 2 (2005): 89.

8. Ibid., 91.

9. Ben H. Bagdikian, *The Media Monopoly*, 6th ed. (Boston, MA: Beacon Press, 2000), vii.

10. One of the best resources for watching the rise of serials prices is the annual "Periodicals Price Survey" (Lee C. Van Orsdel and Kathleen Born, 1993–2009; Kittie S. Henderson and Stephen Bosch, 2010; and Kittie S. Henderson, Stephen Bosch, and Heather Klusendorf, 2011) published each April or May in *Library Journal.*

11. Thomas M. Susman, David J. Carter, Ropes & Gray LLP, and the Information Access Alliance, *Publisher Mergers: A Consumer-Based Approach to Antitrust Analysis*, 23 (Washington, DC: Information Access Alliance, 2003), accessed August 17, 2011, www.information access.org/bm~doc/antitrustwtppr.pdf.

12. Ibid., 29.

13. Albert A. Foer, "Can Antitrust Save Academic Publishing?" (paper, American Library Association annual meeting 2004, Orlando, FL, June 28, 2004; revised July 20, 2004), 14, accessed August 17, 2011, www.informationaccess.org/bm~doc/Bert.pdf.

14. Aaron S. Edlin and Daniel L. Rubinfeld, "Exclusion or Efficient Pricing? The 'Big Deal' Bundling of Academic Journals," *Antitrust Law Journal* 72 (2004): 151–152.

15. Ibid., 139, 141, 147.

16. For journal pricing analysis from Bergstrom and Bergstrom, see Theodore C. Bergstrom, "Free Labor for Costly Journals?" *Journal of Economic Perspectives* 15, no. 4 (Autumn 2001): 183–198, and Carl Bergstrom and Theodore Bergstrom, "The Costs and Benefits of Library Site Licenses to Academic Journals," *Proceedings of the National Academy of Sciences* 101 (2004), accessed July 27, 2011, www.pnas.org/content/101/3/897.full.

17. Edlin & Rubinfeld, "Exclusion," 150–151.

18. Plasmeijer, "Pricing," 348.

19. Ibid., 351, 354.

20. Gibbs, "Walking Away," 93.

21. David Baker, "'Inside Every Fat Man': Balancing the Digital Library Budget," *Interlending and Document Supply* 36, no. 4 (2008): 215.

22. Beth R. Bernhardt, "Purchasing New Journal Subscriptions?: Why? Because We Have Pay-Per-View Usage Statistics That Prove We Need to Own Them!" in *2004 Charleston Conference Proceedings* (Westport, CT: Libraries Unlimited, 2006), 94–99.

23. Baker, "'Inside,'" 216.

24. Edlin & Rubinfeld, "Exclusion," 129.

Chapter 8

EResource Management, Workflows, and Standardization

Negotiation is not finished when the contract is signed. Once a librarian has successfully negotiated a contract for a new eresource product, the task of managing and providing access to this content still awaits. This chapter briefly explores the role of negotiation within the chaotic world of eresource management. The paradigm shift from a primarily print to a primarily electronic world has changed the face of the technical services and collection development realms forever. Moreover, the addition of electronic content has altered almost every nook and cranny of library services. Reference librarians have to evaluate their roles in a digital world while watching relatively new departments—such as web services departments—continually increase in size.

Available statistics for different types of libraries offer hard evidence of the rapid shift from print to digital. According to 2008–2009 Association of Research Libraries statistics, university member libraries are now spending a median of 57.03 percent and a mean of 56.33 percent of their total materials budget on electronic expenditures, with some as high as 85.40 percent. Compare that with 2003–2004 data, which shows a median of 29.81 percent. Much negotiation must occur internally between co-workers and administration in order to accommodate such drastic change, and large institutions, many with hundreds of staff members, are not the most nimble of creatures: Change does not come easy.

Public libraries are seeing similar increases. While many public libraries rely on their state virtual libraries for a large proportion of their electronic content, these libraries are seeing a significant increase in the *users* of these eresources. In 2002, public libraries in the U.S. reported 292,708,000 uses of eresources. In 2007, that number had risen to 357,013,000—a 27.97 percent increase in 5 years.[1]

Multiple Models of Acquisition

New and revised models of acquisition of materials are constantly emerging, each with its own benefits and challenges. Librarians have experimented with pay-per-view models for journal articles for some time, perhaps conducting an analysis triangulating journal subscription prices, usage statistics, and the cost of purchasing articles individually. The library might set up a deposit account for a patron and allow patrons to download articles at the point of need. Emerging now are pay-per-view streaming videos via companies such as Films on Demand or video rental services via companies such as NetFlix, offered through the library. Both of these are "leased" options that allow a library to supplement ownership with temporary access while still serving its patrons.

All of these are models of patron-driven acquisition, but as mentioned, they are not long-term acquisitions for the library. Ebook aggregators and publishers offer patron-driven acquisition of etitles. In her January 2009 "Off the Shelf" column in *Booklist* (www.booklistonline.com/ProductInfo.aspx?pid=3226359), Sue Polanka described the different options available. Whether ownership or leasing options, all of the aforementioned can wreak havoc with traditional acquisitions workflows. Thus, in addition to negotiating contracts with the content providers, library staff must adjust to accommodate these types of acquisitions. These sorts of adjustments necessarily involve negotiation, both inside and outside the library.

New situations and opportunities for negotiation constantly occur. For example, supervisors and staff must negotiate evolving job descriptions that include learning how to use and showing others how to use digital content. Public library administrators must wrestle with policy negotiations such as how long an individual is allowed at a computer terminal. Library administrators must also negotiate with user groups, parents, and library boards about internet filtering for minors. The list goes on.

In addition to the negotiations associated with eresource management and workflow, this chapter will briefly explore standardization initiatives in terms of negotiation and licensing. For the past half-decade or more, eresource management (ERM) has been at the top of the agenda for many specialized professional conferences, such as the Charleston Conference: Issues in Book in Serial Acquisition, Electronic Resources in Libraries, Computers in Libraries, the North American Serials Interest Group, and many more. The Association for Library Collections and Technical Services and other smaller groups continue to sponsor preconferences and online and face-to-face programming about ERM. Why all the attention? The world had hundreds of years to standardize print; the standardization of digital content is a constantly changing landscape.

EResource Workflow and Management

To define our terms, eresources include ejournals, emagazines, ebooks, abstracting and indexing databases, full-text aggregated databases, data sets, free search engines, open access repositories, personal webpages, wikis, blogs, podcasts, vodcasts, and more. The processes for selecting, acquiring, and managing these eresources are nonlinear and nonstandardized. Initially, libraries viewed eresources as add-ons to traditional print processing, and as such, they received little attention. As more and more of the materials budget moved to eresources, however, libraries were forced to re-evaluate the entire notion of collections. Delineation of duties between discrete departments such as acquisitions, cataloging, serials, monographs, and systems blurs. Upper-level administrators may not completely understand the dire situation at hand because the number of eresources continues to explode. One associate dean for collections at a large state institution commented,

"We saw bubbles emerging from our eresources librarian and realized it was her drowning."

The Digital Download on Multiple Formats, Models, and Delivery Options

When purchasing materials, it is easy to reduce the options to a binary: print or electronic. This is, however, a gross oversimplification. Electronic is a vast sea of possibilities. For example, it is possible to purchase an electronic book on a reader, such as a Kindle, to loan to patrons. It is possible to prepopulate the reader or to allow patrons to choose the etexts. It is possible to purchase ebooks on a publisher's platform or on an aggregator's platform. It is possible to purchase directly from the publisher or the aggregator. It is possible to use a book jobber to purchase from the publisher or the aggregator, but not all book jobbers work with every publisher directly or with every aggregator. Some publishers will allow dual access on their platform and on the aggregator's platform, assuming a library has purchased the ebook *somewhere*. Some publishers charge an additional fee to access the ebook on their platform if the ebook was originally purchased from an aggregator.

Negotiations can get quite convoluted. Consider the following scenario: Patrons prefer access to ebooks on a publisher's platform (e.g., ScienceDirect from Elsevier). Depending on the title, the publisher does not allow libraries to purchase one-off titles of their choosing. Libraries can purchase only subject sets of ebooks. Aggregator A, however, does allow purchase of this publisher's titles one by one, but the publisher allows dual access only for an additional fee. The patron wants the access on the publisher platform, but the library cannot afford a subject set. When faced with this sort of situation, the librarian must sort through all the options and negotiate either with the patron or with the publisher.

Without proper administrative support or understanding, employees are left to negotiate duties and areas of responsibility themselves. Even with administrative support, the task of documenting or creating workflows for disparate products and services becomes daunting. One way to begin the process is to conduct a communication audit, such as the one conducted by Celeste Feather when she was at Ohio State University.[2] Feather spearheaded a project to map how staff within her library communicated about eresources, tracking many modes of communication: email, telephone, face-to-face, and more. While time-consuming, such an audit allows an institution to determine who is handling what issues and problems. This allows administration and employees to begin negotiating revised processes.

For example, the eresources librarian's office can become a bottleneck if his or her duties are not regularly assessed. Problems, licenses, requests for trials and usage statistics, other requests for database customizations, and more—they check in but they don't check out. Perhaps an institution eventually realizes that the discrete eresources librarian position was merely a stopgap while the world made the transition from print to electronic. It was still an effort to fit the virtual, nonlinear eresource into a print, linear box. Thus, a renegotiation of duties occurs, and employees are forced to adjust and cooperate again.

One EResource Tool to Rule Them All

With such chaos, it is easy to fall prey to a clever marketing scheme used by some vendors who develop and market the tools to manage and provide access to eresources. There is no simple solution to the complex problems we face as the paradigm shifts from print to electronic publishing. Link resolvers, federated search systems, ERM systems, usage statistic tools, digital content management, next-generation library catalogs, interactive library guides—the list can seem endless, and librarians must navigate among these products to determine what will best fit their organizations.

Advice From an Expert:
Maria Collins

How Negotiation Fits Into an
EResource Manager's Daily Job

Negotiation is a critical component of ERM. Because of the large volume of eresources available in most libraries and the number of personnel involved in their management, negotiation often manifests itself as management of political nuance, perception, and expectation within the organization. As an acquisitions manager of eresource materials, I feel as if most of the negotiations in which I've engaged are for the resources needed to support eresource workflows. These negotiations have occurred with both administrators and ground-level staff.

What are the most common workflow-related negotiations in which I've engaged? Staffing for eresource management has been a constant point of negotiation throughout my career. Within the academic library environments I've worked in, I've advocated distributing eresource management tasks across all serials staffing positions and have promoted the need for additional professional-level positions to assist in the management of this work. Emphasizing the workflow lifecycle and making transparent connections across the entire library environment have been key aspects in communicating the value of this kind of work and winning administrative buy-in for evolving staffing models.

Of course, even after additional positions were obtained and staffing models changed, the real negotiations have often been with the staff slated to pick up ERM responsibilities. Quickly, I discovered that without a broader context and intimate understanding of the entire eresource lifecycle, some staff found the transition from a print to an electronic workflow to be difficult and nonintuitive. Building a sense of security within an eworking environment for staff not comfortable with ambiguity is still something I struggle with on a daily basis. This kind of work requires a different level of engagement that is more holistic and not production or task oriented, and staff work habits are not so easily transformed.

One primary reason for the nonintuitive nature of eresource workflows is the lack of tools to support their management. Anyone weaned on an ILS model for data management quickly understands the inability for these systems to manage the complex relationships that exist across eresource metadata. It should come as no surprise, then, that I have spent an inordinate amount of time negotiating for the appropriate management tools to support eresource workflows. These negotiations have entailed the following actions:

- Advocate for ERM tools that support technical services workflows and not just public display.

- Campaign for consistent programming resources needed for locally developed management tools.

- Explain the necessity for workflow management tools that are interactive and not just a flat, ILS-like construct for data storage.

Often, the discussions surrounding ERM tools have been challenging; the complexity of ERM processes themselves can easily undermine the value of underdeveloped tools that have been tasked with their management. However, eresource workflows should not be over-simplified and management resources should not be downsized until the profession has effective tools designed to simplify their complexity.

Another area of workflow-related negotiations is evaluating legacy workflows that should be abandoned. It is extremely difficult to predict the future information needs of users and make management decisions that not only modify the work but actually transform the work, requiring a new universe of skill sets and staff competencies. Transformative workflow changes that call into question traditional library values require thoughtful evaluation and risk assessment to achieve a careful balance between managing current library needs and shaping future direction. For me, this is why ERM workflow management is so challenging and requires such an intense level of negotiation.

Maria Collins has worked as serials librarian and associate head of acquisitions at North Carolina State University Libraries since 2005, and became head of content acquisitions and licensing in 2011. She previously worked as serials librarian and serials coordinator at Mississippi State University Libraries for 6 years. She is the editor of Serials Review *and does consulting work with OCLC on its web-scale services. Her greatest experience in workflow management comes from raising three children with her husband in Cary, North Carolina.*

As noted in Maria Collins's sidebar, integrated library systems (ILSs) were built for and function properly in a print world. ILS products are not equipped to manage the multitude of variables associated with interrelated eresources. Most ERM systems emerged based on the work of the Digital Library Federation's Electronic Resource Management Initiative (ERMI; www.diglib. org/standards/dlf-erm02.htm); some libraries began to purchase them, and others tried to build their own. Yet the ILS could not be completely abandoned because, among other reasons, many libraries' ILS products are integrated with the larger institution's payment processing. This can leave libraries maintaining two systems—the ILS and the ERM. Had we done a better job of negotiating with the ILS vendors and demanded that they adjust their products to accommodate eresources, we as a community would not be faced with this duplication.

Lest we lose hope, however, the original work of ERMI continues under the auspices of the National Information Standards Organization (NISO) ERM Data Standards and Best Practices Review, whose purpose is to define the next steps for ERM (www.niso.org/workrooms/ermreview). Perhaps this work will assist librarians in negotiating the path of eresources management. Also to watch are other innovative approaches to redefining the quotidian work of libraries, such as OCLC's Web-Scale Management Services (www.oclc.org/webscale) and the Kuali Open Library Environment (kuali.org/ole).

Librarians and information professionals can, however, learn from this experience and advocate better interoperability. If no single eresource tool can manage everything, then we need interoperability among varied systems. The subscription agent system must talk to the ERM and the ILS, and the ERM and ILS must be able to exchange information with each another. The federated search tool needs to integrate with the next-generation library catalog and the link resolver. And these tools should chitchat with one another regardless of vendor. Furthermore, interoperability involves more than the technical processes associated with inanimate objects exchanging information. It also involves people and politics and standards organizations such as NISO.

Standards Are Important

As mentioned earlier in this chapter, interoperability has a great effect on daily eresource workflow, as well as the holistic management of eresources. Greater efficiency is achieved if the tools used to manage and facilitate access to eresources are interoperable. Interoperability requires standards. Groups such as NISO can succeed in guiding the negotiation of standards through shared committees with multiple companies and constituencies represented. Much like a virtual state library has a committee with various representatives (public, school, academic) to determine content interests, NISO can serve as an objective third party to host and advocate standards that allow for greater interoperability and greater cooperation.

One such initiative is the NISO/EDItEUR ONIX for Publication Licenses (ONIX-PL) Working Group (www.niso.org/workrooms/ onixpl). ONIX-PL is a joint effort of NISO and EDItEUR (an international standards organization, www.editeur.org) and hopes to address the automated exchange of license information.

The Digital Library Federation's ERMI articulated a blueprint of sorts for ERM systems such as those offered commercially by companies such as Serials Solutions, Innovative Interfaces Inc., Ex Libris, and EBSCO. The ERMI work paved the way to greater automation and flexibility for eresource management, but librarians were still faced with translating and manually entering licensing information into an ERM system. Some publishers allow remote access; others don't. Some publishers allow certain types of interlibrary loan; others don't. All these variations depend on the license your institution has negotiated. Having such negotiated licensing data in an ERM makes it available in a variety of internal and external ways and thus allows librarians and users alike to know the specific terms of use for specific materials.

In a presentation at the 2006 Center for Networked Information meeting, Christopher McKenzie of John Wiley & Sons summarized the issue.[3] There is significant confusion about who can do what with which licensed resources. Complicating the issue are several elements: license terms and conditions, copyright and contract laws, and varied resource types. McKenzie goes on to suggest that some of the possible responses to the problem are to eliminate copyright and contract law, to agree on a single model license, or to use technology to manage the complexity. Such technology includes digital rights management; rights expression languages; and standards for rights, licenses, and content (e.g., ONIX for Licensing). Clearly, the likelihood of eliminating copyright and contract law or universal agreement on a single model license is very slim. Thus, the License Expression Working Group (www.niso.org/work rooms/lewg) emerged as a group to explore a third option, namely, using technology to manage the complexity. In 2008, this group evolved into the ONIX-PL Working Group. The ONIX-PL group's charge states that it should "actively support and contribute to the continued development of the ONIX-PL standard for license expression to ensure it is fit for use by all types of stakeholders."[4]

The group continues to strive toward greater standardization of license terms, as well as increased automation for the transfer of these terms. It is important to stress that the group is not advocating a standard license; instead, its goal is to standardize the terms themselves and how those terms are represented. For example, if we can all agree on a common definition for remote access and agree that it will commonly be represented as X, then it becomes possible to automate the transfer of this information. The act of negotiating the right of remote access remains with the information professional and the content provider. For more information about ONIX-PL, visit www.niso.org/workrooms/onixpl.

Advice From an Expert:
Steve Black

WTF, or How Ejournals Have Introduced Chaos and Confusion Into the Daily Duties of Everyone I Know

Electronic delivery of journals has blurred the lines between job functions at my library in ways that force us to communicate and cooperate in new and increasingly critical ways. In the future, we may redefine our job descriptions, but for now we're working within frameworks of responsibility formed years ago. The many ways online journals have disrupted our traditional duties have crept up on us sometimes unexpectedly.

Our library director, Peter Koonz, handles all our dealings with our several consortia. This responsibility grew out of his original responsibility as liaison to our regional Capital District Library Council, which provides a union catalog, cooperative collection development, and resource sharing. It was then natural for him to assume responsibility for signing agreements for online databases through consortia. This then led to our director also handling full-text databases, including publisher packages. Packages have created new headaches for budgeting. It was once a fairly clean job to assign titles to departmental funds, but for better or worse, we have chosen not to allocate titles in packages among our various departments.

As we go online-only with more and more titles through package deals, the records I track for journals increasingly originate with the library director. I have been taken a bit by surprise at how often I need to ask for records he keeps, in order to confirm that we have access to titles. During renewal time, to be sure we're not paying twice for a title, I have to reconcile our orders through our subscription agent with the publisher package contracts. So it's essential that we share records. We decided not to buy an ERMS, so we rely on the library director's Access database and my Excel spreadsheet. It's a bit cumbersome for us to keep records in two different formats, but the data can be converted easily enough that we've made it work.

Our vendor rep has tried for years to convince us to order all packages through our subscription agent, but we have chosen to go direct. Going through the subscription agent would definitely have saved some hassle and confusion for the library director and myself, but by ordering through a consortium instead of using a subscription agent, we saved several hundred dollars. But we've not ruled out the option of ordering packages through the vendor in the future if we think it can significantly streamline our processes.

Peter Osterhoudt, our systems librarian, handles the integrated library system and our proxy server. Causes of problems in accessing our online journals can be difficult to pin down. We have to work together to determine whether the problem is an issue with the proxy server database, payment records, our IP addresses registered at the publisher, or something else. It's often the case during troubleshooting that our college's information technology staff has to become involved to resolve network access glitches.

Another area requiring cooperation and collaboration is deciding how we want online journals to appear in the library's catalog. We've worked together to choose the wording and the order of display of the MARC fields. More significantly, we collaborate to decide when to bend cataloging rules. We've chosen to have one bibliographic record for each journal and add MARC 856 in the holdings record rather than follow the correct practice of having separate bibliographic records for print and online. We believe this is best for our patrons, but we remain concerned that fudging the rules may create problems for interlibrary loan, as more and more of our journals are online-only. The ultimate decision will require input from our entire team of librarians.

Sustaining and improving communication among the library director, serials librarian, and systems librarian will continue to be an issue for us. We work well together, but I expect the ongoing transition to mostly online-only journals will require further adjustments.

_____

Steve Black is a professor and librarian at the College of Saint Rose in Albany, New York. His duties include reference, instruction, and managing the serials collection. He is the author of Serials in Libraries: Issues and Practices *(2006) and the magazine reviewer for* Library Journal. *He is also an adjunct instructor in the Department of Information Studies at the University at Albany, New York, where he regularly teaches courses in serials and in information sources and services.*

Understand Shared EResources

What about eliminating certain portions of licenses altogether? This is precisely the goal of another NISO initiative, the Shared Electronic Resource Understanding (SERU). Negotiating contracts for each and every eresource is extremely time-consuming and costly for all sides—vendors, content providers or publishers, and libraries. All sides find it particularly difficult to deal with the "long tail" of smaller publishers who have small title lists. The SERU website summarizes the issue: "In some circumstances bilateral negotiation of a formal license agreement is in the interest of the publisher, the library, or both, but as the number of electronic information products expands and a lower end of the market is increasingly developed, many question whether universal, bilateral license negotiations are scalable."[5]

It is this "lower end" that proves especially difficult for both librarians and publishers. If a harried eresource librarian has X amount of time to negotiate all licenses, how will the librarian prioritize? Will the million-dollar Elsevier deal take top priority, or will the small publisher with two titles on its list rank No. 1? On the other side of the fence, is the smaller publisher with limited staff capable of individually negotiating contracts? Or will that publisher make the decision to offer a single contract or click-through, thus eliminating bilateral negotiation? Then, the librarian is left with either accepting potentially unacceptable terms or blocking content for users.

Of course, this is not a value judgment intended to imply that smaller publishers' content is not valid or important. It is. But publishers and librarians alike, with limited time, have to make difficult choices. SERU addresses this issue by attempting to come to some sort of shared understanding about the use of eresources and eliminate some of the tedious process associated with contracts and licensing.

The SERU document notes, "Libraries and publishers have a long history of cooperating in a non-litigious relationship that predates the introduction of electronic resources."[6] Is this cooperation possible in the electronic world? In certain instances, it just might be. Note that SERU does not attempt to address the business terms of a license, such as price; those terms would still be negotiated, if necessary, by the librarian and the vendor.

The SERU website describes the process:

> Publishers wishing to sell some or all of their products using a SERU approach and libraries wishing to use SERU in acquiring content from selected publishers will be able to sign up on a NISO registry to indicate their willingness to forego a license agreement and rely on the shared expectations expressed in the statements of shared understanding.
>
> Publishers should indicate to serials vendors and to customers their desire to do business in this way. Rather than post terms on their website, publishers should link to the NISO website and SERU documents.[7]

When a library decides to purchase the product, a purchase order is generated and payment is made. (Note: Payment is made between the customer and the provider only; SERU is not involved and does not require a margin.) It may be necessary to negotiate pricing (for instance, if the publisher doesn't use list pricing or if special circumstances for the particular transaction justify an increased or reduced price) or work out other business terms. For instance, if the subscribing institution does not fit the general parameters described in the SERU document section titled the Subscribing Institution and Its Authorized Users, the issue can be resolved through negotiation of a special price or some other accommodation appropriate to the unique situation of the sub-scribing institution. If either the library or the publisher feels that changes should be made to SERU, it is an indicator that perhaps a license should be used.[8]

Ultimately, SERU is one alternative that "offers publishers and libraries the opportunity to save both the time and the costs asso-ciated with a negotiated and signed license agreement by agreeing to operate within a framework of shared understanding and good faith."[9] SERU does not attempt to eliminate all licenses and certainly does not eradicate the need for negotiation. Instead, it attempts to define mutually agreeable common ground and thus streamline the process in certain cases. Having begun in 2006, the SERU initiative is still relatively new, and its success or failure remains to be seen. A full list of participants is available via the SERU registry (www.niso.org/workrooms/seru/registry).

The NISO topic committee and working group members associated with SERU include representation from consortia, publishers, aggregators, special and university libraries, and library organizations. Other cooperative efforts include the Single Sign-On Authentication Working Group (www.niso.org/workrooms/sso), CrossRef (www.crossref.org), and Project Transfer (www.uksg.org/ transfer).

To Infinity and Beyond

First and foremost, what we must do is cease and desist all efforts to treat digital materials as if they were print, just in a different format. The chasm between the print and digital is ever-widening. Specifically discussing ebooks, Eric Hellman noted on his blog, "*Now* is the time for publishers and libraries to sit down together and develop new models for working together in the ebook economy. ... Libraries need to recognize the need for change and work with publishers to build mutually beneficial business models that don't pretend that ebooks are the same as print."[10]

Purchasing, acquiring, processing, and managing ebooks—or any eresources, for that matter—require a commitment to more staff and better training. When the acquisitions librarian or eresources librarian says, "I need more people because we are spending 80 percent of our budget on eresources and have 80 percent of our staff devoted to print," the library administrator needs to listen. Otherwise, any amount of negotiation for digital materials is a waste if there is no one at the library who has sufficient time to manage, troubleshoot, and provide access to the purchased eresources.

Advice From an Expert:
Selden Durgom Lamoureux

Standard Licenses

In the 1990s, when library consortia developed model licenses and John Cox teamed with subscription agents to create a set of standard licenses, there was a general sense that the difficulty of negotiating licenses would ease over time. Licenses would become less idiosyncratic and more predictable, standardized, and routine. The Cox standard license is still used by many publishers today, as are standard licenses developed by the library community, but standardization never really took root. Why not?

For many years, I assumed that license standardization was slowed by legally binding proscriptions against collusion, coupled with new publishers entering the arena and being unaware of the standard license options. But I think there might be a more obvious reason that license standardization has failed: The license is not the appropriate vehicle to achieve the desired ends.

One of those ends is to protect against risk. From the standpoint of the publishers, their investment and their ability to make a profit on future sales are at stake. Another function of the license is to articulate the business model, the sometimes very creative and often unique description of the details of what you get, how much it costs, who gets to use it, and how long you have it. Third, the license usually describes how the resource can be used, something that, in the predigital environment, was regulated by copyright law.

Let's take a look at the license track record:

1. How successful has the license been in curbing abuse? Not very. The license is between the publisher and library, while the greatest risk to the publisher comes from the end user.

2. How essential is the license in cementing the details of the business model? Not at all. Once signed, a license may persist for years whereas business models evolve rapidly. Equally effective is a purchase order, which has the additional advantage of avoiding the need for the labor- and time-intensive proscriptions imposed by universities and states on license negotiations.

3. How successful has the license been in describing the standards of use? There are already standards in place for this. I will not pretend to believe that copyright law is well understood by end users, but I do believe that users in general understand that a copyrighted work cannot be plagiarized or used to make a profit. Beyond that, users will use the resource how they use it. For generations, intellectual property rights and rights of the consumer have been established by copyright law.

In short, I think standard licenses have been doomed precisely because they are the wrong vehicle for the purpose. Risk management is far more effective at using software to detect abuse; there are no standards for business models by design; and standards for terms of use are already well articulated in copyright law, which has a long and successful record of balancing the competing rights of the copyright holder and the end user.

After more than a decade of experience with licensing, it might be time to admit there will never be a standard license, any more than there will ever be a standard business model; that risk is best managed through software and by building on the good relationships between publisher and library; and that terms of use are best left to the standards already in place, copyright law, and new standards being developed for eresources.

Selden Durgom Lamoureux was the eresources librarian at North Carolina State University Libraries and retired in 2011. Previously she worked as the eresources librarian at the University of North Carolina–Chapel Hill. She has taught several licensing workshops and has spoken widely about eresource issues. She is part of the development team of SERU. She and Judy Luther are the recipients of the Coutts 2009 Innovations award for their work on SERU.

Librarians with workflow issues should demand more help from serials agents, book jobbers, and content providers. In the case of serials agents or book jobbers, negotiate a lower service fee if the company will not give you the reports you need to facilitate more efficient workflow. Likewise, librarians should insist on better service and better products from the ILS and ERMS vendors. We are their market. For example, track the amount of time it took your ERMS vendor to resolve a reported problem and use that information when it comes time to renegotiate the renewal.

Insist on more transparent pricing and access models because these models invariably affect eresource workflow and management. The more complicated the access model, the more confused both the librarian and the user will be. If ebook vendor A has a Byzantine access model involving a myriad of variables—time outs, strange "digital loan" periods, an overly complex and prohibitive digital rights management system—then jettison that vendor and look for another. Or use those variables as negotiating points. If the vendor cannot accommodate your library's authentication solution, such as EZ Proxy, then negotiate for a lower subscription price or a lower or waived annual access fee if the purchase is a perpetual one.

Support standardization efforts such as SERU and those sponsored by NISO. Better and more widely adopted standards reduce the chaos. If SERU were more widely adopted, it would reduce the amount of time overtaxed eresource librarians would have to spend negotiating license terms with small publishers who may offer only a very limited number of titles. Ultimately, overtaxed librarians must prioritize, and if it's a choice between negotiating and processing the Elsevier license or the Association of Insect Fisheries license, then, unfortunately, the small association loses.

We've mentioned just a few of the key issues associated with workflow problems and negotiation. To infinity and beyond are the possibilities and problems that eresources offer.

Endnotes

1. For statistics, see www.arl.org/stats/annualsurveys/arlstats/preveds. shtml.

2. Celeste Feather, "Electronic Resources Communications Management," *Library Resources & Technical Services* 51, no. 3 (2006): 204–228.

3. Christopher McKenzie, "Standard License Expression," John Wiley & Sons, Inc., April 4, 2006, accessed August 18, 2011, www.niso.org/workrooms/lewg/CNI.ppt.

4. "ONIX-PL Working Group," NISO, accessed August 18, 2011, www.niso.org/workrooms/onixpl.

5. "SERU Problem Statement," NISO, accessed August 18, 2011, www.niso.org/workrooms/seru.

6. "SERU Version 0.9, Draft Recommended Practice for Trial Use," NISO, accessed December 3, 2011, www.niso.org/workrooms/seru/seru draft0_9.pdf.

7. "SERU Initiative Overview," NISO, accessed December 3, 2011, www.niso.org/workrooms/seru/seru_faq.

8. "SERU Initiative Overview," NISO, accessed August 18, 2011, www.niso.org/workrooms/seru/seru_faq.

9. NISO SERU Working Group, "SERU: A Shared Electronic Resource Understanding," NISO, February 2008, accessed August 18, 2011, www.niso.org/publications/rp/RP-7-2008.pdf.

10. Eric Hellman, "eBooks in Libraries a Thorny Problem, Says Macmillan CEO," go to hellman, March 10, 2010, accessed August 18, 2011, www.go-to-hellman.blogspot.com/2010/03/ebooks-in-libraries-thorny-problem-says.html.

Chapter 9

Negotiating in the Age of Open Access, Open Source, and Free Internet Resources

When we think about negotiation, we think in dollar signs, but the truth is that much of the negotiating we do has nothing to do with money. In a world with an increasing number of "free" resources, such as open access journals, open source software, and social networking tools, many of our user communities expect, or at least espouse, that everything online be free. The term *free* is a scary one in the modern library world. Free resources often come with strings attached. The selection by a library of an open source electronic resource management system may not require payment to a vendor, but it does carry hidden costs, such as the need to hire additional staff to support the product, including an expensive programmer to customize and maintain it.

Vendors might initially offer free access to a resource for a given amount of time, betting that users will become hooked on it and then the library will be forced to subscribe, or a free product might have little actual content value but have great public relations value for the provider. Or *free* might mean that you can use a minimum set of features until you outgrow them and desire the real deal. Or *free*, as in a product or resource so inexpensive compared with the other resources as to make the price seem negligible. In this chapter, the word *free* is used to include most, if not all, of these definitions.

The joys of electronic interlibrary loan and document delivery, internet protocol authentication, and the proxy server propagate this feeling of freedom for our users, even when they are reaching beyond the free web and into the expensive resources and services that libraries provide. This freedom seems like a logical conclusion for users to draw. That is, until librarians remember that long before the internet revolution, users were perfectly aware that someone purchased all the print and media materials found in the library. There was no expectation of a library fairy who magically deposited journals and multivolume sets for free on library shelves. So why the confusion now?

In the hybridized world of the internet, the line between what your library has provided for you and what you are getting as a citizen of the World Wide Web is blurry at best. Moreover, this blur extends well beyond content and into the world of tools. Confirmed Zotero users can attest to the lack of a need for pricey citation software at their institutions. As with many products, average users may find it difficult to tell the difference between a free resource and one users pay for, when they have little experience with either and even less of a notion whether they need to pay a little more for something better. However, when discussing institutionwide purchasing and implementation, the difference between a commercial product and an open source one can be stark, and this includes the impact that each product will have on the bottom line. So one needs to consider the open option right along with the commercial option, and that consideration includes licensing and negotiation.

Read Open License Agreements Carefully

One advantage to negotiating open source and open access materials is the standardized nature of the licenses that usually govern these resources, provided that one is familiar with these types of agreements. The principles behind an open source software product license are defined by the Open Source Initiative (www.open

source.org) and the Open Source Definition (www.opensource.org/docs/osd; see the next section for an explanation of open source). These terms help you understand what makes something open source and can assist you when you are reading the license for a particular open source product. Open source refers to the open nature of the coding behind the product. These licenses can be every bit as intimidating as, if not more so than, those from a commercial vendor. If you want to examine a license for commonly used open source software, check out the Mozilla Public License v.1.1 (www.mozilla.org/MPL/MPL-1.1.html) or visit the Open Source Initiatives library of open source licenses (www.open source.org/licenses).

The most important aspect distinguishing an open source license from licenses for commercial products is that many of the restrictions placed on the user are requirements that govern making changes to the source code public and available under the same terms as the original product, rather than restrictions governing how the end product may be used and by whom. The stark contrast between this approach and the restrictions from commercial vendors is encouraging, but it makes these open source resources far from worry-free.

What Does It Mean to Be Open Source?

The Open Source Initiative requires the following elements be present in order for a resource to call itself *open source*. To learn more about what it means to be open source, visit "The Open Source Definition" Open Source Initiative, last updated July 7, 2006 (www.opensource.org/docs/osd). This content from the Open source.org site is redistributed and licensed under a Creative Commons Attribution 2.5 License (creativecommons.org/licenses/by/2.5).

1. *Free Redistribution.* The license shall not restrict any party from selling or giving away the software as a

component of an aggregate software distribution containing programs from several different sources. The license shall not require a royalty or other fee for such sale.

2. *Source Code.* The program must include source code, and must allow distribution in source code as well as compiled form. Where some form of a product is not distributed with source code, there must be a well-publicized means of obtaining the source code for no more than a reasonable reproduction cost preferably, downloading via the internet without charge. The source code must be the preferred form in which a programmer would modify the program. Deliberately obfuscated source code is not allowed. Intermediate forms such as the output of a preprocessor or translator are not allowed.

3. *Derived Works.* The license must allow modifications and derived works, and must allow them to be distributed under the same terms as the license of the original software.

4. *Integrity of the Author's Source Code.* The license may restrict source-code from being distributed in modified form only if the license allows the distribution of "patch files" with the source code for the purpose of modifying the program at build time. The license must explicitly permit distribution of software built from modified source code. The license may require derived works to carry a different name or version number from the original software.

5. *No Discrimination Against Persons or Groups.* The license must not discriminate against any person or group of persons.

6. *No Discrimination Against Fields of Endeavor.* The license must not restrict anyone from making use of the program

in a specific field of endeavor. For example, it may not restrict the program from being used in a business or from being used for genetic research.

7. *Distribution of License.* The rights attached to the program must apply to all to whom the program is redistributed without the need for execution of an additional license by those parties.

8. *License Must Not Be Specific to a Product.* The rights attached to the program must not depend on the program as being part of a particular software distribution. If the program is extracted from that distribution and used or distributed within the terms of the program's license, all parties to whom the program is redistributed should have the same rights as those that are granted in conjunction with the original software distribution.

9. *License Must Not Restrict Other Software.* The license must not place restrictions on other software that is distributed along with the licensed software. For example, the license must not insist that all other programs distributed on the same medium must be open-source software.

10. *License Must Be Technology-Neutral.* No provision of the license may be predicated on any individual technology or style of interface.

What Does It Mean to Be Open Access?

Most open access resources are defined as such by one of a number of statements including the Bethesda Statement, the Berlin Statement, and the Budapest Statement on Open Access. Peter Suber, an open access advocate, defines open access as "digital, online, free of charge, and free of most copyright and licensing restrictions."[1] Written directly into these statements and into the definition of open access is the right to maintain sustainable and unfettered access to the resource. This can be seen as a direct response to concerns that librarians have about the preservation of access to commercial online resources and the internet in general.

The Budapest Statement, from February 2002 (www.soros.org/openaccess), states:

> By "open access" to this literature, we mean its free availability on the public internet, permitting any users to read, download, copy, distribute, print, search, or link to the full texts of these articles, crawl them for indexing, pass them as data to software, or use them for any other lawful purpose, without financial, legal, or technical barriers other than those inseparable from gaining access to the internet itself. The only constraint on reproduction and distribution, and the only role for copyright in this domain, should be to give authors control over the integrity of their work and the right to be properly acknowledged and cited.

The Bethesda Statement, from June 2003 (www.earlham.edu/~peters/fos/bethesda.htm), states:

1. The author(s) and copyright holder(s) grant(s) to all users a free, irrevocable, worldwide, perpetual right of access to, and a license to copy, use, distribute, transmit and display the work publicly and to make and distribute derivative works, in any digital medium for any responsible purpose, subject to proper attribution of authorship, as well as the right to make small numbers of printed copies for their personal use. ...

2. A complete version of the work and all supplemental materials, including a copy of the permission as stated above, in a suitable standard electronic format is deposited immediately upon initial publication in

at least one online repository that is supported by an academic institution, scholarly society, government agency, or other well-established organization that seeks to enable open access, unrestricted distribution, interoperability, and long-term archiving (for the biomedical sciences, PubMed Central is such a repository). ...

3. Open access is a property of individual works, not necessarily journals or publishers. ...

4. Community standards, rather than copyright law, will continue to provide the mechanism for enforcement of proper attribution and responsible use of the published work, as they do now.

The Berlin Statement, from October 2003 (oa.mpg.de/berlin-prozess/berliner-erklarung) states:

Open access contributions must satisfy two conditions:

1. The author(s) and right holder(s) of such contributions grant(s) to all users a free, irrevocable, worldwide, right of access to, and a license to copy, use, distribute, transmit and display the work publicly and to make and distribute derivative works, in any digital medium for any responsible purpose, subject to proper attribution of authorship (community standards will continue to provide the mechanism for enforcement of proper attribution and responsible use of the published work, as they do now), as well as the right to make small numbers of printed copies for their personal use.

2. A complete version of the work and all supplemental materials, including a copy of the permission as stated above, in an appropriate standard electronic format is deposited (and thus published) in at least one online repository using suitable technical standards (such as the Open Archive definitions) that is

> supported and maintained by an academic institu-
> tion, scholarly society, government agency, or other
> well-established organization that seeks to enable
> open access, unrestricted distribution, interoperabil-
> ity, and long-term archiving.

An interesting wrinkle to the open access model is the growing number of commercial publishers embracing aspects of open access for some of the titles in their catalogs. These hybrid models, such as older issues of a title being made available, will continue to make licensing and linking unpredictable and to leave the door open for librarians to negotiate more favorable terms and to see more creative solutions to access issues, particularly when content is publicly funded and/or journals are published jointly with commercial publishers and professional scholarly societies that can push an open access agenda in the name of equal-opportunity scholarship.

In the U.K., where discussions of open access have made it all the way to Parliament,[2] discussions about bringing commercial publishers into the open access fold affect some of the key negotiations that appear to be shaping the information industry landscape of the future.[3] Librarians' input into these negotiations is important to ensure that open access terms will be both useful to today's researcher and flexible for further negotiations to facilitate the needs of researchers in the future, in areas such as data mining.

Negotiate In and With Open Communities

The need for negotiation and collaboration in open communities is not widely discussed, but it is an essential element behind the success of any open access or open source endeavor. The names may change (Cooperative Agreement, Memorandum of Understanding, General Public License), but the idea remains the same. For open environments to succeed, all members of the community, from developers to distributors to end users, need to understand the goals of the endeavor.

Unlike commercial databases, open access projects often represent collaboration between libraries and content creators. One example is the collaboration between the University of Arizona (UA) and the Society for Range Management (SRM) to digitize and provide open access to back files of the journal *Rangeland*. As described in a 2005 article in the quarterly bulletin of the International Association of Agricultural Information Specialists, the Memorandum of Understanding contains the following provisions:

> Responsibilities for SRM and UA were defined. SRM agreed to provide (a) print copies of volumes and (b) rights to unlimited, free-of-charge use of the digitized data consistent with Title 17 of the US Code on Copyright. UA Library agreed to (a) scan the printed material and create digitized TIFF and PDF files; (b) make this information available over their World Wide Web (WWW) site; (c) provide SRM with 2 free copies of the TIFF and PDF files and make additional copies at cost if requested; d) make the Rangelands information from the UAL web site directly accessible from other web sites that emphasize rangeland information, particularly the SRM home page site."[4]

Whether you are participating in a digitization project or just linking to the resources made available, you should be aware of the memorandum of understanding as it will govern how the resources are developed, used, and preserved in the future.

Note that the open source software and application solutions being developed by user communities also use negotiation skills to ensure the stability of the products they create, distribute, and support. In a paper from the Proceedings of the 38th Hawaii International Conference on System Sciences, Chris Jensen and Walt Scacchi provided a snapshot of the collaboration and conflict negotiation that occur in large-scale open source software development communities.[5] Understanding and researching the community that has developed an open source tool for implementation involves the same sort of due diligence that librarians must have when it comes to researching a vendor.

However, if a resource is free, what is there to negotiate? Actually, free resources require a lot of negotiation, and much of it mirrors the process for a for-cost resource, only with a wider variety of parties involved—both internal and external. Here are a few important points of negotiation for any resource—free or otherwise.

Support: Who you gonna call when something breaks or the resource is not accessible? This is where research about the provider is critical. It is important to know who has developed a resource, the developer's involvement in supporting its use, and whether a user community exists that provides debugging, tech support, and documentation. Occasionally, it might be necessary to negotiate with a third party to support a resource. This could mean purchasing a resource through a free software company or distributor such as LibLime (for the Koha Integrated Library System), Equinox (for the Evergreen ILS), or Media Flex (for OPALS). You could end up hiring an in-house programmer who understands the underlying architecture of the free resource or negotiating with a vendor such as Serials Solutions to act as a go-between to ensure that information is up-to-date, such as when it comes to adding open source journal titles to your library's electronic journal collection.

Development and Maintenance: Would you link to an open access title that stored all of its articles in an archaic file type that would require you to install a special reader? Probably not. How about a resource that was free but required a username and a password? These are questions of development, and while negotiation rarely leads to prognostication, your research should seek to determine how the resource has been developed. This includes finding out what features, if any, are currently under development, what bugs are in the process of being exterminated, and, ultimately, whether the resource continues to be developed at all or if its community has already moved on to the next big thing. While it might be difficult to get any group of developers or open access publishers to commit to continued development, any commitments that do exist should be included in license agreements and clarified in writing. Some free resource developers, such as the browser-based chat service Meebo, are all too eager to keep users apprised of their development activities. This is not uncommon and definitely a good sign. Sure, technology moves at the speed of light, and this week's big thing is next week's "What's that?", but when it comes to development, silence is not golden.

Stability: If a resource is actively being developed, users need to know when major changes are going to occur and what actions, if any, may be required to maintain access for users. Consult license agreements and developers about standard procedures for notifying users of changes; if that information is not available, ask developers for an assurance of notification. If there is an RSS feed for updates, subscribe to it. If there is a listserv for the user community, monitor it. Developers and publishers want users, and libraries can deliver them, often on a grand scale. Sending out an email before the server goes down is a small price to pay for free mass marketing. But before libraries can begin providing all of this free publicity, they need to know what they are advertising.

Deliverables: A librarian wouldn't purchase a quarterly journal that came out only once a year or a citation software that doesn't do American Psychological Association style. We need to know exactly what a resource promises and then test whether it delivers. This aspect, like maintenance, may require some internal negotiation as well in order to develop workflows and mechanisms to check that resources are working properly and fulfilling the need they are supposed to fill. It can be tough to anticipate whether a resource will come through on its promises, and there isn't always much recourse if it doesn't, other than to simply discontinue use of the resource.[6]

What Are the Costs of Free Resources?

In many cases, free isn't really free for libraries. Outsiders would see a large donation of books or materials as a stroke of luck, but the acquisition librarian understands what it will cost to add these materials to the collection. The same can be said for even the best free online resources. When an institution is deciding whether to use a free resource or choosing between a commercial and an open source product, an internal negotiation needs to take place to make sure that the institution is making the best choice. With the advent of such venues as the Directory of Open Access Journals and Code4Lib, and with the number of homegrown publishers and software developers that have recently emerged from libraries, the proper evaluation of open resources will only become more important in the future. Some of the elements that must be considered in negotiations include the following:

Implementation: Will this implementation consist of turning on a package of open access titles in your A-to-Z journal list, or will you need a programmer who knows open source databases MySQL and PHP to customize an interface? These two endeavors have wildly different costs associated with them and often the costs of implementation will prove to be a deal breaker when it comes to choosing a free resource.

Maintenance: Many resources will need to have maintenance performed in-house, whether this includes updating software, patches for debugging, updating holdings information, or updating URLs. Depending on the size and complexity of a resource, this could be a formidable task and might require some deal-making within the organization to ensure that the resource can be sufficiently maintained to make it useful and reliable. Remember, it doesn't take many bad experiences to lead users to decide that a resource is not worth their time. Internal negotiations to ensure sufficient staff for the maintenance of resources is an important issue, one often forgotten when staring at the low, low price of $0. For example, if a library is integrating its online holdings into its catalog, the inclusion of a collection of open access titles could be highly unstable and might not be worth the costs associated with maintaining it in the catalog. Like many of the costs associated with electronic resources, the recurring nature of maintenance can put its price well beyond that of print resource costs such as binding and shelving. Internal negotiations must occur when deciding how to distribute staff to support the maintenance of a new free resource. In many organizations, the number of staff once devoted to the acquisition and processing of print materials has led to lopsided staffing between print and electronic resources. Incorporating maintenance of new free resources into workflows can challenge mindsets that do not perceive those resources as assets deserving continued attention. Librarians may also find themselves negotiating with colleagues outside their institutions to create a user community that can develop and maintain free resources. The same collaboration and negotiation that created the first library consortia and union catalogs can be repurposed to create user communities of open resource development.

Marketing: For any product to succeed, it needs marketing to a targeted community of users. Commercial products often come with a slick interface, branded within an inch of its life and, more and more, customized to reflect the library that has purchased the product for its users. And don't forget the bookmarks, pencils, and tutorials that vendors create to assist libraries in training users and making them aware of the product's strengths. However, in the case of open source and open access resources, there is generally no marketing budget or flashy interfaces, and libraries must foot the bill, which can add extra strain to already stressed systems and reference and instruction departments. Internal negotiations with public services staff to ensure that they can properly support a new resource are critical to its success in your user community.

Assessment: The natural outgrowth of good marketing and training should be use, but unless librarians follow users around all day, it's hard to assess the use of and user satisfaction with a resource. While some internal measures, such as web statistics and user surveys, can shed some light on this activity, true user assessment needs to be a partnership between developers and libraries. Access to statistics compliant with Counting Online Usage of NeTworked Electronic Resources (COUNTER) standards for open access journals or the number of sessions conducted on open source software should be necessary components in the choice of resources, whether commercial or open source. Implementing a resource without the means to assess its use can become a black hole of time and money.

But Is It Asking Too Much?

If the idea of negotiating with the providers of free resources still seems foreign and overreaching, let's look at a couple of unique collaborations between libraries and a free resource provider that have put libraries in a position to negotiate. One reason these examples are so compelling is that they are instances of librarians negotiating with Google—the librarian's best friend or the angel of death for our profession, depending who you talk to. It is this spectrum of experience in regard to Google that makes it the ideal example of a free negotiation partner, or to put it another way, keep your friends close and your enemies closer—and don't forget to negotiate a good deal with both of them.

Google Scholar and Library Holdings

Google Scholar launched in 2004 and offered libraries an opportunity to use one of the latest tools in their arsenal, link resolution, to both enhance one of the open web's most popular search engines and put their often expensive resources in the hands of users. As one might imagine, this opportunity had librarians rubbing their eyes and pinching themselves. Could it be true that a giant search engine such as Google, one that many patrons use to begin their research (OCLC has said that as many as 62 percent of those surveyed named Google as their most recently used search engine[7]), could also become a tool for putting users in touch with the appropriate copy of the resources their libraries purchase for them? A caveat quickly emerged: Librarians needed to share their holdings information with Google. Rather than simply acting as an origin for library link resolvers, in the same way that link resolvers were interacting with citation databases, Google wanted to know each library's holdings in order to prioritize the links offered to a user based on the availability of the chosen article. For some libraries, this seemed like a small price to pay for access, but for others, it was a disturbing request from a supposedly benign partner. Let the negotiations begin!

But negotiations didn't begin, or at least they didn't get any-where. Where did libraries go wrong when it came to negotiating with Google about library holdings? As John McDonald, acquisi-tions librarian at the California Institute of Technology, stated in a 2006 interview for a *Searcher* magazine article on Google Scholar, librarians "felt that it was a free resource and anything they required we would just have to submit to." Now, there's nothing wrong with knowing a good thing when you see it, but an oppor-tunity could have been missed when libraries chose not to negoti-ate with the library holdings requirement for linking from Google Scholar. As McDonald points out, "I really didn't think Google Scholar could be a success without partnering with libraries, and so these holdings didn't turn out to be a big deal."[8] But what librar-ians seemed to have missed is the amount of leverage that their holdings and link resolution to those holdings gave them in deal-ing with Google. These negotiations could have been less about libraries wanting compensation for providing holdings and more about becoming fuller partners in the development of Google Scholar and creating a real, free alternative to commercial article-indexing databases. It is a matter of opinion whether allowing Google to have access to library holdings in exchange for link res-olution to resources was a missed opportunity.

Sometimes in negotiation our biggest or most galling losses can seem pretty insignificant through the lens of time. Other times, losing a battle can put one in a position to win a war or at the very least give one a better position from which to negotiate the next time parties meet, which, in the case of Google and libraries, was not far off.

Google Book Search and Library Book Scanning

In 2006, Google announced that it was partnering with some major academic libraries to take on the ambitious endeavor of scanning the web's final content frontier: books. This represented a much greater partnership between the individual libraries and Google than the passing of library holdings for link resolution to Google Scholar. The agreements that have led to Google's scanning millions of titles currently held in libraries for its Google Book Search Project are far more complex than a handshake and a warm fuzzy feeling of cooperation. The contracts signed by libraries take into account a variety of variables and rights that both Google and the providing library wanted to be sure to include. For an example, see the cooperative agreement between the University of Michigan and Google (www.lib.umich.edu/mdp/um-google-cooperative-agreement.pdf), and the amendment to that agreement (www.lib.umich.edu/mdp/Amendment-to-Cooperative-Agreement.pdf).

It is important to note that each Google partner has its own agreement with Google that reflects the constraints of the institution. The University of Michigan, as a public institution, has laws governing its partnership that are different from the laws governing a private institution such as Harvard; the University of Michigan's agreement was released to the public because Michigan laws mandate open access to contracts with public agencies. The agreements are also unique in that each institution has its own digitization plan. Some institutions may have agreed to the digitization of only public domain collections versus digitizing collections regardless of copyright status. Moreover, some of the institutions that became Google partners more recently may not enjoy all the advantages of early partners (e.g., receiving a library digital copy), but they also do not have the same sweeping digitization of their collections. Instead, Google is cherry-picking, coming in with lists of what it wants to digitize.

Regardless of preference for Google Book Search, the Open Content Alliance, or other book digitization initiatives, all parties need to get something for the costs they will incur. Those costs continue to be substantial, not only because of the high price for scanning a book, but also because of the sheer number of volumes involved. In order for a negotiation and any partnership that results from it to succeed, each party must feel comfortable with the investment being made, as well as with the products being delivered. At the time of this writing, the settlement being reached between Google and the Association of American Publishers and the Authors Guild is expected to work out a veritable cornucopia of negotiation issues that copyright brings into any digitization project. Questions such as who has the right to digitize this material, who retains the rights to the digital copy, and what rights other parties have to the digital copy should get some answers in the Google settlement agreement.

Even with copyright issues squared away, the following meat-and-potato issues remain:

- Which collections are to be scanned (what does Google want, and what are the libraries willing to provide)?

- How will both physical and digital copies be transported between the two institutions?

- How long does each party have to execute its activities in the partnership (for libraries, determining and preparing collections for scanning, and for Google, scanning and preparing digital copies)?

- What guarantees does either party have to hold up its end of the bargain?

While the rights issues likely took up the lion's share of the negotiating time, it is just as likely that many of these other issues proved to be deal breakers for libraries' participation. However, the ever-growing number of library partners demonstrates that mutually beneficial agreements can and will be achieved with Google and other digital partners. Once the Google settlement is accepted, new issues, and therefore new points for negotiation between partners, will probably crop up.

As reported in the December 2008 issue of *American Libraries*, Harvard University Library, amid concerns that the current settlement did not properly define the rights of library users regarding the scanned in-copyright materials that other libraries are providing, decided to maintain its policy of providing only out-of-copyright materials to Google for scanning. Robert C. Darton, director of the Harvard University Libraries, wrote in a letter to library staff, "As we understand it, the settlement contains too many potential limitations on access to and use of the books by members of the higher education community and by patrons of public libraries. ... The settlement provides no assurance that the prices charged for access will be reasonable, especially since the subscription services will have no real competitors [and] the scope of access to the digitized books is in various ways both limited and uncertain."[9]

The Digital Download on Open Resources

If there is one area where negotiation can reap big benefits for librarians and users, it is in the arena of open resources. Many librarians, as early adopters of new technology, are creative in their identification and use of the latest Web 2.0 technologies. But there is room for librarians to take a step further.

The user communities that libraries represent can often be the same audiences that open developers seek. Particularly when resources are funded through advertising, the more users [you have], the more income can be brought in to keep the development going. Libraries can use this strategy as a negotiation tool to get in on the ground floor of building resources that can improve library services and collections. Consider this three-pronged approach:

- Let the open resource developers know that librarians and library users like their work and how they are using it. Find out how many libraries are using the tool and give the developers examples of how libraries are implementing their resource.

- Let the developers know what would make the tool even more attractive to libraries and their users. Even if you can't think of a way that you would improve the resource, consider asking about their plans for future development and whether they have done any piloting with libraries for new versions.

- Offer to create partnerships with the developers to help them introduce new users to their resource and pilot new versions. In exchange, ask for a seat at the table when discussing new developments, as well as the ability to brand the resource for your library.

Open resource developers often share the same service-oriented attitude that many librarians hold dear. They see a need in the digital marketplace and have the know-how to fill that need. By supporting their development, librarians can be on the cutting edge of useful new technologies and may also create valuable partnerships long before a successful product goes commercial.

So negotiations are far from over for this currently "free" resource. Whether because of vague language governing library use in the final settlement, an outright rejection of the current settlement agreement by the courts, or the ever-changing landscape of internet resources, there will be a need to renegotiate the way individual libraries and libraries as a group interact with Google Book Search as providers of content, users of the resource, and possible licensees of the content. Moreover, library-based activities such as the HathiTrust (www.hathitrust.com) will play a role in how libraries use Google products in the future, as well as giving libraries a bit of leverage when it comes to further negotiations with Google.

Use Free Resources as Leverage

Depending on who you talk to, free resources are either no competition or completely antithetical to existing information and software markets. While Microsoft may not be panicking over the popularity of Linux, the compatibility of free programs such as Google Docs with more traditional resources such as Microsoft Word certainly leaves the door open for users to make informed choices. And where users go, institutions often follow. Debbie Schachter, in a June 2007 article in *Searcher*, described the introduction of free and open access resources as having a discernible effect on the negotiation environment. "Look at R. R. Bowker LLC's Books In Print (BIP) and Amazon. Librarians can simply use Amazon as a free service for identifying materials in print. Bowker's response to this competitor in its traditionally dominant field has been to enhance its product to try to differentiate BIP for its customers by clearly defining customer value for the subscription price, from that offered by the free service."[10] Using a free alternative to negotiate a better price is another aspect of how these resources change negotiations. Free resources have also provided a measuring stick by which to judge the functionality of purchased resources.

Tools such as Google and Google Scholar and the algorithms that power them function in contrast to the integrated library system and the article database search interfaces that libraries provide to their users. When the difference between these resources becomes stark enough in the favor of the free tools, it can be difficult to rationalize the purchase of commercially available tools no matter how much tradition tells us that we need them. Even with no comparable free resource available to the commercial resource under consideration, the lack of a sufficient search interface and algorithm can be a tool to negotiate a better price for a resource that does not quite meet your users' expectations—yet.

When weighing the pros and cons of making an open access or open source tool available to your users, just as with commercial resources, look at those cons as points for possible negotiation. Free resources can easily become stagnant or irrelevant if their developers are not keyed into the market they serve. In many ways, this danger can make their developers friendly to suggestions for improvements, particularly since many of these resources have their origins in community-based initiatives. Becoming a part of that community, while a responsibility, entitles you to have a say in the development of a resource, as well as keeping you abreast of where things are heading and whether you want to travel that road. All too often librarians take what they are given and happily run away. Even in the world of "free resources," negotiation has a place; librarians need not be afraid to take a page from the book of that perennially cheerful singing orphan (no, the other one) and say, "Please, sir, I want some more."

Endnotes

1. Peter Suber, email message to Beth Ashmore, July 5, 2009.

2. House of Commons (U.K.), Select Committee on Science and Technology, "Science and Technology—Tenth Report," *UK Parliament Website*, July 20, 2004, accessed July 28, 2011, www.publications. parliament.uk/pa/cm200304/cmselect/cmsctech/399/39902.htm.

3. Graham Walton, "Negotiation in Health Libraries: A Case Study of Health Information and Libraries Journal and Open Access Publishing," *Health Information and Libraries Journal* 22 (2005): 161–163.

4. Yan Han, Jeanne Pfander, and Marianne Stowell Bracke, "Digitizing Rangelands: Providing Open Access to the Archives of Society for Management Journals," *IAALD Quarterly Bulletin* 50, no. 3/4 (2005): 107.

5. Chris Jensen and Walt Scacchi, "Collaboration, Leadership, Control, and Conflict Negotiation and the Netbeans.org Open Source Software

Development Community," in *Proceedings of the 38th Hawaii International Conference on System Sciences* (Los Alamos, CA: IEEE Computer Society Press, 2005), 1966.

6. For more information about open source evaluation and implementation, see Karen Schneider's, "The Thick of the Fray: Open Source Software in Libraries in the First Decade of this Century," *Bulletin of the American Society for Information Science and Technology* 35 no. 2 (December 2008/January 2009),: 15–19, accessed July 28, 2011, www.asis.org/Bulletin/Dec-08/DecJan09_Schneider.pdf; and E. Balnaves, "Open Source Library Management Systems: A Multidimensional Evaluation," *Australian Academic & Research Libraries* 39 no. 1 (March 2008): 1–13.

7. OCLC, *OCLC Perceptions of Libraries and Information Resources*, (Dublin, OH: OCLC Online Computer Library Center, 2005): 1–18.

8. Beth Ashmore and Jill E. Grogg, "Google and OCLC Open Libraries on the Open Web," *Searcher* 14, no. 10 (Nov./Dec. 2006): 44–52.

9. G. Flagg, "Google Settles Scanning Suit With Authors, Publishers," *American Libraries* 39 no. 11 (December 2008): 30.

10. Debbie Schachter, "Negotiating in Areas Where End-User Services Dominate," *Searcher* 15, no. 6 (June 2007): 47–48.

How to Research a Forthcoming Negotiation

Librarians would seem to be the last people to need advice on how to research any given topic, but sometimes the high stakes associated with a particular negotiation can make it difficult to know where to begin in researching a company, employer, or funding agency. You must always know as much as you can about the other party before entering a negotiation so that you can understand the other side's interests and needs. This appendix offers a few tools and tips that can put you in a position to feel confident about understanding the party across the table. Since this book covers a wide variety of negotiation situations that a 21st-century librarian will likely encounter over the course of his or her career, this appendix includes information on preparing for negotiations with all kinds of parties, including vendors, employers, and funding agencies.

Company and Industry Research

When negotiations involve purchasing a product or license, researching the company that provides that product, as well as the product itself, is key to successful negotiations. In addition to knowing about competing products and their pricing, you want to know about the company itself and its relationship to the industry. The following tools are useful for company and industry research:

- Hoover's Company Records (www.hoovers.com/free): Hoover's company records include contact information, company history, top executives, products and operations, and competitors. Hoover's provides a skeletal, free version at the web address above, but your library may have access to more information through a subscription to Hoover's data through ProQuest.

- MarketResearch.com (www.marketresearch.com): MarketResearch.com provides market forecasts and analyses for a wide variety of industries. These reports contain information on the top companies in a given field, as well as what trends appear to be affecting the overall market. Reports can be purchased individually, or you can subscribe to the entire database.

- Mergent Online (www.mergentonline.com): While Mergent Online is generally geared toward prospective investors, many of the tools it offers can be useful in discovering what place a company holds within a given industry, particularly in the face of the amount of market consolidation that has taken place in the information industry over the past few years. Tools such as a history of mergers, acquisitions, and joint ventures, lists of subsidiaries, and annual reports can help determine where a company is looking to develop in the future. Mergent Online is a subscription database.

- ReferenceUSA (www.referenceusa.com): ReferenceUSA is a subscription database that contains information about more than 14 million U.S. businesses. Company profiles include competitor reports, management directories, and historical data on employees and sales.

- ValueLine (www.valueline.com): Like Mergent Online, ValueLine is geared to investors, but its short (usually just a couple of paragraphs) and current analyses can give you an idea of what a company faces in the coming quarter and where its priorities might lie in the near future. ValueLine is both a print title and a subscription database.

Business and Trade Journal Databases

Article databases such as ABI/INFORM (ProQuest), Business Source (EBSCO), Business and Company Resource Center (Gale), and LexisNexis Academic can provide the currency necessary to really know what a company is facing in the immediate future, particularly if new developments in mergers, acquisitions, or legislation have thrown the industry a curveball. These databases also include trade publications for the information industry, which contain product reviews that can take some of the guesswork out of determining how a resource measures up against its competition.

Company Websites and Webinars

While information from a company may seem like an unlikely source for straight talk, the claims made in promotional materials or demonstrated in webinars can provide an excellent foundation for knowing which questions to ask during negotiations. If a claim sounds too good to be true, be sure to ask the company how it is able to accomplish this difficult achievement.

Fellow Librarians and Listservs

The generally communicative nature of the library profession tends to work in our favor when it comes to research for negotiations. While contracts may prohibit a fellow librarian from disclosing the terms of a deal, the nature and quality of the negotiations can be shared, and, often on listservs such as LIBLICENSE, it is possible to find accounts of librarians struggling with the tactics or terms of a particular vendor or group and coming to the listserv for help. Learn from the mistakes and triumphs of others.

Employer–Employee Research

For employers and employees who may not have databases chock-full of information about potential employees and employers, the internet provides a wealth of information about your potential new co-workers. In addition to Googling institutions and job applicants, be sure to look for the personal websites and curriculum vitae of potential supervisors and co-workers to identify their research interests, service interests, and previous institutional affiliations. Knowing the previous institutions of prospective co-workers increases the pool of people who might provide you information. Once you have contacted all the people you know who might have some information about an organization or person, be sure to look at any mission statements or planning documents available. While these documents are not always entirely indicative of how an organization really functions, they may give you an idea of the institution's priorities. Databases of trade journals may not always have information about a person or institution, but be sure to do the search, because if a person or institution does something newsworthy, you will want to know about it.

Funding Agency Research

Researching a library board or trustees is in many ways similar to researching a prospective employee or employer. Searching for information about the backgrounds of each of the board members or trustees can help you better understand their priorities and interests. It can also help you identify anyone you may know who knows these individuals personally and could give you greater insight into how to frame your needs or proposals in a light that would work in your favor. These funding agencies are, after all, those who get the budgets for eresources and much more. Presenting them with relevant facts, figures, and convincing usage stats will only help in any negotiation regarding budgeting or staffing for a digital library.

What to Look For

Sometimes there can be so much information that it can be difficult to know what is relevant and what is extraneous. The key
things to look for when researching a company or institution are
people, products, and problems. In terms of people, be sure to
find out whom you may already know within an organization, and
this includes people who others in your organization or consortia
might know as well. These are all possible contacts for the inside
scoop on the organization. In addition, figure out to whom your
sales representative or negotiation contact reports and to whom
that person reports. Understanding the organizational structure
can help you determine who the deal makers are and, if necessary,
when you might need to go to the next level in negotiations. If the
representative you deal with doesn't have the power to make the
concessions or license changes you need, get the next person up
the ladder in on the negotiations.

In terms of products, you want to know what the vendor's product line is and the general consensus on that line. How many customers does the vendor have, and are those customers similar to
you in their needs and users? If a particular product is dramatically
different in price from its competitors, do product reviews help
explain why? Do personal or listserv conversations with other
librarians shed any light on what type of negotiations a particular
company or sales representative takes part in? In short, try to put
together a picture of what a typical negotiation with this company
looks like. Although this picture is not likely to be 100 percent
accurate, it may help you dodge any tactics a sales representative
might use to throw you off your game.

In terms of problems, is anyone screaming? With all the listservs, trade publications, blogs, and so forth available to us, we can
find plenty of opinions on products and organizations. Some of
this vitriol should be taken with a grain of salt, but it may suggest
topics that need to be brought up in negotiations. If librarians are
lambasting a vendor for lack of prompt help desk service, than a
new license with that vendor should include explicit information

about expectations for help desk response time and what redress the library has if those expectations are not met. By identifying potential red flags prior to negotiations, librarians can know where to spend their time during contract negotiation.

Competitive intelligence, as defined by Larry Kahaner, author of *Competitive Intelligence: How To Gather, Analyze, and Use Information to Move Your Business to the Top*, is a "systematic program for gathering and analyzing information about your competitors' activities and general business trends to further your own company's goals."[1] In other words, all the little pieces of information you turn up need to form a bigger picture in order to be useful. It is easy to get caught up in the gathering activities and forget about the analysis. When reviewing the information you have found, ask yourself these questions: What does this information tell me about the institution or the representative with whom I'm dealing? To whom does this information give leverage? For example, if you discover that your library's peer institutions subscribe to a particular resource, this information can be seen as leverage on the side of the vendor. However, a *Library Journal* review stating that the vendor's resource overlaps with resources already in your library can be used as leverage on your side.

Endnote

1. Larry Kahaner, *Competitive Intelligence: How to Gather, Analyze and Use Information to Move Your Business to the Top* (New York: Touchstone, 1997), 16.

Useful Resources

The resources listed below delve into many aspects of the negotiation process. Some of the materials are from the librarian's perspective, and others are from outside the field but provide insights into negotiation that information professionals will find useful. Many of the resources listed below are cited in the chapters of this book and provide in-depth analysis of the negotiation process beyond the scope of this book. Other resources listed below are from some of the top negotiators in the library and information industry, some of whom have contributed to this book. These titles focus largely on the process and mechanics of negotiating and managing electronic resources and provide a variety of perspectives on how to manage the electronic resource acquisition and management process.

Albitz, Becky. *Licensing and Managing Electronic Resources.* Oxford, UK: Chandos, 2008.

   Albitz, chair of the Copyright Committee of the Association of College and Research Libraries, provides guidance on the copyright issues associated with licensing, in addition to advice on selection and management of resources and understanding license agreements and other license alternatives.

Anderson, Rick. *Buying and Contracting for Resources and Services: A How-to-Do-It Manual for Librarians.* New York: Neal-Schuman, 2004.

   Neal-Schuman is known for its excellent how-to-do-it manuals, and *Buying and Contracting for Resources and Services* is no exception. Anderson gets down to the nitty-gritty of creating requests for proposals and approval plans and tackles big issues such as tracking vendor performance and evaluating library–vendor relationships over time.

Black, Steve. *Serials in Libraries: Issues and Practices.* Westport, CT: Libraries Unlimited, 2006.

Black is a recognized expert in serials and workflow management. This book traces serials from the earliest of publications through the turmoil of the past 20 years. Black says he is considering proposing an updated edition because this area of librarianship changes so quickly.

Camp, Jim. *Start With No: The Negotiating Tools That the Pros Don't Want You to Know.* New York: Crown Business, 2002.

Of all the titles in this appendix, librarians may find Camp's the most difficult to put into practice. Camp provides a lot of information about getting neediness and the other emotions that come up in negotiation under control, which can be key for librarians who feel very strongly about their institutions and users and bring those feelings into the negotiation process.

Christensen, Stan. "The Art of Negotiation." Stanford Technology Ventures Program podcast, Stanford University, Palo Alto, CA, October 31, 2007. ecorner.stanford.edu/authorMaterialInfo.html? mid=1819.

In a lecture in Stanford University's Entrepreneurial Thought Leaders series, Stan Christensen provides insight into the serial nature of the negotiation process, particularly from an entrepreneur's perspective, which can be similar to a library perspective. Christensen is funny and experienced, and he dispels some of the myths and fears surrounding negotiation.

Conger, Joan. *Collaborative Electronic Resource Management.* Westport, CT: Libraries Unlimited, 2004.

Conger offers a refreshing and philosophical look at the chaotic world of electronic resource management. She delves into the murky waters of management and applies concepts of organizational development to our profession. She has a section specifically devoted to negotiation through cost and benefit. This is one of the best books available on the topic.

Durrant, Fiona. *Negotiating Licences for Digital Resources*. London: Facet, 2006.

Durrant, now Fiona Fogden, provides an excellent timeline of the negotiation process, from assessing organizational needs to communicating the outcomes of negotiation to your organization. Fogden's unique perspective as head of large special libraries in the U.K. provides insight into the motives and needs of commercial entities that many outside the for-profit world will find enlightening.

Fisher, Roger, and Daniel Shapiro. *Beyond Reason: Using Emotions As You Negotiate*. New York: Penguin Books, 2005.

Fisher and Shapiro tackle the difficult issue of managing the emotions that can sometimes sabotage even the most well-intentioned negotiator. The very nature of conflict management can require the management of emotions that arise from the conflict. This book seeks to identify how emotions can damage a negotiation by diverting attention, affecting relationships, and exploiting parties, as well as looking at how emotions can be used to build rapport and address and satisfy each party's interests.

Fisher, Roger, and William Ury. *Getting to Yes*. 2nd ed. New York: Penguin Books, 1991.

Fisher and Ury's research on negotiation came out of the Harvard Negotiation Project, a program designed to develop best practices in negotiation and mediation. The book's examples range from hostage negotiations to landlord trouble, and it can seem difficult to apply the information to a particular library situation, but this short, well-organized study provides the logic behind the techniques.

Gregory, Vicki L., with assistance by Ardis Harrison. *Selecting and Managing Electronic Resources: A How-To-Do-It Manual for Librarians.* Rev. ed. New York: Neal-Schuman, 2006.

Particularly for practicing electronic or acquisitions librarians, Gregory and Harrison offer practical advice about workflow, policy creation, budgeting and acquisitions, and more. A chapter is devoted to digital rights management and intellectual property, including discussions of licensing issues.

Harris, Lesley Ellen. *Licensing Digital Content: A Practical Guide for Librarians.* 2nd ed. Chicago: ALA Editions, 2009.

Harris provides an excellent global perspective on licensing. In addition to providing practical resources for negotiating and organizing licensing information, she brings expertise in copyright law, an area that can involve some of the most confusing elements associated with electronic content acquisition. Harris also offers online and in-person seminars that can provide important continuing education opportunities for your organization or library community. A blog for discussion of this book and issues of digital content licensing can be found at www.licensingdigitalcontent. blogspot.com.

Johnson, Peggy. *Fundamentals of Collection Development and Management.* 2nd ed. Chicago: ALA Editions, 2008.

Electronic resources and other electronic media are changing the face of collection development and management, necessitating the second edition of this book originally published in 2004. If your negotiation responsibilities coincide with any acquisitions, collection development, or management work, this book is a comprehensive guide.

LibLicense, www.library.yale.edu/~llicense/index.shtml

The LibLicense listserv is a must-have for any librarian involved in license negotiation. In addition to keeping you up-to-date on the advances and setbacks that librarians have experienced in negotiating with vendors and publishers, the LibLicense community can serve as a sounding board and source of support, particularly for "army of one" librarians.

Licensingmodels.org, www.licensingmodels.org

If you are new to the world of licenses and aren't even sure what one would look like, this website, developed by John Cox in conjunction with major subscription agents such as EBSCO, Harrassowitz, and Swets, will provide you with six standard license agreements for a variety of organizations. Sample licenses for a single academic institution, an academic consortium, a public library, a corporate or special library, an ebook or journal archive purchase, and a 30/60-day free trial include not only the license but also guidance on how to use it and what to look out for.

Phillips, Kara. Deal or No Deal series:

- "Licensing and Acquiring Digital Resources," October 15, 2006, LLRX.com, www.llrx.com/columns/deal1.htm

- "Licensing and Acquiring Digital Resources: License Negotiations," November 22, 2006, LLRX.com, www.llrx.com/columns/deal2.htm

- "Licensing and Acquiring Digital Resources: License Negotiations Reprise," January 15, 2007, LLRX.com, www.llrx.com/columns/deal3.htm

- "Licensing and Acquiring Digital Resources: Deal Breaking License Clauses," March 18, 2007, LLRX.com, www.llrx.com/columns/deal4.htm

Phillips's article series for LLRX.com, a website devoted to law and technology resources for legal professionals, provides practical advice from a legal perspective written in plain English and designed to demystify some of the terms commonly found in resource licensing.

Shapiro, Ronald, and Mark A. Jankowski. *The Power of Nice: How to Negotiate So Everyone Wins—Especially You!*. New York: Wiley, 2001.

Shapiro and Jankowski's title may appeal to many librarians as our desire to be nice, helpful, and accommodating threatens to become a major strike against us at the negotiation table. In addition to basic instruction in negotiation, the authors provide a number of worksheets that can be used or modified to help librarians integrate some negotiation best practices into their resource acquisition workflows.

Shell, G. Richard. *Bargaining for Advantage: Negotiation Strategies for Reasonable People*. London: Penguin Books, 2006.

Shell's approach to negotiation relies heavily on taking advantage of your own personal style and growing as a negotiator from what is most comfortable to you. This can be a welcome approach for those who don't care for the idea of becoming a shark in the conference room. Shell also provides excellent information on how to deal with tricky situations that may tempt you or your opponent to be less than ethical.

Survey of Library Database Licensing Practices. New York: Primary Research Group, 2008.

Data crunchers out there will find this title useful in providing the big picture of the amount and character of licensing going on in our industry. The data can be useful in negotiating for particular licensing terms (e.g., alumni access, perpetual access, interlibrary loan). This title can also help you prioritize which issues might be the most likely to require future consideration (e.g., service interruption, shortfalls in content, lawsuits).

Sample Licensing and Negotiation Checklists

Any licensing or negotiation checklist will need modification for given organizations. The following sample licensing and negotiation checklists are not meant to be comprehensive but rather a starting place. Some of the books in Appendix B: Useful Resources, particularly those specifically addressing how-tos for licensing, contain more comprehensive examples of licensing checklists. Leslie Ellen Harris, in an April 2008 *Information Outlook* article, offers her thoughts about striving for consistency in digital content licensing policies, including elements for a licensing checklist.[1] Harris advocates including the following items on a checklist, as do many other licensing experts, such as Becky Albitz, Rick Anderson, Trisha Davis, Fiona Fogden, Ann Okerson, and others:

- The name of the licensor and licensee

- The name of the person in your organization who has negotiating and signing authority for agreements

- A description of the content being licensed

- The duration for which the content is licensed

Harris goes on to list several other policylike items, such as definition of authorized users and jurisdiction. Licensing and other checklists can serve a number of different purposes and come in all shapes and sizes, so outlining your goals for a particular checklist makes the process more fruitful. If your organization is large enough to have a general counsel's office or purchasing department, make sure to consult with that unit to see whether some licensing checklists are already in existence—there's no use reinventing the wheel!

Licensing Checklist

Library's rights (should all be yes):

- Content can be printed, downloaded, and copied for scholarly purposes. Content can be used by Organization X's definition of authorized user for remote access and walk-in users.

- Content is available for interlibrary lending.

- A period of at least 30 days will be granted to mend any breach of contract.

- The licensee will have a right to terminate a contract with at least 30 days' notice if the provider breaches the contract.

- The licensee will have a right to a prorated refund if the provider breaches the contract.

Library's responsibilities (should all be no):

- Library is required to make other than "reasonable" efforts to notify its users of terms and conditions.

- Library is required to adhere to terms between the vendor and a third party without detailing all the terms.

- Library is required to indicate that the terms are subject to terms in another license (including click-through links).

- Library is required not to disclose the terms of the agreement.

Vendor responsibilities (should all be yes):

- Vendor will give 90 days' notice of a change in the terms of a license.

- Vendor agrees to specific performance terms and to pay penalties in the case of a failure to meet these levels of agreed-on performance.

- Vendor gives library notice of any suspected or alleged use violations and gives library "reasonable time" to solve the problem before suspending access.

- Vendor gives library usage data compatible with Counting Online Usage of NeTworked Electronic Resources (COUNTER) standards.

- Vendor holds library blameless for any misuse of information.

- Vendor is required to respect the confidentiality of personal use information.

Unacceptable terms:

- Library does not agree to indemnification of licensor.

- Library does not agree to jurisdiction or governing law other than its own state.

- Library does not agree to binding or mandatory arbitration.

- Library does not agree to the assignment of licensor rights to a third party.

- Library does not agree to pay any licensor attorney fees, late payment fees, or finance charges.

- Library does not agree to any personal liability of the signer or of any other library/institutional employees.

- The contract should not allow price or other terms to be unilaterally changed in the future.

Negotiation Checklist

- Library conducted background and other research appropriate to negotiation.

- Library identified alternatives or articulated a Best Alternative to a Negotiated Agreement, which can be as complex or as simple as a given situation warrants. (While addressed in some library literature, information about the Best Alternative to a Negotiated Agreement abounds in nonlibrary negotiation literature.)

- Library determined deal breakers. (List only those items that truly will cause you to walk away.)

- Library distinguished less important points from deal-breakers.

- Library communicated with appropriate personnel within the organization, particularly if negotiating on behalf of someone else, which is the case for most information professionals; we represent our users!

Endnote

1. Lesley Ellen Harris, "Striving for Consistency in Your Digital Content Licensing Policy," *Information Outlook* 12, no. 4 (2008): 38–39.

Digital Tools, Netiquette, and Negotiation

Digitized Communication

Digital tools have changed the way we negotiate with each other. This appendix is a list of some of those tools, with brief comments about how they affect negotiation communication and strategy.

Email and Chat

One of the great advantages of email and chat, particularly chat, is that both modes potentially have the speed of a phone conversation but also allow each party to carefully craft messages. Certainly, chat requires less care because the other party expects a certain degree of quick response, but without the pressure of a humming phone line or a blank stare across a room. With email, there is also the added advantage of being able to attach documentation. Email, however, can be quite asynchronous. With no expectation of an immediate response, time lapses between emails vary wildly. Both chat and email have a general lack of context, and owing to a lack of facial or verbal expression, the possibility of misunderstanding and misreading remains ever present. Such misunderstanding can often be cleared up in the space of a phone call.

Videoconferencing Via the Internet

With the ubiquity of tools such as Skype, the videoconference is now available to an increasingly broad audience. Video reintroduces visual cues into the conversation, although the quality can vary depending on the connection, camera, screen, and so forth.

Many companies and institutions have invested in proprietary clients for teleconferencing, either with or without video, but plenty of free options exist as well. For the cash-strapped individual, such technology imitates face-to-face communication without the accompanying cost. Additionally, such clients can provide critical continuing education to librarians and other interested parties, again without the accompanying travel costs.

File Sharing

Google Docs has made file sharing available to anyone with an internet connection. Some companies and libraries might be uncomfortable sharing drafts of legal contracts in the cloud, so they instead opt to exchange Microsoft Word or Adobe Acrobat documents via email or otherwise. Documents are more malleable than ever. With Word's Track Changes and other markup and commenting tools, both parties can trace the evolution of a negotiation and reduce any chance of misunderstanding. Many copy machines come with a scan feature, which brings the fax ever closer to extinction. Shifting paper via snail mail or intra- and interdepartmental mail is still around, however. Even if a given institution or company doesn't require the original signed contract, most, if not all, require a scanned version of an actual signature.

Web-Based Applications for Account Administration

Whether administering access to databases, getting usage statistics, downloading or viewing training materials, or renewing subscriptions, the ability to administer accounts has never been easier. Unfortunately, each vendor usually has its own account, so the library must maintain some sort of record of usernames and passwords, either in an eresource management system or in an Excel spreadsheet. Renewing a product online or via email, either directly or through a consortium, is convenient, but it can also leave one feeling disconnected from the sales and customer service representative. Librarians and vendors alike must make a particular effort to communicate in a variety of ways in order to regularly revisit contract terms and pricing structures.

Automated Data Sharing

Electronic Data Interchange, the Standardized Usage Statistics Harvesting Initiative, ONIX-PL, and other forms of automated data sharing can make negotiations much easier. The ability to let the machines do the talking when it comes to making purchases and keeping accounts gives everyone a clearer picture of accounts, usage, and license terms. The combination of price and usage via automated processes adds another variable to allow the librarian to make an even more informed decision. As any good negotiator knows, informed negotiation is good negotiation.

Websites

There is no greater or possibly cheaper tool for the dissemination of information than the basic website. Part of developing a good relationship is becoming informed about the other party, as well as giving feedback to the other party, and this has never been easier. Website comment forms, social networking tools, and web-based surveys only enhance our understanding of one another.

These examples are only a sample of the types of tools that have altered negotiation in the digital age, but they offer a general cross-section.

Netiquette

Unfortunately, netiquette is one of those topics that seem like common sense but often are not so common. Just like the lamentable dearth of people who say "please" and "thank you," lack of attention to netiquette still roams the binary world. Here are just a few of the major offenses, tips, and tricks.

Reply and Reply All

Who hasn't had the heart-stopping moment when you fear you just broadcast sensitive or inappropriate information to a waiting world? One of the most convenient communication tools to hit the human race can quickly become a nightmare. Especially during sensitive negotiations, stop, breathe, and read. You certainly don't want internal communication about a particular deal landing in the wrong hands. Negotiations, especially during times of economic stress, can be quite tense. Stop, breathe, read, and then let a colleague reread, if necessary. There is a significant chance of misunderstanding via email, so use the time it affords to craft appropriate responses. Last, use discretion when choosing to include others in your emails, especially those above you on the ladder. Most of us are bombarded with email on a daily, if not hourly, basis, so be a good employee and choose carefully who you decide to include in any correspondence.

Plain Text or HyperText Markup Language

The choice between using plain text or HyperText Markup Language (HTML) in emails and other digital communications is a matter of taste, but be tasteful. Plain text is always a good way to go, but if you use HTML or other flourishes, be professional. This is especially true of the signature line. The pithy phrase that just "sums you up" is often more appropriate for personal correspondence.

Privacy

If it's out there on the open web, then those with whom you are negotiating can find it. The line between what is personal and what is professional can blur easily on favorite social networking sites, so be aware of mixing the two. Use the privacy options available to you, and if you choose to be "friends" with professional colleagues, either create sections within one social networking environment or use two networks, such as Facebook for personal and LinkedIn for professional.

Being Professional

Speaking of being professional, tread carefully in personal waters. This is a business relationship, not a budding friendship. Vendors are not your friends; they are your business colleagues. It is perfectly acceptable to be friendly and personable, but there's a difference between being friendly and personable and being overly familiar.

The Usual Suspects

The usual suspects bear repeating: Don't use capital letters. Avoid emoticons in professional communication. Be aware of the size of your attachments—not everyone has unlimited bandwidth and storage space. Always include a meaningful subject line, especially with vendors. Simply referring to the "upcoming contract" may have meaning for you, but it's likely the vendor receives many, many contracts. Spell-check your emails, and brush up, if necessary, on your grammar. A haphazard email or other correspondence suggests a haphazard approach to the serious business at hand. If you want to be taken seriously, give your writing the attention it deserves.

Theory in Practice: Understanding Communication

It is impossible to negotiate without communicating, and it is helpful if the evolving negotiator grasps a bit of history and understands a few basic concepts. For hundreds of years, the apex was the printed book. Then, in the 19th century, the world became wired. First the telegraph and, soon after, the telephone allowed for—demanded—instantaneous point-to-point global communication. Consider the ways in which instant communication changed the art of negotiation. In the world of politics and diplomacy, for example, leaders became more susceptible to the immediate passions of the masses. Decisions that had once come through leisurely debate now pushed through at the speed of a telegrapher's finger. It was the first real glimpse of the information glut in which we are currently mired. Radio and television made the world smaller still, and quicker, but it was not until the late 20th century that reality shrank to the size of a home computer, and scholars began wondering what it meant to communicate in a world where space and time had lost much of their limiting tyranny.

Computer-mediated communication (CMC) became a hot and fertile research area, an academic rain forest teeming with life in the form of research questions, hypotheses, and theories. After all, CMC can be online or offline, synchronous or asynchronous. It can be one-to-one, many-to-one, one-to-many, or many-to-many. It can be wholly textual, wholly audio or video, wholly still image, persistent or transitory, vetted or shot from the hip. It can be some hybrid stew, mixed and matched from ever-developing digital media and shifting social norms. There was, and remains, much to discover about how all this impacts the ways in which messages are transmitted, received, and understood.

Researchers began examining CMC in earnest during the 1980s. Among their first topics of inquiry were computer efficiency, cost, and technical capabilities. Other studies sought to illuminate CMC impact in libraries and other organizations and the ways in which various communication channels influenced comprehension and message impact. Researchers found that audible and visual cues from a likable person can enhance the effectiveness of a message, while unlikable people can argue just as persuasively when the message is exclusively textual. Around the middle of that decade, questions about social and psychological issues emerged, as did questions about group processes and consensus building.

Much of what was groundbreaking in the 1980s has become accepted wisdom today. Common experience demonstrated early on that the absence of an in-the-flesh communication partner made people much more likely to misinterpret messages and, behind the veil of internet anonymity, freely vent the ill will this misinterpretation sometimes caused. To use the vernacular, people flamed one another. Much of this problem can be traced to the lack of visual or auditory cues embedded in face-to-face communication. Without an ironic tone of voice, a wink, shrug, or playfully raised eyebrow, an off-the-cuff or joking comment can be received as a threat or insult. Further, the anonymity inherent in many CMC transactions levels social hierarchies and lends participants the power to bluster with little chance of real retribution from the other party.

The 1990s saw a preoccupation with the study of email as a means of CMC and of issues related to internet usage. There were studies on conferencing via computer, about emerging CMC norms, and about user attitudes toward cultural differences. As the 21st century dawned, researchers delved more deeply into social networking and looked hard at the ways in which CMC fit into the burgeoning online education movement. Away from the ivory tower, everyone from grade-school children to great grandparents surfed the web, joined sites such as Myspace and Facebook, and spent and stored large chunks of their lives in the digital realm. A once-esoteric medium was now an indispensable part of the world landscape.

No matter how it is conducted, communication is an inherent quality of sentient life, encompassing far more than outwardly directed verbal or written messages. Indeed, understanding the general attributes of a basic communication transaction can improve one's chances of communicating effectively in a broad range of environments. The most basic, of course, is face to face. Experts agree that in face-to-face communication, more information may pass between people through body language than is exchanged through words. An individual's posture, their willingness—or not—to make eye contact, whether their arms are crossed or open, and many, many other signals help people form decisions about the speaker's intended message. This holds true in situations such as television broadcasts, in which a speaker sees only the people and equipment on set, while millions of viewers watch from the comfort of their homes. Among the most famous examples of body language working to help viewers decide their opinion on an important issue is the 1960 televised debate between senator John F. Kennedy and vice president Richard M. Nixon. Many observers believe that Nixon's answers were, in fact, more substantial than Kennedy's, but the charismatic, telegenic, and confident senator easily won the body language war against his uncomfortable and sweaty opponent. It was a brave new world of mass media and visual politicking, and poor Nixon did not grasp what it took to win in this arena. He did not have the necessary tools, and thus, on that night, he never had a chance.

Other research about the messages relayed during nonverbal communication can inform our understanding of negotiation as well. Such research has permeated the popular culture and popular news sources. In a CNN.com post from 2010, CNN included material from a story by Jonathan Vatner that was originally published in *O, The Oprah Magazine*, "Why Copycats Win." "During business negotiations: A Northwestern University study found that

negotiators who copied their counterparts' gestures and manner-
isms (such as running their fingers through their hair or leaning
back in their chair) were able to secure a better deal."[1] If "copycats
win" in the face-to-face world of negotiation, what is the digital
equivalent? Perhaps copying common phrases or emoticons will
help negotiators secure a better deal. Yet copying phrases or emoticons assumes that negotiation in the digital world is entirely asynchronous: text or email-based. This view is entirely too limited.
With the widespread availability of voice and video calling via
technology such as Skype, the digital negotiation begins to more
closely resemble the physical. Nor are we limited to Skype. Many
internet teleconferencing products, free or commercial, offer
asynchronous voice and video components, allowing multiple
people to participate in a single negotiation.

As librarians, we are routinely called upon to communicate and
negotiate in an array of situations; it is incumbent upon members
of the profession to understand the elements of effective communication and to recognize potential blocks to optimal message
construction, delivery, and interpretation. Contemporary communication theory elucidates the ways in which effective, robust
negotiation takes place. Seen from a librarian's perspective, such
theory can help us to understand why we win some, lose some,
and sometimes fight to a draw.

To begin at the beginning, let's dredge up a concept that many
people encounter during their undergraduate, or perhaps even
high school, career and then probably rarely think of again:
Maslow's hierarchy of needs, articulated in "A Theory of Human
Motivation," published in *Psychological Review* in 1943.[2] Simply
put, the hierarchy moves upward from the need for basic life-
sustaining elements—nourishment, air, sex, and so forth—
through ever more rarefied needs. Safety, love and belonging,
esteem, and finally self-actualization make up the remainder of
Maslow's model.

Effective negotiation requires that we understand where we and
the opposite negotiator land on Maslow's scale at all times. A tired,
lonesome, and hungry negotiator with shaky self-esteem will offer

challenges that are fundamentally different from those of negotiators who have their lower bases covered and are working on self-actualization. Different mental and physical states demand different negotiation strategies.

Once upon a time, people who thought much about communication believed that it was a fairly straightforward activity with highly predictable outcomes. Some of these people called this idea the bullet theory or the hypodermic needle theory because they believed that communication went from the source to the person receiving it like a bullet to the gut or a shot in the arm. Receipt of the message was unavoidable, and the receiver would act on the message as intended by the sender. This idea developed from behaviorist research conducted in Germany in the 1930s, influenced by propaganda studies and the perceived implications of propaganda techniques on the outcome of World War I. The trouble is, while propaganda surely has an effect, like all messages, it can and does affect different people in different ways. This is not to say that well-crafted or effectively delivered messages do not have a reasonable chance of convincing their audience. Good courtroom lawyers who have argued before a jury can point to times when they have used logic or oratory to convince a jury of the rightness of their client's case. But juries don't always buy what a lawyer says. After all, there are two sides to every case, and one side has to lose. And then there are hung juries, in which some of the jurors, having heard the same evidence, come to a conclusion at odds with others on the panel. Closer to home, a library director might ask one civic group for support and be turned down cold. The next day, that director might deliver the same pitch to a different group and walk away with enough capital to break ground on that essential new building.

One of the reasons that different people can arrive at different conclusions based on the same message is the imposition of "noise" on message reception. This remarkably descriptive idea can be traced to a 1948 model of communication proposed by Claude Elwood Shannon in an article in the *Bell System Technical Journal* and later made popular in a book Shannon wrote with collaborator Warren Weaver, *The Mathematical Theory of Communication*, published in 1963 by the University of Illinois Press. Though the Shannon-Weaver model, as it is commonly known, was constructed to describe communication by telephone, communication researchers quite rightly latched onto it as a convenient way to explain communication in general. This model can be applied to anything from an internal monologue to private emails and to a network television broadcast being watched by millions of viewers. The basic elements of the Shannon-Weaver model are information source, transmitter, channel, sources of noise, receiver, and destination.

Noise can be literal sounds, as anyone who has ever tried to carry on a conversation with an adult while a 2-year-old screams in the background knows. But more broadly defined, the concept refers to any stimulus that gets between the message and its intended receiver. Noise could result from the appearance of the messenger. People are less likely to take investment advice from an unwashed person in ragged clothing than they are from someone sporting a business suit and a hundred-dollar haircut. Noise can be hunger or exhaustion. It could be a preconceived belief, a strong emotion, or an entrenched value system. It could be apathy or mental illness, a desire to win at all costs, or any number of impediments to the message getting from the sender to the receiver in the pristine fashion the sender intended.

Noise, however, is not an impenetrable wall to effective communication, and one of the reasons for this is feedback. Let's pretend that you and I are walking along a sidewalk in a busy city on a windy day. I am a sales representative from a major vendor, and you are a serials librarian who decides what ejournal package, if any, your library might license. It is my job to make you want to do business with my company, and the bigger the business, the better it will be for me. You, however, are not an ideal receptor for my message. You had a big fight with your spouse last night and had to sleep on a hard, lumpy couch. You overslept and missed breakfast, and now it is past noon and you haven't eaten all day. You are hungry, tired, sad, and grumpy. On top of all this, you have decided that my weak chin makes me appear untrustworthy, and the racket from traffic and our fellow pedestrians is loud and distracting. Noise of all sorts abounds. My only hope for success in our business dealings on this day lies in maintaining and artfully using the feedback loop that binds our communication and, through the skillful use of this feedback, reducing or eliminating the noise that distracts you from my message.

Feedback works like this: I deliver my message and you receive it. The ways in which you react to my message are your feedback to me. My response to your feedback is my feedback to you. Together they make a loop, and this loop can go around and around, again and again, clarifying, expanding, editing, or negating the original message. As this is happening, myriad messages may be delivered back and forth between the two of us, each now a sender and receiver. For example, I make my sales pitch to you. You tell me thanks but no thanks, because you think my prices are too high. I tell you that I can make you a special offer that will knock your socks off. You tell me that you'd like to hear more. I have effectively limited the noise that was keeping you from fully appreciating my message. It becomes easy to see that the feedback loop contains the give and take that make up successful negotiation.

Let's apply the artful use of the feedback loop to the example given above about the grumpy serials librarian. A skilled sales representative might gauge the mood and reaction of the librarian—verbal and nonverbal—and discontinue the sales pitch. The representative might invite the librarian to lunch and veer the conversation toward the personal, perhaps commiserating about high housing prices or other common ground. Having connected on a personal level and helped elevate the librarian's mood, the representative continues the sales pitch. A savvy negotiator understands that keeping the feedback loop vital, effective, and interesting to the other party enhances one's chance for success.

In the decades since Shannon and Weaver introduced their model, communication theorists have tinkered with its basic concepts in a variety of ways, for the most part making things more complex and sometimes dizzyingly obscure to lay readers, though perhaps more valuable to scholars. The purpose of this book, however, is not to tease out the esoteric nuances of increasingly rarified ideas on how messages get from point A to point B with the least resistance to reception, interpretation, and acceptance. For our purposes, a basic understanding of the contributions Shannon and Weaver gave the world is sufficient.

Endnotes

1. Jonathan Vatner, "Why Copycats Win," CNN Living, June 14, 2010, accessed August 26, 2011, www.cnn.com/2010/LIVING/wayoflife/06/14/o.mirror.effect/index.html.

2. A. H. Maslow, "A Theory of Human Motivation," *Psychological Review* 50, no. 4 (July 1943): 370–396.

Bibliography

Alderman, Lesley. "Bargaining Down the Medical Bills." *New York Times*, March 14, 2009. www.nytimes.com/2009/03/14/health/14patient.html?emc=eta1.

Ashmore, Beth, and Jill E. Grogg. "Google and OCLC Open Libraries on the Open Web." *Searcher* 14, no. 10 (Nov./Dec. 2006): 44–52.

Bagdikian, Ben H. *The Media Monopoly*. 6th ed. Boston, MA: Beacon Press, 2000.

Baker, David. "'Inside Every Fat Man': Balancing the Digital Library Budget." *Interlending and Document Supply* 36, no. 4 (2008): 213–217.

Balnaves, E. "Open Source Library Management Systems: A Multidimensional Evaluation." *Australian Academic & Research Libraries* 39, no. 1 (March 2008): 1–13.

Bates, Mary Ellen. "Living Large in Lean Times." *Searcher* 17, no. 3 (2009): 22–27.

Bergstrom, Carl, and Theodore Bergstrom. "The Costs and Benefits of Library Site Licenses to Academic Journals." *Proceedings of the National Academy of Sciences* 101 (2004). www.pnas.org/content/101/3/897.full.

Bergstrom, Ted, and Preston McAfee. "Summary Statistics." *Journal Cost-Effectiveness 2006-8 BETA*. www.mcafee.cc/Journal/Summary.pdf.

Bergstrom, Theodore C. "Free Labor for Costly Journals?" *Journal of Economic Perspectives* 15, no. 4 (Autumn 2001): 183–198.

Bernhardt, Beth R. "Purchasing New Journal Subscriptions?: Why? Because We Have Pay-Per-View Usage Statistics That Prove We

Need to Own Them!" In *2004 Charleston Conference Proceedings*, 94–99. Westport, CT: Libraries Unlimited, 2006.

Botero, Cecilia, Steven Carrico, and Michele R. Tennant. "Using Comparative Online Journal Usage Studies to Assess the Big Deal." *Library Resources & Technical Services* 52, no. 2 (2008): 61–68.

Brantley, Peter. "Libraries Re-Shaping." Peter Brantley's Thoughts and Speculations. blogs.lib.berkeley.edu/shimenawa.php/2007/09/09/libraries_re_shaping.

Brevig, Armand. "Getting Value From Vendor Relationships." *Searcher* 16, no. 9 (2008): 28–34.

Camp, Jim. *Start With No: The Negotiating Tools That the Pros Don't Want You to Know*. New York: Crown Business, 2002.

Cohen, Patricia. "Library Leader in Era of Change to Step Down." *New York Times*, November 19, 2009, C1, 8.

Deyrup, Marta Mestrovic. "Is the Revolution Over? Gender, Economic and Professional Parity in Academic Library Leadership Positions." *College & Research Libraries* 65, no. 3 (2004): 242–250.

Doctorow, Corey. "Philadelphia Free Library System Saved!" Boing Boing, September 21, 2009. boingboing.net/2009/09/21/philadelphia-free-li-1.html.

Duranceau, Ellen Finnie. "Cornell and the Future of the Big Deal: An Interview With Ross Atkinson." *Serials Review* 30, no. 2 (2004): 127–130.

Ebert, Loretta. "What's the Big Deal? 'Take 2' or, How to Make it Work for You ..." *Serials Librarian* 48, no. 1/2 (2005): 61–68.

Edlin, Aaron S., and Daniel L. Rubinfeld. "Exclusion or Efficient Pricing? The 'Big Deal' Bundling of Academic Journals." *Antitrust Law Journal* 72 (2004): 151.

"Executive Notes." *JSTORNews* 13, no. 1 (March 2009). news.jstor.org/jstornews/2009/03/march_2009_no_13_issue_1_execu.html.

Feather, Celeste. "Electronic Resources Communications Management." *Library Resources & Technical Services* 51, no. 3 (2006): 204–228.

Feick, Tina, Gary Ives, and Jo McClamroch. "The Big E-Package Deals: Smoothing the Way Through Subscription Agents." *Serials Librarian* 50, no. 3/4 (2006): 267–270.

Fisher, Roger, and William Ury. *Getting to Yes: Negotiating Agreements Without Giving In.* 2nd ed. New York: Penguin Books, 1991.

Flagg, G. "Google Settles Scanning Suit With Authors, Publishers." *American Libraries* 39, no. 11 (December 2008): 30.

Foer, Albert A. "Can Antitrust Save Academic Publishing?" Paper presented at the Annual Meeting of the American Library Association Annual Meeting, Orlando, FL, June 28, 2004 (revised July 20, 2004). www.informationaccess.org/bm~doc/Bert.pdf.

Frazier, Kenneth. "The Librarians' Dilemma: What's the Big Deal?" *Serials Librarian* 48, no. 1/2 (2005): 49–59.

Gibbs, Nancy J. "Walking Away From the 'Big Deal': Consequences and Achievements." *Serials* 18, no. 2 (2005): 89–94.

Han, Yan, Jeanne Pfander, and Marianne Stowell Bracke. "Digitizing Rangelands: Providing Open Access to the Archives of Society for Management Journals." *IAALD Quarterly Bulletin* 50 no. 3/4 (2005): 105–110.

Harris, Lesley Ellen. "Striving for Consistency in Your Digital Content Licensing Policy." *Information Outlook* 12, no. 4 (2008): 38–39.

House of Commons (U.K.), Select Committee on Science and Technology. "Science and Technology: Tenth report." www.parliament.uk.www.publications.parliament.uk/pa/cm200304/cmselect/cmsctech/399/39902.htm.

Jensen, Chris, and Walt Scacchi. "Collaboration, Leadership, Control, and Conflict Negotiation and the Netbeans.org Open Source Software Development Community." In *Proceedings of* the 38th Hawaii International Conference on System Sciences, 196b–206b. Los Alamitos, CA: IEEE Computer Society Press, 2005. www.computer.org/comp/proceedings/hicss/2005/2268/07/22680196b.pdf.

Kahaner, Larry. *Competitive Intelligence: How to Gather, Analyze and Use Information to Move Your Business to the Top.* New York: Touchstone, 1997, 16.

Kenney, Kristine. "Negotiating With Vendors." *Public Libraries* 45, no. 5 (2006): 11–14.

Krause, Donald G., and Miyamoto Musashi. *The Book of Five Rings for Executives.* London: Nicholas Brealey, 1998.

Kretzmann, John, and John McKnight. *Building Communities From the Inside Out: A Path Toward Finding and Mobilizing a Community's Assets.* Evanston, IL: The Asset-Based Community Development Institute, Institute for Policy Research, Northwestern University, ACTA, 1997.

Krumenaker, Larry. "A Tempest in a Librarian's Teapot: EBSCO, ProQuest, Gale Exclusive and Unique Titles." *Searcher* 9, no. 7 (July/August 2001). www.infotoday.com/searcher/jul01/krumenaker.htm.

Kuang, Cliff. "Burning Question: Can Recession Be a Bargaining Chip?" *Wired* (April 2009). www.wired.com/culture/culturereviews/magazine/17-04/st_burningquestion.

Maslow, A. H. "A Theory of Human Motivation." *Psychological Review* 50, no. 4 (July 1943): 370–396.

Oder, Norman. "ALA 2010: Library Journal Helps Launch LosingLibraries.org." *Library Journal* June 25, 2010. www.libraryjournal.com/lj/community/ala/885525-264/ala_2010_library_journal_helps.html.csp.

Oder, Norman. "Nebraska's OCLC Network Dissolves, Libraries Move to BCR." *Library Journal* (April 22, 2009). www.libraryjournal.com/article/CA6653492.html.

Ojala, Marydee. "Reed Elsevier (Finally) Divests U.S. Trade Pubs: Facts and Fallout for Information Professionals." *NewsBreaks* (May 27, 2010). newsbreaks.infotoday.com/NewsBreaks/Reed-Elsevier-Finally-Divests-US-Trade-Pubs-Facts-and-Fallout-for-Information-Professionals-67457.asp.

OCLC. *OCLC Perceptions of Libraries and Information Resources.* Dublin, OH: OCLC Online Computer Library Center, 2005.

Phillips, Kara. "Deal or No Deal: Licensing and Acquiring Digital Resources: License Negotiations." LLRX.com. www.llrx.com/columns/deal2.htm.

Plasmeijer, Henk W. "Pricing the Serials Library: In Defence of a Market Economy." *Journal of Economic Methodology* 9, no. 3 (2002): 337–357.

Powell, Chris. "Library Controversy Isn't About Censorship," *Connecticut Post Online*, October 30, 2009. www.allbusiness.com/society-social-assistance-lifestyle/censorship/13361709-1.html.

Poynder, Richard. "Interview With Derk Haank, CEO, Springer Science+Business Media: Not Looking for Sympathy." *Information Today* 28, no. 1 (January 2011). www.infotoday.com/it/jan11/Interview-with-Derk-Haank.shtml.

Public Agenda. *Long Overdue: A Fresh Look at Public and Leadership Attitudes About LIBRARIES in the 21st Century.* New York: Public Agenda, 2006. www.publicagenda.org/files/pdf/Long_Overdue.pdf.

Quint, Barbara. "Searcher's Voice: Long Thoughts, Big Dreams." *Searcher* 18, no. 6 (July/Aug 2010). www.infotoday.com/searcher/jul10/voice.shtml.

Quint, Barbara. "Six Rules of Engagement: Negotiating Deals With Vendors." *Bottom Line* 10, no. 1 (1997): 4–10.

Rose, Carol M. "Bargaining & Gender." *Harvard Journal of Law & Public Policy* 18, no. 2 (1995): 547–563.

Satin, Seymour. "Negotiating: From First Contact to Final Contract." *Searcher* 9, no. 6 (2001): 50–55.

Schachter, Debbie. "Negotiating in Areas Where End-User Services Dominate." *Searcher* 15, no. 6 (June 2007): 46–49.

———. "The Rules of Negotiation." *Information Outlook* 10, no. 9 (2006): 8–9.

Schneider, Karen. "The Thick of the Fray: Open Source Software in Libraries in the First Decade of this Century." *Bulletin of the American Society for Information Science and Technology* 35, no. 2 (December 2008/January 2009): 15–19. www.asis.org/Bulletin/Dec-08/DecJan09_Schneider.pdf.

Shapiro, Ronald, and Mark A. Jankowski. *The Power of Nice: How to Negotiate So Everyone Wins—Especially You!* New York: Wiley, 1998.

Shell, G. Richard. *Bargaining for Advantage: Negotiation Strategies for Reasonable People.* New York: Viking Penguin, 1999.

"SOLINET Successfully Negotiates Zero Price Increase and a Flat Renewal With LexisNexis on Behalf of ICOLC." SOLINET press release (February 11, 2009). www.lyrasis.org/News/SOLINET%20and%20PALINET%20Archives/SOLINET%20Press%20Releases/~/media/Files/Lyrasis/News/Press%20Releases/2009/LexisNexis%20Academic%20Fee%20Waiver%20Release.ashx.

Srodin, Sharon. "'Let's Make a Deal!': Tips and Tricks for Negotiating Content Purchases." *ONLINE* 28, no. 4 (2004), 16–19.

Susman, Thomas M., David J. Carter, Ropes & Gray, LLP, and the Information Access Alliance. *Publisher Mergers: A Consumer-Based Approach to Antitrust Analysis.* Washington, DC: Information Access Alliance, 2003. www.informationaccess.org/bm~doc/antitrustwtppr.pdf.

Tennant, Roy. "Metasearch Options." Slide show presented at the Association for Library Collections & Technical Services Symposium, American Library Association Midwinter Meeting

2009, Denver, CO, January 22, 2009. wikis.ala.org/midwinter 2009/index.php/ALCTS.

Wade, Rona. "The Very Model of a Modern Library Consortium." *Library Consortium Management* 1, no. 1/2 (1999): 5–18.

Walker, Rob. "Take It or Leave It: The *Only* Guide to Negotiating You Will Ever Need." *Inc.* 25, no. 8 (August 2003): 75–82.

Walsh, Mary Williams, and Jonathan Glater. "Contracts Now Seen as Being Rewritable." *New York Times*, March 31, 2009. www.ny times.com/2009/03/31/business/economy/31contracts.html?_ r=1&emc=eta1.

Walton, Graham. "Negotiation in Health Libraries: A Case Study of Health Information and Libraries Journal and Open Access Publishing." *Health Information and Libraries Journal* 22 (2005): 161–163.

About the Authors

Beth Ashmore is a librarian, writer, and avid TV watcher with an interest in researching whatever happens to be bugging her in her own little library world at the moment, including learning to be a better negotiator. Currently she is a metadata librarian at Samford University where she does cataloging, eresources, and serials management and a little bit of database building, when necessary.

Prior to moving into metadata, she worked as an instruction and reference librarian at Samford and Mississippi State University. She has an MS in library and information science from the University of Illinois, Urbana–Champaign (2000). She has also written articles for a variety of journals, including *Searcher* and *College & Research Libraries*. She also maintains the website The Researching Librarian at www.researchinglibrarian.com.

Jill E. Grogg is the eresources librarian at the University of Alabama Libraries. She has published widely on topics such as reference linking, eresource management, digital libraries, and negotiation in a variety of publications, including *Searcher, College & Research Libraries, Computers in Libraries*, and *The Serials Librarian*. Her work has been cited both inside and outside her field, including in *Science*. She is a member of the editorial board of *Serials Review* and has presented nationally and internationally.

She has an MS in information science from the University of Tennessee (2001), where she was mentored by Dr. Carol Tenopir. She also has an MA in English from the University of Mississippi (1998).

Jeff Weddle is an associate professor in the School of Library and Information Studies at the University of Alabama. Before settling into the academy, he served as a public library director in Mississippi and Maine. His previous books include *Bohemian New Orleans: The Story of the Outsider and Loujon Press* (University Press of Mississippi, 2007) and a poetry collection, *Betray the Invisible* (OEOCO, 2010). He has an MS in library and information science from the University of Kentucky (1988) and a PhD in Communications from the University of Tennessee (2003).

Index

A

AALL Spectrum (magazine), 124

access. *See also* free (open) resources; open access (OA); open source
consortial agreements providing cross, 46
economic stress affecting, 74–75
exclusivity agreements on, 68, 135–137
library acquisition *vs.* internet availability, 90–91
long-term (perpetual), 39–40, 48, 80, 81, 127–128
title transfers between publishers and, 79–80

Accessible Archives, 112

acquisitions. *See also* budgets; collection development
content and community access, 90–91
economic stress impacting, 64, 66–68
electronic, statistics, 163
free and good enough *vs.*, 70
grant-proposal reports supporting, 91

multiple models of, 164
time *vs.* evaluations of, 30

Adobe Acrobat, 12

Against the Grain (magazine), 123

AISTI, 58

ALA (American Library Association), 93, 94

Alabama Virtual Library (AVL), 98–99

alternatives, best, 2–3, 12–13, 30

Amazon, 70, 202

American Library Association (ALA), 93, 94

Americans for Libraries Council, 101

Ancestry.com, 112

Anderson, Ivy, 46, 56

Anderson, Rick, 32, 35–36, 38–39, 42

Antitrust Law Journal (magazine), 152

archiving, 40, 80

ARL (Association of Research Libraries), 61, 78, 79, 137, 141, 163

Armstrong, Kim, 46–47, 55, 60

article writing, as negotiation leverage, 123

assessment costs, and open resources, 195–196

Association of American
    Publishers, 199
Association of Research
    Libraries (ARL), 61, 78, 79,
    137, 141, 163
Atkinson, Ross, 146
attitude, 37, 107–108
Austin, Terry, 47–48, 54
authority approvals, 129–131
Authors Guild, 199
Aversa, Elizabeth, 115–116

B

Bagdikian, Ben H., 149
Baker, David, 157
Bargaining for Advantage
    (Shell), 14, 15, 17–19
Bates, Mary Ellen, 63
BATNA (Best Alternative to a
    Negotiated Agreement),
    2–3, 12–13, 30
Bayou La Batre public library,
    111
Bergstrom, Carl, 153, 159
Bergstrom, Theodore C., 141,
    153, 159
Berlin Statement, 187, 189–190
Best Alternative to a Negotiated
    Agreement (BATNA), 2–3,
    12–13, 30
Bethesda Statement, 187,
    188–189
Big Deal Contract Project, 141
big deals (periodical pricing
    model)
    advantages and disadvan-
        tages, 144–146,
        158–159
    budget cuts and challenges,
        155–158

confidentiality clause con-
    troversies, 141
during economic stress,
    76–77
economic stress and negoti-
    ation of, 65–66
negotiating strategies for,
    159–160
overview and definition, 144
publisher consolidation and
    antitrust law, 148–155
and usage statistics, 156–157
BIP (Books in Print), 70, 202
Black, Steve, 173–174
blogs, 29
Booklist (review website), 164
Book of Five Rings, A
    (Miyamoto Musashi), 119
*Book of Five Rings for
    Executives, The* (Krause),
    119–121
Books in Print (BIP), 70, 202
Boston Public Library (BPL)
    Foundation, 113–114
Botero, Cecilia, 144
Bottom Line (magazine), 29–30
brainstorming, 7–8
branding, customized, 112
Brantley, Peter, 21
Brevig, Armand, 30
bribery, 132
Budapest Statement, 187, 188
budgets
    acquisition decision making
        vs. timelines, 30
    big deals and, 144, 146–147,
        152, 155–158
    community allocation of
        resources and, 86
    community support and
        negotiating, 95–98, 101

consortial agreements and financial hardship, 60–61
economic stress forcing changes to, 66–67, 72–76
electronic expenditure statistics, 163
hardball negotiation for, 121–122
library reputation and misuse of, 88
public awareness of, 101
public campaigns to limit, 95
bundling, 147, 156. *See also* big deals
Burke, Jane, 34, 66, 70

C

California Digital Library, 58, 61, 82, 146
Cambridge Scientific Abstracts (CSA), 81
Camp, James, 10, 12, 14, 16, 17
CARLI (Consortium of Academic and Research Libraries), 49, 58
Carrico, Steven, 144
Carter, David J., 151
censorship, 89
Center for Networked Information, 172
chambers of commerce, 87
Charleston Review (magazine), 123
Cheshire Public Library, 89
children, 92–93, 105, 165
CIC, 58

circulation policies, 89–90
Clark, Larra, 71–72
Clennon, Cynthia, 49, 53
collection development
community challenges to, 89–90
consortia sharing, 58
of eresources, 165
evidence-based decision making in, 64
policy knowledge in, 31
College & Research Libraries (magazine), 138
Collins, Maria, 168
Columbo effect, 16–17
combat analogies, 119–121
communication
authority approval requirements as ineffective, 129–131
community relationship building with, 104
in consortia models, 50, 53
listening skills, 10, 100, 108–110, 115
online options for, 4, 6, 12, 25–26
peer sharing, as leverage, 123
preparation and identification of strengths in, 4
and professionalism, 35–36
as success component, 107, 110
community. *See also* patrons
budget allocations within, 86–87
budget crises and support from, 95–98, 101
campaigns against libraries, 94–95

communication skills
    enhancing relation-
    ships with, 104–106
competing interests bal-
    anced within, 111
content access and acquisi-
    tion issues, 90–91
as funding sources, 97
library policies and bill of
    rights, 93–94
library reputation within,
    88–90
lobbying support from, 87,
    98–99, 101
competition, vendor, 29
complaints, 90, 109
confidence, 26, 29, 85, 122
confidentiality clauses, 141
conflict-management styles, 15
consistency traps, 17–18
consolidations, 64, 81, 148–155
consortia
    advantages of, 46–47, 53–54
    big deal agreements, 145
    deal-acceptance criteria, 55
    disadvantages of, 41–42,
        57–58
    economic stress and cre-
        ative solutions, 69
    existing contracts and join-
        ing, 30–31
    group selection and mem-
        bership levels, 48–50,
        55–56
    international coalitions for,
        59
    libraries and history of,
        47–48
    listings of, 58–59
    membership fees, 59–60
    negotiation levels, 61
    networks *vs.*, 50–52

overview of model, 45–46
    personnel hiring and nego-
        tiation skills required
        for, 52–55
    policies and organization,
        50
    pricing flexibility, 40, 41
    small library memberships,
        challenges to, 60–61
Consortium of Academic and
    Research Libraries
    (CARLI), 49, 58
contracts
    amendments to existing,
        30–31, 128
    economic stress and rene-
        gotiations of, 66–68, 70,
        73–74, 76–77
    nonnegotiable elements in,
        34
    online advantages, 6
    opt-out clauses, 60
    oral *vs.* written, 126–127
    overview and advice on,
        27–28
    personnel assignments and,
        25, 126
    remaining silent *vs.* revising,
        128
    reviewing, 125–126
    unacceptable terms and risk
        transfer, 128–129
cooperation, 137–138, 175–176
copyright, and open access,
    188–190, 199
Cornell University Libraries,
    146
counteroffers, 14
Counting Online Usage of
    Networked Electronic
    Resources (COUNTER),
    54, 77, 196

Courant, Paul, 141
Cox, John, 26, 42–43, 178
creative solutions
    during economic stress,
        68–71, 77–78, 82
    for financial hardship and
        consortial agreements,
        61
    for mutual gain, 7–9
    as success component, 103
CrossRef, 177
culture clashes, 133–135
customers. *See* patrons

D

Darton, Robert C., 200
Davis, Denise, 70, 71–72, 74,
    75–76
deadlines, 3–4, 36
deliverables issues, 193
development of open
    resources, 192–193,
    200–201
Digital Library Federation, 170,
    171
direct marketing, 133
discrimination, and open
    source, 186–187
divestments, 64
document delivery (DD), 30, 39
donors, 112–114
Doyle, Greg, 50, 53, 57
Dyrup, Marta Mestrovic, 138

E

Ebert, Loreeta, 145
ebooks, 177

EBSCO, 79, 81, 135
economic stress
    budget cuts and renegotia-
        tions, 66–68, 70, 72–77
    creative solutions during,
        68–71, 77–78, 82
    free and good enough *vs.*
        acquisition, 70
    impact of, 63–66
    negotiation responsibility
        shifts, 72
    official statements on, 77–78
    online support during,
        72–73
    title transfers and access
        challenges during,
        79–80
EDItEUR, 171
Edlin, Aaron S., 152–153, 156,
    159, 160
education, 22, 25, 26, 116, 117
Electronic Resource
    Management Initiative
    (ERMI), 170, 171
Elsevier, 152
email communications, 4, 6,
    12, 25–26
empathy, 100, 107–110, 115
employees
    communication skills and
        negotiating with, 108
    eresource management and
        workflow, 164–165, 167,
        168–169, 177, 179–180
    hiring terms and written
        documentation, 127
    salary negotiations, 123–124
    signatory authorization as
        negotiation barrier,
        129–131
employers, 124, 127
Equinox, 192

eresource management (ERM)
  acquisition models, multiple, 164
  as conference agenda topic, 165
  electronic expenditures, statistics, 163
  eresource user statistics, 164
  job responsibilities and workflow issues, 164–165, 167, 168–169, 177, 179–180
  licensing initiatives and shared, 175–177
  licensing standardization for, 171–172
  management reform focused on, 177, 179–180
  tools for, 66–67, 167, 168–169, 170–171
  usage statistics data from, 54
eresources
  and big deal arrangements, 65–66, 148
  collection development policies regarding, 165
  defined, 165
  multiple formats, models and delivery options, 166
  pricing structures for, 40–41
ERM. *See* eresource management (ERM)
ERMI (Electronic Resource Management Initiative), 170, 171
Estabrook, Leigh S., 124
ethics, 85, 100, 108, 113–114, 131–132, 136

exclusivity agreements, 68, 135–137
EZ Proxy, 180

F

Facebook, 92
Facts on File, 64
fear, 22, 43, 71
Feather, Celeste, 167
Ferguson's Career Guidance Center (Facts on File), 64
Fields, W. C., 85
Films on Demand, 164
Fisher, Roger, 7, 8, 9–10, 17, 33
flexibility
  budget cuts and big deal agreements, 157
  consortia agreements and, 41, 57
  as economic stress solution, 78, 80, 82
  as negotiation quality, 100, 107, 108, 115
  ordered, as conflict tactic, 120
Foer, Albert A., 151–152
Fogden, Fiona, 27–28
Frazier, Kenneth, 145–146
Free Library of Philadelphia (FLP), 96–97, 97–98, 122
free (open) resources. *See also* open access (OA); open source
  costs of, 183, 194–196
  definitions of, 183
  development partnerships with libraries, 200–201
  economic stress and purchases *vs.*, 70

as leverage, 202–203
library purchased *vs.* patron
    free access, 184
negotiation tips, 203
social networking and
    minors, 92–93
Fund for America's Libraries, 95
funding sources, public
    community partnerships as,
        97
    donors, 112–114
    relationship building with,
        87–90, 94–95, 104–106
fundraising, 96

G

Gadsden Public Library, 109
Gale's Career Library, 64
Galileo (virtual library), 98–99
gender, 137–138
Getting to Yes (Fisher and Ury),
    7, 8, 9–10, 17, 33
"Getting Value From Vendor
    Relationships" (Brevig),
    30
Gibbs, Nancy J., 146–147, 156
goals
    alternatives for, 2–3, 12–13,
        30
    consortial agreements, 50,
        55
    creative solutions for, 7
    knowledge of, as success
        component, 107
    mutual gain approaches,
        7–9, 17–19, 33–34
    negotiation preparation and
        identification of, 4–5,
        36, 37–38, 100, 115

Go Ask Alice (anonymous), 95
good enough revolution, 70
Google, 112, 196–197, 202
Google Books, 70
Google Book Search Project,
    198–200, 201–202
Google Docs, 202
Google Scholar, 112, 196–198,
    202
grant-writing reports, 91
Greater Western Library
    Alliance (GWLA), 55, 58

H

Haank, Derk, 158–159
handshake agreements,
    126–127
Hane, paula, 70
hardball negotiations
    aggressive actions and tim-
        ing examples, 124–125
    barriers to, 129–131
    combat analogies, 119–121
    culture clashes, 133–135
    elements of, 122–123
    and ethics, 131–132
    exclusivity agreements,
        135–137
    gender roles and, 137–138
    personality affecting skills
        in, 123
    respectfulness, 138–141
    salary negotiation examples,
        124
    skills for, 121–122
    written documentation
        requirements, 126–129
Harten, Ramona, 90
*Harvard Journal of Law &
    Public Policy,* 137

Harvard University Libraries, 146, 200
HathiTrust, 201–202
Hellman, Eric, 177
Hinds, Isabella, 34
hiring terms, 127
honesty, 85, 100, 108, 113–114, 131–132, 136
Hoover's Online, 29, 64
hypotheticals, 11

I

ICOLC (International Coalition of Library Consortia), 59, 77–79, 137
ILL (interlibrary loan), 39
ILS (integrated library system), 66–67, 168–169, 170
implementation costs, 194
Information Access Alliance, 151
Information Outlook (magazine), 30
in-person communication, as communication method, 4
integrated library system (ILS), 66–67, 168–169, 170
integrity, 43
intellectual property, 34
interests
    balancing, 111
    consortia memberships and common, 55–56
    creative solutions for, 7
    negotiation preparation and clarification of, 3
    negotiation responsibilities and understanding, 21–22

Interlending and Document Supply (magazine), 157
interlibrary loan (ILL), 39, 47, 54
International Coalition of Library Consortia (ICOLC), 59, 77–79, 137
internet. *See also* eresource management (ERM); eresources; free (open) resources; open access; open source
    access controversies, 92–93, 95, 165
    advantages and disadvantages of, 5–6
    and big deal developments, 147–148
    budget cuts and support organized through, 72–73
    communications through, 4, 6, 12, 25–26
    community expansion of, 91
    for negotiation education opportunities, 25
    researching information on, 5–6, 29
intimidation, 32
Ives, Gary, 144

J

Jankowski, Mark A., 2–5, 7–8, 10–12, 13, 17, 85–86
Jensen, Chris, 191–192
Journal of Economic Methodology, 143
journals. *See also* big deals; open access (OA)

article writing for leverage, 123
electronic, impact of, 173–174
nonprofit *vs.* for-profit pricing, 154
pay-per-view acquisition models for, 164
JSTOR/ITHAKA, 79
judgment, premature, 7

K

Katterjohn, Anna, 90
Kenney, Kristine, 31, 37
Knapp, Mandy, 63–64
knowing thyself principles, 15–17, 29–31
knowledge requirements
asking questions, 10–12, 16, 33, 43
contracts and licensing details, 29
for hardball negotiations, 121–122
in-house library policies and organization, 29–31
interests and patron needs, 3, 21–22, 30, 104
negotiation procedures and skills, 22, 25, 26, 116, 117
overview, 102–103
personal negotiation style, 15–17
product information, 5–6, 53
state library laws, 102
vendor information, 5–6, 29
Koonz, Peter, 173
Krause, Donald G., 119–120
Krumenaker, Larry, 135

Kuali Open Library Environment, 170
Kuang, Cliff, 68

L

Lamoureaux, Seldon Durgom, 178–179
laws, state library, 102
Lebrun, Corinne, 56
LeClerc, Paul, 104
leverage
article writing and presentations for, 122–123
and big deals, 156
communication and peer sharing as, 123
community relationships, 87, 101
consortia business models and, 41
during economic stress, 68–69
free (open) resources as, 202–203
of libraries, 14–15
maintaining, 36–37
neediness *vs.*, 14
respectfulness, 139–140
sales representative tactics for, 133–134
Lexington public library, 88
LexisNexis, 79
LibLime, 192
libraries, overview
business, for product information and research, 29
core policies and bill of rights documents, 93–94

libraries, overview (*cont.*)
   electronic expenditures, statistics on, 163
   public *vs.* academic, negotiation comparisons, 102
   reputation and public perception of, 87–90, 94–95, 104–106
   selling points supporting, 101, 121
Library Bill of Rights, 94–93
Library Consortium Management (magazine), 47
Library Journal, 63–64, 90, 95
Library Resources and Technical Services (Botero, Carrico, and Tennant), 144
License Expression Working Group, 172
licensing
   as add-on responsibility, 25
   challenges in, 39–40
   consortia advantages in, 46–47
   consortial agreements and opt-out clauses, 60
   cooperative efforts simplifying, 39, 175–177
   economic stress and issues with, 65
   eresource management and, 171–172, 175–179
   online communications for, advantages of, 6
   open access/commercial hybrid models and, 190
   open source, 184–187
   researching information on, 29
   standardization of, 178–179

listening skills, 10, 100, 108–110, 115
listservs, 29
"Living Large in Lean Times" (Bates), 63
LLRX.com, 33
lobbying, 87, 98–99, 101, 121
logic traps, 17–18
"Long Overdue" (Public Agenda), 104
LosingLibraries.org, 64, 73
Lots of Copies Keep Stuff Safe, 80, 127–128
Louisiana State University, 72–73
LYRASIS, 49, 51, 52, 59, 79

M

maintenance issues, 192–193, 194–195
Manchester Journal-Inquirer (newspaper), 89
manipulation, 32, 35
Margolis, Bernard, 110, 111–112, 113–114, 116, 139–140
marketing costs, 195
McAfee, R. Preston, 141, 153
McBride, Ed, 46, 50–52, 53, 54
McDonald, John, 197
McKee, Anne, 45–46, 55, 58, 60, 131–132
McKenzie, Christopher, 172
media, 87, 89, 95–98, 122–123
Media Flex, 192
Media Monopoly, The (Bagdikian), 149
Medina, Sue, 25, 37, 71, 74, 98–99

Meebo, 193
Memorandum of
    Understanding, 190, 191
mentors, 25, 116, 117
Merck, 152
Mergent Online, 29
Microsoft Word, 12
Mitchell, Rebecca, 107–110
Miyamoto Musashi, 119–121
monopolies, 144, 149, 150–153
Morgan, Candice, 90
Mozilla Public License, 185
mutual gain approaches, 7–9,
    17–19, 33–34, 107–108,
    116–117
Myspace, 92

N

NAAL (Network of Alabama
    Academic Libraries), 59
National Information
    Standards Organization
    (NISO), 170, 171, 175–177
Nature Publishing Group, 7
NEBASE, 52
neediness, 14
negotiation, overview. *See also*
    related topics
  classes of external, 106–107
  knowledge requirements for,
      102
  library success and impor-
      tance of, 21
  obstacles to, 38, 103,
      129–131
  preparation elements of,
      2–5, 85–86
  qualities required for, 43,
      100
  skills required for, 122

NELINET, 49, 52, 59
NetFlix, 164
NetLibrary, 81
Network of Alabama Academic
    Libraries (NAAL), 59
networks, 50–52
New York Times (newspaper),
    68–69, 76
NISO (National Information
    Standards Organization),
    170, 171, 175–177

O

OA. *See* open access
objectives. *See* goals
observation, 116, 117, 122
OCLC (Online Computer
    Library Center), 51, 52,
    75, 81, 170, 196
offers, 13–15, 115
"Off the Shelf" (Polanka), 164
OhioLink, 59
Ojala, Marydee, 64–65
Okerson, Ann, 34, 38, 39, 42
ONIX Publication Licenses
    Working Group, 171, 172
Onkst, Wayne, 102–103, 107,
    117
ONLINE (magazine), 31
Online Computer Library
    Center (OCLC), 51, 52, 75,
    196
open access (OA)
  collaborative negotiation
      examples, 190–191
  costs of, 194–196
  definitions, 187–190
  internet technology and big
      deal development, 148

open access (*cont.*)
  as leverage, 202–203
  negotiation points with, 192–193
  negotiation tips, 203
  publishers offering hybrids of commercial and, 190
Open Content Alliance, 70, 199
Open Letter to Licensed Content Providers (California Digital Library), 61, 82
open source
  collaborative negotiation in, 191–192
  costs of, 194–196
  definitions, 185
  elements of, 185–187
  as leverage, 202–203
  license agreements for, 184–185
  negotiation points with, 192–193
  negotiation tips, 203
Open Source Definition, 185
Open Source Initiative, 184–185
opponents, overview. *See also specific types of opponents, i.e., publishers, patrons, vendors, employees, etc.*
  classes of external negotiations, overview, 106–107
  combat analogies, 119–121
  mutual gain approaches with, 7–9, 17–19, 31, 33–34
  professional behavior and, 32, 35–37

relationship analysis as negotiation preparation, 2
opt-out contract clauses, 60, 74, 78
Orbis Cascade Alliance, 50, 59
Osterhoudt, Peter, 174
outcomes. *See* goals

P

PALINET, 49, 52, 59
Parable of the Orange, 7
parental substitutions, 92–93
Partnership Among South Carolina's Academic Libraries (PASCAL), 73–74
Pasteur, Louis, 85
patience, 43
patrons (customers). *See also* community
  child discipline issues, 92
  and collection development policies, 89–90
  complaints and procedures, 90, 109
  interests based on needs of, 3
  internet access policies and children, 92–93, 95, 165
  policy issues, 92–93
  research information and knowledge of, 30, 103–104
  usage statistics, 54, 64, 77, 156–158, 159, 163–164, 195–196
pay-per-view, 30, 157–158, 164
peer sharing, 123
periodicals. *See* big deals; journals

personality and personal style, 4, 15–17
Phillips, Kara, 33
phone calls, as communication method, 4
Plasmeijer, Henk W., 143, 155, 159
poise, 122
Polanka, Sue, 164
Portico, 80, 127–128
positional bargaining, 33
Powell, Chris, 89
Power of Nice, The (Shapiro and Jankowski), 2–5, 7–8, 10–12, 13, 17, 85–86
practice, 19, 87–88, 116
precedents, identification of, 2
preparation
  benefits of, 86
  education and training, 22, 25, 26
  elements of, 2–5, 85–86
  for face-to-face meetings, 100
  goal identification, 4–5, 36, 37–38
  for hardball negotiation, 121
  lack of, as cause of negotiation failure, 38
  research as, 5–6, 29–31
  strength and confidence from, 85, 100
presentations
  conference, as negotiation leverage, 123
  face-to-face meetings, 26, 100
  for library public relations, 87, 88
  practicing sales, 87–88
pricing
  and big deals, 144–145, 150, 151–155

consortia agreements and, 46
haggling, 32
lack of flexibility in, 40
nonprofit *vs.* for-profit journal comparisons, 154
research information on, 29
vendor structuring of, 40–41
product information, 5–6, 29, 53
professionalism, 35–36, 37, 91, 138–141
Project Transfer, 177
ProQuest, 112, 135
Public Agenda reports, 104
Public Libraries (magazine), 31
Public Library of Science, 156
public relations, 87–90, 94–95, 104–106
publishers. *See also* big deals
  consolidations of, 64, 81, 148–155
  economic stress and content access, 61, 74–75, 79–80
  economic stress challenges, 64, 81
  eresource management and licensing standards, 171
  and eresources, 166
  open access/commercial hybrids, 190
  periodical copyright monopolies, 143
purchasing departments, 21–22, 34–35

Q

questions, asking, 10–12, 16, 33, 43

Quint, Barbara, 29–30, 33, 34, 37, 91, 134

R

Rangeland (journal), 191
Readex, 112
reciprocity traps, 18
Reed Elsevier, 64
relationship building
    hardball approach choices
        and, 139–140
    library public relations with
        user communities,
        87–90, 94–95, 104–106
    professional behavior,
        35–37, 138–139
    trust, establishing, 110–111,
        125
renegotiations, 66–68, 70,
    73–74, 76–77
report writing, 91
repository deposits, 47, 48
reputations, library, 87–90
research, as preparation, 5–6,
    29–31, 103–104, 133
respectfulness, 138–141
"Review of the Year 2009 and
    Trends Watch—Part 1"
    (Hane), 70
Robinson, Curtis, 37–38,
    105–106
Rose, Carol M., 137
Rubinfeld, Daniel L., 152–153,
    156, 159, 160
rudeness, 139

S

SAGE Publications, 81
salary negotiations, 124
sales representatives, 26, 34, 35,
    57–58, 133–134
samauri combat principles,
    119–121
Sanville, Tom, 49, 57
Satin, Seymour, 33, 36
Scacchi, Walt, 191–192
Schachter, Debbie, 30, 33, 202
Schlessinger, Laura, 94
Scholarly Publishing and
    Academic Resources
    Coalition, 156
Searcher (magazine), 30, 33, 63,
    135, 197, 202
self-interests, 103
Serials (magazine), 146
Serials Solutions, 171, 192
Shapiro, Ronald, 2–5, 7–8,
    10–12, 13, 17, 85–86
Shared Electronic Resource
    Understanding (SERU),
    39, 42, 175–177, 180
Shell, Richard, 14, 15, 17–19
Sherman Antitrust Act, 152
signatory authority, 129–130
silent, remaining, 128
Single Sign-On Authentication
    Working Group, 177
Skype, 5
Small Business Reference
    Center (EBSCO), 64
social networking, 92–93
Society for Range Management
    (SRM), 191
soft bargaining, 33
SOLINET, 49, 52, 59, 79
Soloman, Laura, 63–64
source codes, 186

Srodin, Sharon, 31, 34–35
stability issues, 193
staff. *See* employees
Start With No (Camp), 10, 12,
    14, 16, 17
Statewide Electronic Library, 63
strategies *vs.* tactics, defined,
    119–120
strengths, personal, 4
Suber, Peter, 187–188
subscription agents, 42,
    173–174
suggestion boxes, electronic,
    8–9
Sunflower County Library, 95
support issues, 192
Susman, Thomas M., 151
SWOT (Strengths, Weaknesses,
    Opportunities, Threats)
    analyses, 4

T

tactics, 16–17, 119–120, 120,
    128
Tavaska, John, 40
teachers, 87
teams, 5, 16
Tennant, Michele R., 144
Tennant, Roy, 66
Thoughts and Speculations
    (blog), 21
time, 30, 36, 57
timing, as negotiation skill, 122
title transfers, 79–70
Tonkery, Dan, 34
tough economic times (TET).
    See economic stress
Toys-R-Us, 95
training, 22, 25, 26, 116, 117

Transfer Code of Practice, 80
Triangle Research Libraries
    Network (TRLN),
    146–147, 156
trust, 110–111, 125
Twain, Mark, 122

U

U.K. Serials Group conference,
    146
UNILINC, 59
University of Arizona, 191
University of Michigan, 198
University of Missouri Library
    Systems, 59
Ury, William, 7, 8, 9–10, 17, 33
usage statistics
    acquisition decision making
        based on, 64
    big deals purchasing models
        and, 156–158, 159
    economic stress and agree-
        ment reforms based
        on, 77
    eresources providing, 54,
        163–164
    as open resource cost,
        195–196

V

values, 111–112
vendors
    consortia arrangements
        with, 46, 53, 54, 57–58
    cultural clashes with,
        133–135

vendors (*cont.*)
    during economic stress, 67–68, 70–71
    ending negotiations and relationship with, 37
    and exclusivity agreements, 68, 135–136
    free resources from, 183
    price structuring, 40–41
    researching information on, 5–6, 29
    sales representatives of, 26, 34, 35, 57–58, 133–134
    soft bargaining and relationships with, 33–34
video conferencing, as communication style, 5
Virgil (Roman poet), 85

walking away, 30, 37, 54–55, 138, 139, 140
weaknesses, personal, 4, 16
Web-Scale Management Services, 170
WHAT (questioning technique), 10–12
win-win approaches, 7–9, 16–19, 33–34, 107–108, 116–117
Wired (magazine), 68, 70
workflow and responsibility
    contract negotiations and, 25, 126
    eresource management and, 164–165, 167, 168–169, 177, 179–180
WorldCat.org, 75, 112
written documentation, 126–129

W

Wade, Rona, 47, 60
Walker, Rob, 16

Z

Zotero, 184